Red Fighting Blue

The national electoral map has split into warring regional bastions of Republican red and Democratic blue, producing a deep and enduring partisan divide in American politics. In *Red Fighting Blue*, David A. Hopkins places the current partisan and electoral era in historical context, explains how the increased salience of social issues since the 1980s has redefined the parties' geographic bases of support, and reveals the critical role that American political institutions play in intermediating between the behavior of citizens and the outcome of public policy-making. The widening geographic gap in voters' partisan preferences, as magnified further by winner-takes-all electoral rules, has rendered most of the nation safe territory for either Democratic or Republican candidates in both presidential and congressional elections - with significant consequences for party competition, candidate strategy, and the operation of government.

David A. Hopkins is Associate Professor of Political Science at Boston College. He is coauthor of *Asymmetric Politics: Ideological Republicans and Group Interest Democrats* (with Matt Grossmann) and *Presidential Elections: Strategies and Structures of American Politics*, 14th edition (with Nelson W. Polsby, Aaron Wildavsky, and Steven E. Schier). His research has been the subject of a feature by Ezra Klein of Vox.com and cited by a number of other prominent journalists and analysts of American politics.

Red Fighting Blue

How Geography and Electoral Rules
Polarize American Politics

DAVID A. HOPKINS
Boston College

CAMBRIDGE
UNIVERSITY PRESS

CAMBRIDGE
UNIVERSITY PRESS

University Printing House, Cambridge CB2 8BS, United Kingdom

One Liberty Plaza, 20th Floor, New York, NY 10006, USA

477 Williamstown Road, Port Melbourne, VIC 3207, Australia

4843/24, 2nd Floor, Ansari Road, Daryaganj, Delhi – 110002, India

79 Anson Road, #06-04/06, Singapore 079906

Cambridge University Press is part of the University of Cambridge.

It furthers the University's mission by disseminating knowledge in the pursuit of education, learning, and research at the highest international levels of excellence.

www.cambridge.org
Information on this title: www.cambridge.org/9781107191617
DOI: 10.1017/9781108123594

First published 2017

Printed in the United States of America by Sheridan Books, Inc.

A catalogue record for this publication is available from the British Library.

ISBN 978-1-107-19161-7 Hardback
ISBN 978-1-316-64214-6 Paperback

For Monica

Contents

List of Figures   *page* viii

Acknowledgments   xi

1   A Nation Votes, Ohio Decides   1

2   Solid States: The Regional Bases of the American Parties   29

3   The Geographic Roots of Party Strength and Cohesion   64

4   Mapping the Cultural Battlefield: How Social Issues
    Fuel the Regional Divide   99

5   Regional Polarization and Partisan Change in the
    U.S. Congress   146

6   Rural Red, Big-City Blue, and the Pivotal Purple Midwest   193

7   A Locked-Up Nation   213

Index   237

Figures

1.1 State partisan alignments in the 2016 presidential
     campaign   *page* 8
1.2 State-level partisan consistency in the 2012
     and 2016 presidential elections   9
1.3 The decline of split partisan constituencies in presidential
     and congressional elections, 1968–2016   20
1.4 The five political regions of the United States   27
2.1 The 2000 presidential election (the original
     "red-versus-blue" map)   33
2.2 Popular and electoral vote winning percentages in
     U.S. presidential elections, 1968–2016   40
2.3 Average state popular vote margins in presidential
     elections, 1968–2016   46
2.4 Average state popular vote deviation in presidential
     elections, 1968–2016   47
2.5 The decline of electorally representative states, 1968–2016   49
2.6 The shrinking electoral battleground, 1976–2016   51
2.7 State partisan alignments in presidential elections,
     2000–2016   55
2.8 State-level partisan consistency across five consecutive
     presidential elections, 1880–2016   56
2.9 Regional polarization in U.S. House elections, 1968–2016   58
2.10 Regional polarization in U.S. Senate elections, 1968–2016   60
3.1 Total number of presidential victories per state by
     Franklin D. Roosevelt (D), 1932–1944   72
3.2 Total number of presidential victories per state by
     Republican or independent candidates, 1968–1988   84

3.3 Share of southern congressional seats held by Republicans, 1960–2016 — 90

4.1 Comparison of the 1976 and 1992 presidential elections by state — 110

4.2 The increasing partisan divide over abortion, 1980–2012 — 116

4.3 The emergence of the "God gap," 1980–2012 — 118

4.4 The growing partisan divide over Christian fundamentalism, 1988–2012 — 119

4.5 Regional differences in economic and cultural attitudes, 1988–2012 — 130

4.6 Relationship between state religiosity and party shift in presidential elections, 1988–2016 — 138

5.1 The decline of ideological moderates in the U.S. House of Representatives, 1972–2016 — 173

5.2 The decline of ideological moderates in the U.S. Senate, 1972–2016 — 174

5.3 Party and ideology among House and Senate members in Red America, 1972–2016 — 175

5.4 Party and ideology among House and Senate members in Blue America, 1972–2016 — 175

5.5 Constituency partisanship and member ideology, 1972–2016 (average across House and Senate) — 176

5.6 Reelection rate in the U.S. House of Representatives by incumbent ideology, 1972–2016 — 178

5.7 Reelection rate in the U.S. Senate by incumbent ideology, 1972–2016 — 178

5.8 Most House moderates are replaced by nonmoderates from the opposite party — 179

5.9 Most Senate moderates are replaced by nonmoderates from the opposite party — 180

5.10 The fundamental Republican advantage in House elections — 184

5.11 The fundamental Republican advantage in Senate elections — 185

5.12 The regional polarization of the U.S. House of Representatives, 1932–2016 — 190

5.13 The regional polarization of the U.S. Senate, 1932–2016 — 191

6.1 The geographic polarization of the Northeast and Pacific Coast, 1980–2016 — 196

6.2 The geographic polarization of the South and interior West, 1980–2016 — 200

6.3 The representativeness of the Midwest in presidential elections, 1968–2016 — 205

6.4   The representativeness of the Midwest in House elections,
       1968–2016   206
6.5   The persistence of split Senate delegations in the Midwest,
       1968–2016   207
6.6   The geographic polarization of the Midwest, 1980–2016   209

Acknowledgments

This book has taken shape over a long period of time, and many people have helped along the way. My interest in American political geography, which dates back to an era before anyone had even heard of red states and blue states, first assumed academic form as an undergraduate thesis at Harvard University with the incisive assistance of advisor David E. Campbell. During my graduate studies at the University of California, Berkeley, I was fortunate to benefit from a dedicated group of faculty mentors. Eric Schickler served as an uncommonly thoughtful dissertation advisor, and Rob Van Houweling, John W. Ellwood, and J. Merrill Shanks graciously shared their considerable expertise. I am especially grateful to the brilliant Laura Stoker for her advice and generosity.

While at Berkeley, I spent countless hours at the Institute of Governmental Studies in the company of talented colleagues who were a constant source of intellectual enrichment, perceptive feedback, and personal camaraderie, including Melissa Cully Anderson, Justin Buchler, Devin Caughey, Brendan Doherty, Casey Dominguez, Brent Durbin, Patrick Egan, Angelo Gonzales, Jill Greenlee, Matt Grossmann, Rebecca Hamlin, John Hanley, Peter Hanson, Amanda Hollis-Brusky, Iris Hui, Matt Jarvis, Amy Lerman, Mark Oleszek, Sarah Reckhow, Keith Smith, and Rachel Van Sickle-Ward. Special thanks to Darshan Goux and Alison Gash for their suggestions and encouragement during a critical phase of research.

Since arriving at Boston College, I have once again found myself in an exceptionally stimulating scholarly environment inhabited by gifted colleagues and students. I am particularly indebted to Ken Kersch, Marc Landy, Shep Melnick, Kay Schlozman, Peter Skerry, David Karol, and

David Mayhew, all of whom read a draft of the manuscript with great care and assembled on a spring day in Boston to share an assortment of valuable critiques that vastly improved the final product. Thanks to Marissa Marandola for providing excellent research assistance and to Jennifer Erickson for kindnesses too numerous to detail. I also express my appreciation to Sara Doskow of Cambridge University Press for skillfully shepherding this book into print.

The pages that follow reflect the profound influence of the late Nelson W. Polsby. Nelson was a teacher, mentor, collaborator, and friend whose analytical gifts and playful wit remain as vivid as ever in my mind, and whose dedication to the study of political life in every imaginable form and context still inspires me today. I extend thanks as well to Linda, Emily, Lisa, and Dan Polsby for their continued friendship.

I owe my own lifelong fascination with American politics to my parents, Allen and Joan Hopkins, who have always remained true to their belief that the civic health of a community depends upon the dedication and service of well-informed and public-spirited citizens. Along with Finnegan Hopkins, Caitlin DeAngelis, and Molly and Sam Hopkins, as well as my official and unofficial extended family and friends, they have provided me with boundless love and support for which I cannot adequately convey my appreciation.

Finally, I wish to express my deepest affection and gratitude to Monica Soare. The academic life is often challenging and uncertain; the shared life of two academics can be exponentially more so. She has remained steadfastly enthusiastic, patient, and good-humored throughout, and she has always believed in me. As the dedication page proclaims, this book is for her.

A Nation Votes, Ohio Decides

BATTLE IN THE BUCKEYE STATE

According to a formerly well-established American political tradition, the Labor Day holiday once marked the "official" beginning of the campaign season in every presidential election year. Candidates enjoyed the now-unthinkable luxury of departing the campaign trail for a few weeks after the summer nominating conventions in order to conserve their energy and make strategic preparations for the two-month national sprint that awaited them in the fall, habitually reappearing in public view on the first Monday in September. Like many other bygone campaign rituals, this practice has been rendered obsolete by technological change, reforms to the presidential nomination process (which now produces *de facto* party nominees by the preceding spring, well in advance of their formal selection at the conventions), and a progressively intensifying tactical arms race that has encouraged candidates to spare no opportunity to court and mobilize popular support. While presidential aspirants no longer wait until Labor Day to begin hunting for votes, however, they still find a way to commemorate the holiday by planning campaign activities intended to convince the electorate of their unshakable devotion to the interests and concerns of hardworking Americans.

The 2016 election was no exception. Democratic presidential nominee Hillary Clinton observed Labor Day by attending an outdoor festival in the company of several national leaders of the labor movement, including Richard Trumka of the AFL-CIO and Randi Weingarten of the American Federation of Teachers. Her Republican opponent Donald Trump hosted a roundtable discussion with union members before making an afternoon appearance at a county fair, stopping en route to greet lunchtime customers at a local diner. The most newsworthy aspect of the day was that Clinton and Trump had found themselves in close mutual proximity among the environs of northeastern Ohio; as press photographers snapped pictures, the two candidates' logo-emblazoned airplanes even sat in clear view of each other on the tarmac of Cleveland Hopkins International Airport. In a nation of more than 300 million people spread over nearly 3.8 million square miles, the two prospective presidents had found themselves in the very same place at the very same time.[1]

While the simultaneous timing of the candidates' Labor Day visits to Cleveland was coincidental rather than coordinated, it was hardly surprising that Trump and Clinton both independently chose to spend the holiday personally seeking the votes of Ohioans rather than Texans, Alaskans, or New Yorkers. The strategy pursued by presidential campaigns predictably reflects the incentives presented to candidates by the electoral system itself. Presidents are chosen not by a simple national popular vote but rather by a majority of the electoral college, whose members are selected via a set of 51 simultaneous elections held in each state and the District of Columbia. In every state but two, a slate of electors pledged to a specific party's presidential nominee is elected in a winner-take-all fashion by a statewide plurality vote (Maine and Nebraska instead award two electoral votes apiece to the state-level winner and one electoral vote to the winner of each congressional district within the state). Candidates therefore direct their attention to the residents of states, especially populous states such as Ohio, where they believe either side has a chance of placing first in the statewide popular vote – and thus of receiving the state's entire cache of presidential electors – while virtually ignoring the rest of the nation.

The electoral college has existed since the ratification of the Constitution more than 225 years ago, while the selection of electors pledged to candidates via winner-take-all popular vote has been the procedural norm among states since the 1830s. But the influence of these structural features on the behavior of candidates and the outcomes of national elections has perhaps never been greater than it is today. Electoral rules may remain formally stable over decades or even centuries of history and yet vary considerably in practical importance from one period to the next

---

[1] David Jackson, "Trump, Clinton Launch Fall Campaigns on Same Ohio Tarmac," *USA Today*, September 5, 2016, www.usatoday.com/story/news/politics/elections/2016/2016/09/05/donald-trump-labor-day-cleveland-hillary-cliinton-ohio/89879896/.

due to changes in the direction and distribution of voting preferences within the mass public. Two important trends have emerged over the past quarter-century that have combined to bolster the influence of American electoral institutions – and, indeed, to define the essence of the current political era.

The first key development is the geographic polarization of electoral outcomes in the United States. While the two major parties once fiercely battled each other for popular supremacy across wide swaths of the continent, Republicans and Democrats today both maintain sizable regional bastions that reliably deliver majority support to the nominees of their favored party from one election to the next. The geographic scope of electoral competition has narrowed to a shrinking slice of territory where the parties remain evenly matched and where winner-take-all popular contests are still open to potential capture by either side.

Secondly, the rise of regional polarization over the past few decades has been accompanied by a parallel emergence of persistent electoral parity between the parties at the national level. The margin separating the two major-party presidential nominees in the national popular vote was less than 9 percentage points in each of the eight elections between 1988 and 2016, and did not exceed 4 points in four of the last five. Since 1994, narrow seat margins have also become commonplace in Congress, with majority control of the Senate, House of Representatives, or both chambers often open to serious contestation from one congressional election to the next.

American politics has therefore entered an age in which a close balance between the Democratic and Republican parties in the nation as a whole contrasts with the reliable electoral dominance of most congressional districts, states, and even entire regions by one party or the other. While the national outcome of presidential and congressional elections now frequently remains in doubt until the votes are counted late in the evening on election night, most Americans reside in electoral constituencies where the identity of the winning party can be predicted with confidence well before the campaign even begins. Many of these voters maintain an intense and deeply felt rooting interest in the results of national elections, but they remain spectators on the sidelines of a competition that is being actively waged elsewhere, in the few remaining corners of the nation where neither party can count on certain victory.

More than any other state, Ohio has come to symbolize the shrinking geographic battleground where America's perennially close elections are repeatedly decided: the bloody front lines of the national partisan war. Trump, Clinton, and their vice presidential running mates visited Ohio a collective 48 times between the nominating conventions and the November 2016 election, while the candidates, parties, and allied groups spent over $65 million on advertising designed to persuade the state's voters.[2] Four years before, Republican presidential nominee Mitt Romney and his running mate Paul Ryan made 51 visits to Ohio between them over the final two months of the 2012 race (compared to 28 combined visits by Democratic incumbent Barack Obama and Vice President Joe Biden), while Obama opened 131 Ohio campaign field offices, stretching from Ashtabula in the state's northeast corner to Ironton near its southernmost point (compared to 40 state offices maintained by Romney).[3] Some Ohioans report becoming weary of the incessant attention every four years. "I'm very tired of the ads, and it's only July," complained one state resident to a reporter several months before the 2012 election, while another sighed that "the phone rings three or four times a night and I'm screening calls."[4] But a hardworking activist conducting door-to-door canvassing observed that "I don't ever get anybody saying 'I'm not interested,'" and, as Cincinnati City Council member P. G. Sittenfeld put it, "People do like being the center of the universe."[5]

Any American casually scanning news stories or flipping television channels when a contemporary presidential campaign is in progress will encounter numerous journalistic reports attesting to the massive electoral clout of swing states such as Ohio. Ubiquitous headlines inform their readers about "Ohio – the Heart of the Election Battle,"[6] explaining "Why Ohio Will Decide the Presidential Election"[7] and "Why Ohio Is the

---

[2] "Two-Thirds of Presidential Campaign Is in Just 6 States," nationalpopularvote.com, www.nationalpopularvote.com/campaign-events-2016; Carrie Dunn, "Pro-Clinton Battleground Ad Spending Outstrips Trump Team by 2-1," NBC News, November 4, 2016, www.nbcnews.com/politics/first-read/pro-clinton-battleground-ad-spending-outstrips-trump-team-2-1-n677911.

[3] Field office figures from Elspeth Reeve, "What We Know About Obama and Romney's Ground Games", *The Wire*, October 25, 2012, www.thewire.com/politics/2012/10/what-we-know-about-obama-and-romneys-ground-games/58348/; Obama Ohio field office location information from P2012, www.p2012.org/obama/ofaohfield.html.

[4] Dan Eggen and T. W. Farnam, "Swing States to Weather Brunt of Deluge of Ad Spending," *Washington Post*, July 29, 2012, p. A07; Jonathan Lemire and Celeste Katz, "The 90M Voter," *New York Daily News*, October 14, 2012, p. 13.

[5] Gail Collins, "Guess Who It's All Up To?" *New York Times*, November 1, 2012, p. A31.

[6] "Welcome to Ohio – and the Heart of the Election Battle," *The Economist*, May 8, 2004, p. 27.

[7] Alex Altman and Michael Scherer, "Why Ohio Will Decide the Presidential Election," *Time*, October 25, 2012, http://swampland.time.com/2012/10/25/why-ohio-will-decide-the-2012-presidential-election/.

Most Important State in the Country."[8] News accounts proclaiming the state's outsized influence over American electoral politics have become sufficiently familiar standards of contemporary campaign coverage that readers and viewers might be forgiven for suspecting media organizations of reprinting or rebroadcasting the same story every four years, merely substituting the names of the current candidates. Ohio's key electoral role has even become well-known enough to serve as the basis of wry, referential humor from reporters and comedians assuming that media consumers had gotten the message many times over. "Have we mentioned that it's all up to Ohio?" joked Gail Collins of the *New York Times* in the first line of a column filed from Cincinnati several days before the 2012 election, while the late-night television comedian Stephen Colbert titled his live election night broadcast "A Nation Votes, Ohio Decides."[9]

Colbert's wisecrack actually contains a great deal of truth. Donald Trump's larger-than-expected Ohio victory in 2016 mirrored his unanticipated strength in other key midwestern states, allowing him to defy media predictions to engineer an upset defeat of Hillary Clinton in the electoral college. The winner of the 2012 election similarly became clear at the moment that the major broadcast networks projected a narrow victory in Ohio for Obama shortly after 11:00 P.M. eastern time on the night of the election – a decision that prompted a memorable (and awkward) moment of spontaneous live television when Fox News Channel election analyst Karl Rove, a former presidential advisor to George W. Bush and the nation's best-known Republican political operative, responded by openly disputing his own network's decision to award the state, and with it the presidency, to the Democratic ticket.[10] (In response to Rove's objections, Fox News producers dispatched broadcast co-anchor Megyn Kelly down a back hallway off the studio set to conduct an impromptu, live, on-camera interview with two members of the network's data analysis team, who assured Fox viewers of their confidence in the ultimately correct Ohio projection.) Ohio also gave then-senator Obama a crucial

[8] Chris Cillizza, "Why Ohio Is the Most Important State in the Country," The Fix blog, *Washington Post*, October 11, 2012, www.washingtonpost.com/blogs/the-fix/wp/2012/10/11/why-ohio-is-the-most-important-state-in-the-country/.

[9] Collins, "Guess Who It's All Up To?".

[10] Jeremy W. Peters and Brian Stelter, "On Fox News, a Mistrust of Pro-Obama Numbers Lasts Late Into the Night," *New York Times*, November 7, 2012, p. P13; Gabriel Sherman, "How Karl Rove Fought with Fox News over the Ohio Call," *New York*, November 7, 2012, nymag.com/daily/intelligencer/2012/11/how-rove-fought-with-fox-over-ohio.html.

victory in 2008 over his first Republican opponent, Senator John McCain of Arizona, who lost the state by a margin of 51 percent to 47 percent even after adopting Samuel Joseph Wurzelbacher, a plumber's assistant from the Toledo suburbs who became known as "Joe the Plumber," as a campaign sidekick of sorts to personify his identification with blue-collar Americans. In 2004, Ohio had quite literally decided the presidency, delivering a narrow victory to Republican incumbent George W. Bush in the early hours of the morning that secured his reelection over the Democratic nominee, Senator John Kerry of Massachusetts; just 120,000 more votes in the state – out of more than 5.6 million cast – would have sent Kerry to the White House instead.

The reduction of the active electoral battleground to a decreasing number of swing states such as Ohio has not merely led to the increasingly concentrated deployment of candidate resources or a decline in the proportion of American neighborhoods exposed to active persuasion and mobilization efforts by campaigns, parties, and interest groups. The solidification of large Democratic and Republican territorial strongholds over the past several decades has also worked to render each party more ideologically homogeneous by reducing the size and influence of regionally based moderate party factions such as southern Democrats and northeastern Republicans. Thus the geographic polarization of American elections has played a key role in advancing the ideological polarization of American parties.

The existence of electoral rules and institutions in which geographically defined constituencies serve as the fundamental component units also allows American elections to be decided simply by the ways in which Democratic and Republican voters happen to be dispersed across the political boundaries of the nation. The specific spatial configuration of the parties' regional coalitions is particularly critical for determining the control of the executive and legislative branches when the support for each party in the electorate varies significantly across geographic boundaries and when the national balance between the parties is close to even – two durable characteristics of our contemporary political age. Fully understanding the state of American electoral politics in the early twenty-first century thus requires a thorough examination of the causes and consequences of the two parties' increasingly entrenched geographic polarization.

The 2016 election provides an especially striking example of this phenomenon. The narrow margin of the national presidential vote and the particular state-level distribution of the parties' supporters interacted with the institutional attributes of the electoral college to provide Donald Trump with the majority of state electors necessary to assume the presidency even though he received nearly 3 million fewer popular votes nationwide than did Hillary Clinton. This was the second time in the previous five presidential elections that the national popular vote winner had been denied the White House; meanwhile, the candidate carrying Ohio has become president in each of the past fourteen consecutive elections, dating back to Lyndon B. Johnson's victory in 1964. The quip "A nation votes, Ohio decides" may have been meant as a humorous poke at the well-known idiosyncrasies of the electoral college, but recent history suggests that it is not a wholly inappropriate characterization of how the American electoral system operates today.

DO POLARIZED MAPS REQUIRE POLARIZED VOTERS?

Perpetually vigorous competition between two closely matched parties that each maintain reliable electoral dominance over a significant, and roughly equal, proportion of the nation's geographic territory has become a signature characteristic of American politics in the twenty-first century. The appearance of distinct and stable geographic alignments on the contemporary electoral map thus serves as an apt visual symbol of an era defined by the emergence of intense partisan conflict among leaders and citizens alike. With the vast majority of voters now providing consistent support to the candidates of a single party in national elections, and with Democratic and Republican politicians collectively shifting toward opposite ends of the ideological spectrum, the United States has entered a political age characterized by the dual trends of mass-level partisanship and elite-level polarization – a development that has inspired a series of major academic studies and has received increasing attention from journalists, news media commentators, and the politically attentive public. Under these circumstances, it is only fitting that cartographic representations of recent election results have repeatedly revealed large, comparably sized territorial bastions of opposite partisan affiliations, with a smaller bloc of swing states holding the narrow balance of power between them – just as a dwindling number of voters who remain open to persuasion by either party now find themselves caught between two sizable populations of increasingly fervent, and mutually antagonistic, loyalists to the Democratic or Republican cause.

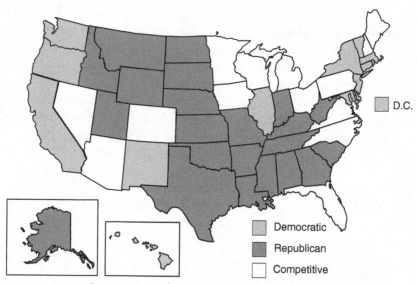

FIGURE I.I. State partisan alignments in the 2016 presidential campaign.

In a particularly eye-catching development, the states providing reliable support to each party are not scattered haphazardly across the nation, but are instead arranged in an increasingly familiar regional pattern. As Figure I.I demonstrates, 14 states (plus the District of Columbia) were considered securely Democratic in the 2016 presidential election and thus virtually ignored by the campaigns of both candidates; nearly all of these "blue states" – as they are known in American political parlance – are located either in the Northeast or along the Pacific Coast (including the island state of Hawaii). Except for noncontiguous Alaska, the 22 "red states" that were considered safely Republican by the Trump and Clinton campaigns lie within in a single *L*-shaped expanse stretching west from South Carolina and southwest from West Virginia through Missouri, Arkansas, Louisiana, and Texas, then turning north to the Dakotas and heading west once more to Idaho and Utah.

The 2016 election was unique in many respects: Clinton was the first woman in American history to receive the presidential nomination of a major political party, while Trump was a newcomer to electoral politics who found particular success in appealing to white working-class voters. Yet the state-level coalitions formed by the two candidates did not differ dramatically from those of preceding presidential elections contested by different nominees. In fact, the relative Democratic or Republican lean of each state in the 2016 election closely matched the 2012 results

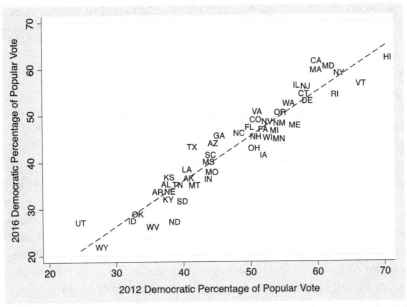

FIGURE 1.2. State-level partisan consistency in the 2012 and 2016 presidential elections.

(see Figure 1.2). The Pearson correlation coefficient between the 2012 and 2016 Democratic vote shares was .96 (on a scale in which 0 represents no statistical association and 1 represents perfect correlation). Trump successfully assembled an electoral majority in 2016 by winning six swing states (Florida, Iowa, Michigan, Ohio, Pennsylvania, and Wisconsin) that Obama had carried in 2012, while the remaining 44 states (and the District of Columbia) supported the same party's candidates in both elections.

The division of the electoral map into large blocs of reliably "red" and "blue" partisan territory has come to symbolize the contentious character of contemporary politics in the eyes of many Americans. But while few experts dispute the conclusion that the elected leaders of the Democratic and Republican parties have become more ideologically dissimilar, procedurally aggressive, and personally hostile since the 1970s and 1980s, the question of whether these developments reflect similar trends or preferences within the mass public remains unresolved – and energetically contested – among scholars of American public opinion. Are strategically minded candidates simply responding to electoral incentives by appealing to increasingly polarized voters? Or, alternatively, does the rise of polarization in government represent a failure of the democratic system, with elected officials in both parties rapidly abandoning a political middle ground on which most citizens still firmly stand?

One school of thought, principally identified with Morris P. Fiorina of Stanford University, contends that elite-level polarization has proceeded without the instigation or approval of the American public at large. Fiorina argues that Democratic and Republican politicians have moved respectively to the ideological left and right in response to intensifying pressure from party activists, interest groups, influential media sources, and primary electorates, leaving most voters with an unappealing choice in general elections between two increasingly extreme options. "There is little evidence that Americans' ideological or policy *positions* are more polarized today than they were two or three decades ago, although their *choices* often seem to be," he writes, proposing a memorable analogy: "The bulk of the American citizenry is somewhat in the position of the unfortunate citizens of some third-world countries who try to stay out of the crossfire while Maoist guerillas and right-wing death squads shoot at each other."[11] To Fiorina, the advent of polarization has created an ominous "disconnect" between the populace and its political leadership that constitutes a veritable "breakdown of representation in American politics."[12]

Other scholars, most prominently Alan I. Abramowitz of Emory University, view the trend of ideological polarization as extending beyond the political leadership class into the mass public as well, especially among the nation's most attentive and engaged citizens. "To a considerable extent," Abramowitz argues, "the divisions that exist among policymakers in Washington reflect real divisions among the American people."[13] Nor should observers worry that politicians have become less responsive to the preferences of the average voter, according to Abramowitz. "Polarization is not a result of a failure of representation; it is a result of successful representation," he writes. "... If concerned citizens want to understand the root cause of polarization and government gridlock, they should ... look in a mirror."[14]

---

[11] Morris P. Fiorina with Samuel J. Abrams and Jeremy C. Pope, *Culture War? The Myth of a Polarized America* (New York: Pearson, 2005), p. 5 (italics in original).

[12] Morris P. Fiorina with Samuel J. Abrams, *Disconnect: The Breakdown of Representation in American Politics* (Norman: University of Oklahoma Press, 2009).

[13] Alan I. Abramowitz and Kyle L. Saunders, "Is Polarization a Myth?" *Journal of Politics* 70 (April 2008), pp. 542–555, at 554.

[14] Alan I. Abramowitz, *The Polarized Public? Why American Government Is So Dysfunctional* (New York: Pearson, 2013), p. xiii.

Both sides of this intellectual debate support their respective conclusions by presenting a series of empirical comparisons between the issue positions of political leaders – such as members of Congress – and those of the mass public. Abramowitz describes the behavior of elected officials as sensitive to the political preferences of voters, with the progression of elite-level polarization merely reflecting a comparable change over time in the demands of the electorate (especially its most active and influential members). In contrast, Fiorina perceives a vast and widening gulf between the policies of politicians and the collective preferences of the public, arguing that most citizens are no longer adequately represented by elected officeholders. He concludes that the primary responsibility for this lapse in representation lies with the Democratic and Republican parties, which he characterizes as effectively captured by ideologically extreme activists and thus unwilling to provide many Americans with an electoral option that suitably corresponds to their political beliefs.

These scholarly disagreements over the strength of the connection between the issue positions of incumbents and the views of their constituents have not always placed much emphasis on the process by which representative democracy is realized in the United States. Analysts sometimes hold the Democratic and Republican parties solely responsible for the task of ensuring that the policies proposed by elected officials reliably reflect the distribution of public opinion in the electorate, but this assumption risks ignoring the critical intermediary role played by the electoral system itself. The preferences of individual citizens are converted into the composition of elective institutions – and, by extension, the development of public policy – by means of a highly complex set of electoral rules and constitutional structures that interact with the two major parties to provide the American polity with representation in government. Among these important institutional characteristics are single-member districts, winner-take-all elections, staggered terms of office, the electoral college, and the distinctive apportionment of the Senate and the House of Representatives.

Geography is thus a fundamental component of the mechanics of democratic representation. Because representatives are chosen via a series of winner-take-all elections held within states and congressional districts defined by geographic borders, the distribution of votes – and the political opinions that influence those votes – across these spatial boundaries fundamentally affects electoral outcomes and thus the policy positions and political incentives of partisan officeholders. It is only sensible to suppose a connection between the recent growth of polarization among political elites and the emergence of strong and persistent geographic bastions of partisan support in the wider electorate.

American political history provides several key illustrations of how the relative strength and cohesion of both major parties reflects the nature of their respective regional coalitions. For several decades in the mid-twentieth century, the Democratic Party maintained a dominant national majority that yet contained significant internal divisions between a conservative southern faction and a more liberal northern wing, convincing some political scientists to propose reforms designed to improve the efficiency and responsiveness of the political system by bolstering party unity and discipline. From the late 1960s until the early 1990s, frequent ticket-splitting by American voters produced a persistent national Republican advantage in presidential elections that was matched by a stable Democratic majority in Congress, prompting widespread concerns among a later generation of academic experts that the apparent decline of party strength in the mass public would increase the frequency of partisan gridlock at the federal level.

Over the past quarter-century, a new party system has emerged – characterized by resurgent party loyalty in the electorate, closely balanced national competition in both presidential and congressional elections, and growing partisan polarization among candidates and elected officials – alongside the increasing proclivity of citizens in the Northeast and coastal West to favor the Democratic Party while electoral outcomes across the South and interior West have shifted decisively toward the Republicans. As a result, once-common scholarly dissatisfaction with the apparent weakening of the parties has given way in recent years to increasingly vociferous concerns that American politics has become excessively partisan and polarized, frustrating the pursuit of bipartisan compromise and jeopardizing the effective performance of the federal government. "The parties had less in common in terms of the territorial basis of their campaigns as the twenty-first century began than they did in the middle of the last century," observed James G. Gimpel and Jason E. Schuknecht in 2003. "This move toward rival geographic bases of support may coincide with the growing partisan intransigence in American politics."[15] These trends have only further intensified in the succeeding decades.

---

[15] James G. Gimpel and Jason E. Schuknecht, *Patchwork Nation: Sectionalism and Political Change in American Politics* (Ann Arbor: University of Michigan Press, 2003), p. 13.

The composition of the geographic coalitions represented by Democratic and Republican officeholders exerts a sufficiently strong influence on the relative size and policy positions of the two parties in government that achieving a full understanding of the latter requires careful examination of the former. Significant and enduring developments in elite-level politics seldom occur without parallel evolution in the behavior of American citizens as aggregated within the boundaries of electoral constituencies. The reliable sensitivity of candidates and elected officials to their own perceived self-interest suggests that fundamental, long-term changes in the nature of the party system – such as the advent of polarization – are likely to occur in tandem with changes in the political behavior of at least a significant fraction of the electorate.

At the same time, the effects of popular trends on the identities or actions of political leaders are not necessarily those consciously intended by voters (in the sense of a "mandate" from the electorate directing victorious politicians to implement specific policies). For example, residents of the South and interior West who increasingly replaced moderate Democrats with conservative Republicans in office over the past three decades did not necessarily do so in order to polarize the national parties, even though this change in their collective electoral preferences indeed produced that very effect. Moreover, the manner in which winner-take-all electoral rules systematically enhance the political power of popular majorities – since the supporters of a candidate placing first with 50 percent plus one of the vote (or even less, in a multicandidate race) receive 100 percent of the elected representation from the state or district – should caution against the assumption that electoral results in any particular section of the country can be easily interpreted as simply revealing the collective popular will of the entire citizenry within its boundaries.

By broadening the examination of the relationship between the preferences of voters and the polarization of politicians to encompass the crucial intermediating role played by the interaction between political geography and electoral institutions, this book arrives at a series of conclusions that can help to resolve ongoing debates over the nature of the contemporary party system. First, it demonstrates that geographic divisions in national elections have indeed become more distinct and more stable since the 1980s in a manner that increases the proportion of congressional districts, states, and even entire regions providing dependable support to the candidates of a single party. The emergence of these consistent partisan alignments on the national map has produced a series of close-fought presidential elections while endangering the electoral viability of moderate congressional candidates running for office outside their party's newfound territorial base. In addition, while some skeptics dispute the claim that the American public has become engaged in a "culture war" over government policies relating to such topics as religion and sexual morality, the rising salience of social issues in the electorate since the 1980s has in fact played a critical role in fueling the rise of regional differences in federal elections. The polarization of party leaders has thus been propelled to a significant extent by the changing electoral habits of American citizens.

Yet the formation of regionalized party coalitions over the past three decades cannot be interpreted as simply reflecting an equivalent ideological divide within the American public. The opinions of voters are seldom guaranteed to correspond directly to the behavior of public officials, in part because of the complex means by which the choices of individual citizens in the voting booth are translated into collective electoral outcomes. Winner-take-all methods of vote aggregation within geographically defined constituencies (such as states and congressional districts) magnify the electoral consequences of what can be, and often are, relatively modest variations in mass-level preferences from one place to the next. For example, the electorates of two particular states might in fact agree far more than they disagree about political matters, thus failing to exhibit significant mutual polarization, yet this limited aggregate difference can still produce sufficiently distinct electoral results to render one state safely Democratic (and therefore consistently fertile ground for the election of liberal officeholders) and the other securely Republican (and thus reliably represented by strong conservatives). Polarized *outcomes* do not require the presence of equally polarized *voters*.

Moreover, a political system in which votes are aggregated within the borders of states and congressional districts systematically bolsters the electoral impact of issues that divide voters along geographic boundaries compared to those on which opinion is dispersed in a more uniform manner. The spatial distribution of the public's views on various political matters substantially affects the strength and direction of their effect on the outcomes of elections. The contemporary regional pattern of party support evident in Figure 1.1 particularly reflects the increased partisan salience of social issues beginning in the 1990s, which divided the culturally liberal Northeast and coastal West from the culturally conservative South and interior West. Yet studies have shown that social issues remain less important than economic concerns in shaping the partisan preferences of individual voters, and the growing influence of cultural concerns over the voting behavior of the national electorate does not itself demonstrate the existence of a polarized public – even as it furthers the trend of collective ideological extremity among elected officials. In a political system based upon winner-take-all elections within multiple geographic subunits, even minor changes over time or differences across district, state, and regional boundaries in the mass public can easily produce much more significant effects on the size, composition, and ideological complexion of the parties in government.

The American electoral system is unlikely to allow an opaque barrier to be dropped between the opinions of voters and the actions of politicians – who, after all, remain sensitive to the perceived demands of the citizens whose support they require to gain office. At the same time, it does not guarantee that mass preferences are simply mirrored in proportional measure among elected leaders. The system instead resembles a lens that can magnify or even distort differences in voters' political views and identities as they are translated into electoral outcomes and the membership of elective offices. Partisan or ideological conflict between factions of political elites seldom entirely lacks a corresponding division within the voting public, but the degree of the conflict's severity and the relative sizes of the two engaged sides often differ at the mass and elite levels. Today, the electoral process converts the relatively muted reddish and bluish hues of the various state populations' collective partisan affiliations into the boldly contrasting colors of the contemporary regional alignment of election results, which in turn has produced two sets of partisan officeholders with sharply diverging policy agendas and little ability to find common political ground.

While they encompass definitional, methodological, and empirical disputes, current debates over the existence and extent of mass polarization also contain an important normative element. For scholars who argue that the American people remain collectively moderate in their views and pragmatic in their style, the presence of an increasingly polarized population of elected officials raises disconcerting questions about the health of representative democracy in the contemporary United States. According to this perspective, most citizens are harmless victims of a politically corrosive demand for ideological purity and knee-jerk partisanship visited upon political leaders by a small population of disproportionately influential activists. In contrast, experts who contend that the trend of polarization also extends to the mass public do not perceive such a troubling gap between the preferences of voters and the actions of politicians – though they may still acknowledge the ways in which the existence of strongly polarized parties can create serious impediments to the competent functioning of government, due to the multiplicity of institutional veto points within the American constitutional structure. To the extent that polarization is a threat to the political system, however, these analysts argue that voters indeed bear significant responsibility for its persistence.

Yet it is once again possible to identify a middle path between these differing perspectives. On one hand, the rise of social issues as a significant but secondary dimension of policy-related partisan conflict in the electorate has contributed to elite-level polarization somewhat accidentally, due to the fact that opinions on these matters happen to be distributed less evenly across regional lines than the positions on economic policy that still remain most central to the partisan preferences of individual citizens. Americans may not have intended to strongly push the parties in opposite ideological directions by increasingly voting on the basis of their cultural views, yet the regional variation in their attitudes exerts a disproportionate effect on the outcome of elections due to the prevalence of winner-take-all rules. At the same time, voters in every region of the nation have increasingly turned moderate incumbents out of office in favor of more party-loyal and ideologically doctrinaire candidates nominated by the partisan opposition. Most members of the public may not hold political opinions that are as polarized as those of most politicians, but they have still become less likely in recent years to reward candidates for taking relatively centrist positions even when they have had the opportunity to do so. Though voters are not wholly liable for the growth of partisan polarization, neither are they entirely innocent of it.

It is important to note points of intellectual agreement as well as areas of dissent. Broad consensus exists among scholars that American citizens have become more likely over the past few decades to align with the party that best fits their ideological orientation, thus markedly reducing the formerly sizable ranks of liberal Republicans and conservative Democrats – a phenomenon often characterized as partisan "sorting."[16] In what may well be a related development, few analysts dispute that party members (and nominal independents who express a consistent preference for one of the major parties) have become more likely to consistently support their favored party's nominees for federal office.[17] These trends, alone

---

[16] Matthew S. Levendusky, *The Partisan Sort: How Liberals Became Democrats and Conservatives Became Republicans* (Chicago: University of Chicago Press, 2009).

[17] Larry M. Bartels, "Partisanship and Voting Behavior, 1952–1996," *American Journal of Political Science* 44 (2000), pp. 35–50.

and in combination, would be expected to produce significant and stable geographic differences in electoral outcomes as long as the partisan and ideological affiliations of voters continued to vary from one place to the next. Because some regional populations are collectively and persistently more liberal or conservative – and, increasingly, more Democratic or Republican – than others, the emergence of geographically polarized electoral outcomes can be seen as a natural consequence of the increasingly well-sorted and party-loyal American public.

ONE ELECTORAL MAP, TWO PARTISAN MAJORITIES

It is difficult to fully evaluate the adequacy of democratic representation in the United States without taking into account the distinctive complexity of American-style democracy. The presidency is filled via the electoral college, an institution that has had the effect in recent elections of limiting the active campaign to a small fraction of the nation's territory and that can deny the office to the winner of the national popular vote. The House of Representatives is elected from a set of single-member districts drawn by state governments pursuing a variety of goals, from ensuring the fair representation of racial minority groups to pursuing partisan advantage via the intentional manipulation of district boundaries. The Senate guarantees each state an equal number of seats regardless of population, leading to the systematic overrepresentation of some voters, opinions, and interests at the expense of others. In both chambers, the party winning the most votes nationwide may fail to gain a majority of seats, while House and Senate terms of office are neither perfectly coincident with the presidency nor with each other – presenting obstacles to the ability of either party to gain and hold unified control of both elective branches of government.

Many of these abundant departures from pure democratic majoritarianism are embedded within the constitutional structure itself, ensuring the substantial influence of political geography over the translation of party votes into party seats – and seats into policy outcomes.[18] In presidential and congressional elections alike, the relative influence of an American citizen's ballot depends upon where it is cast. At a time in which many observers express substantial dissatisfaction with a political

[18] See Robert Dahl, *How Democratic Is the American Constitution?* (New Haven, CT: Yale University Press, 2001).

climate characterized by growing ideological polarization and incessant partisan warfare among the nation's elected officials, it is especially important to understand how the behavior of voters and politicians interacts with a multifaceted electoral system in which geography is a foundational element.

The existence of closely balanced national parties with distinct regional bases of support can also account for the otherwise curious continued frequency of divided partisan control of the federal government in an age of rampant party-loyal voting – a phenomenon that exacerbates the widely perceived drawbacks of party polarization by increasing the likelihood of legislative inaction and regular governing crises. Many critics lament the institutional dysfunction that frequently arises from the mismatch between a polarized party system and a constitutional apparatus that divides power among multiple independent actors. Ideologically unified parties, they argue, are inherently incompatible with a governmental system designed to force broad compromise among independent actors via a set of checks and balances.[19] Yet polarization encourages gridlock only if institutional control is divided between Democrats and Republicans. When a single party holds both Congress and the presidency, increasing cohesion would be expected to render governing stasis *less* likely today than it was in the age of more internally factionalized and less substantively coherent parties.

For several decades in the late twentieth century, a significant proportion of American voters split their tickets in federal elections, usually supporting Republican presidential nominees alongside Democratic congressional candidates. Divided government was therefore a natural occurrence of citizens' collective balloting preferences during a period of weakened party allegiance. Remarkably, however, the resurgence of mass party-line voting after the 1980s has not eliminated, or even sharply reduced, the prevalence of divided government. Of the current president's three most recent predecessors, both Bill Clinton (served 1993–2001) and Barack Obama (2009–2017) faced a Congress in which at least one house was controlled by the Republican opposition for all but the first two of their eight years in office, while Democratic opponents of George W. Bush (2001–2009) held a congressional majority in one or both chambers for

---

[19] See, for example, Thomas E. Mann and Norman J. Ornstein, *It's Even Worse Than It Looks: How the American Constitutional System Collided with the New Politics of Extremism* (New York: Basic Books, 2012).

nearly half (three years and six months) of his own two-term administration.[20] If congressional Republicans manage to retain majorities in the House and Senate after the 2018 midterm elections, the GOP will be the first party to keep control of both Congress and the White House for a full presidential term since the Democrats under Jimmy Carter (1977–1981), who took office four full decades ago.

To be sure, considerable partisan change has occurred in federal elections since the 1970s and 1980s. While frequent ticket-splitting once resulted in two durable national majorities – a strong cross-regional Republican advantage in presidential elections counteracted by an equally persistent coast-to-coast Democratic edge in congressional voting – the two parties have increasingly converged from opposite directions onto a single regional alignment that now dominates electoral outcomes for both branches of government. On balance, the emergence of geographic polarization worked to the net advantage of Democratic presidential nominees by providing the party a set of electorally safe states – including California, New York, New Jersey, Maryland, and Washington – that had previously been open to persuasion by Republican candidates, allowing Democrats to achieve regular success in competing for the White House in the years since Bill Clinton's 1992 election to the presidency.

In House and Senate elections, however, the contemporary regional divide has provided Republicans with a significant systematic benefit. After decades out of power in the legislative branch, the Republican Party gained majorities in both houses of Congress in 1994 due especially to significant electoral advances in the South and interior West, and subsequent elections have contributed to the party's popular ascendancy within what is now a formidable geographic base (the two regions collectively elect 44 percent of the House and 54 percent of the Senate). The long span of perpetual Democratic rule during the mid- to late twentieth century has given way to a new, very different partisan era in which Republicans have not only been able to compete effectively for control of both chambers, but have usually served as the majority party in Congress.

These two symmetrical shifts in opposite partisan directions – toward the Democratic Party in presidential voting, toward the Republicans in House and Senate elections – have thus combined to produce a single

[20] The Republican Party controlled the Senate between January and June 2001, when the decision of Senator James M. Jeffords of Vermont to switch parties shifted control of the chamber to the Democrats. Senate Republicans regained a majority in the midterm elections of 2002, ruling the chamber for the next four years.

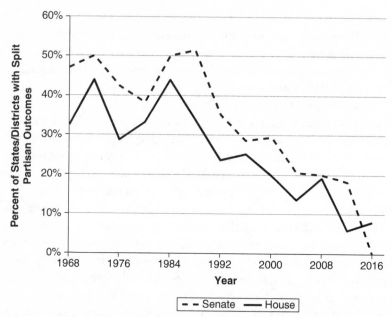

FIGURE 1.3. The decline of split partisan constituencies in presidential and congressional elections, 1968–2016.

national electoral map that predominates in contests for both branches. The vast majority of states and House districts now reliably align with the same political party in presidential and congressional elections alike. In the 2012 election, either the Democratic or Republican candidate placed first in both the presidential and Senate vote in 82 percent of the states holding Senate elections; in 2016, all 34 Senate races nationwide were won by the party carrying the state in the concurrent presidential election.[21] Elections for the lower chamber resulted in an equally strong association between presidential and congressional outcomes, with 94 percent of the nation's congressional districts voting the same way for president and the House of Representatives in 2012 and 92 percent doing so in 2016 – the highest rate in at least 50 years (see Figure 1.3).

Remarkably, this increasing convergence of electoral outcomes since the 1980s has still produced divided party government more often than unified control. One explanation for this apparent puzzle lies in the close partisan balance now evident in American politics; each party maintains

[21] Victorious independent candidates Angus King of Maine and Bernie Sanders of Vermont are counted as Democrats because they joined the Democratic caucus in the Senate.

a significant and comparably sized geographic base and is increasingly unable to make electoral inroads into the base of its rival. Even if the vast majority of constituencies support presidential and congressional candidates of the same party, the near-even electoral strength of the two parties nationwide can allow the relatively small proportion of politically ambivalent states or congressional districts to produce divided partisan control of the presidency and Congress even without universally high rates of split-ticket voting by American citizens. The usual losses incurred by the president's legislative allies in congressional midterm elections – since 1934, the party out of power in the executive branch has gained seats in the House of Representatives in every midterm except 1998 and 2002 – can be sufficient, when the parties are closely divided, to reverse partisan control of Congress, as occurred in the House in 2010, the Senate in 2014, and both chambers in 1994 and 2006.

But the interaction of the spatial location of partisan support in the mass public with the boundaries of geographic constituencies can also provide one party with a structural advantage in the transformation of votes into electoral victories. The lopsided Democratic leanings of voters residing in the populous metropolitan areas of the North and coastal West has benefited the party in presidential elections by rendering large states such as California, New York, New Jersey, and Washington safe territory for Democratic candidates. Yet the more efficient distribution of Republican voters across House districts, when combined with the disproportionate Republican tinge of small states that cast few electoral votes but receive equal representation in the Senate, provides the Republican Party with a pronounced advantage in competing for control of Congress. Although Barack Obama prevailed over Mitt Romney in the national popular vote by nearly 4 percentage points in 2012, he carried only a bare majority of states (26 of 50), while Hillary Clinton won the popular vote four years later over Donald Trump by more than 2 points while winning just 20 states. Romney and Trump also placed first in a majority of House districts nationwide (Romney 226, Obama 209; Trump 230, Clinton 205) despite their overall losses in the popular vote.

Recent election results also illustrate the link between the geographic polarization of the American electorate and the ideological polarization of the congressional parties. As a greater proportion of constituencies become dependable partisan territory, fewer incumbent officeholders face a strong electoral incentive to maintain a moderate voting record. Historically, the centrist bloc in Congress has been mostly populated by Democrats from the South (or interior West) and Republicans from the metropolitan North (or coastal West). Over the past three decades, both of these factions have been decimated by the deepening of regional divisions; even moderate candidates who separate themselves from the leadership of their party on key issues in order to "vote their district" (or state) have become increasingly endangered in congressional elections. In the 2012 Massachusetts Senate election, for example, incumbent Scott Brown lost his seat to the ardently liberal Harvard Law School professor Elizabeth Warren despite compiling a centrist voting record during his three years in Washington and maintaining considerable personal popularity (60 percent of Massachusetts voters reported holding a favorable impression of Brown on the day of the election, compared to just 38 percent who viewed him unfavorably, even as he was defeated by a margin of 8 percentage points).[22] Likewise, moderate Democratic senators Kay Hagan of North Carolina, Mark Pryor of Arkansas, Mary Landrieu of Louisiana, and Mark Begich of Alaska all suffered defeat in 2014 at the hands of sharply conservative Republican challengers who promised to move the congressional GOP even further to the ideological right.

This trend has occurred within both parties, but is especially damaging to Democratic congressional ambitions. The structural disadvantage faced by congressional Democrats due to the overconcentration of their partisan supporters within a minority of districts (in the House) and states (in the Senate) renders the party much more dependent than the opposition Republicans on the ability to compete effectively in marginal or even fundamentally unfriendly electoral constituencies. At times, Democratic candidates have achieved success by taking ideologically moderate positions in order to personally distance themselves from their party label and increase their popular appeal; this approach allowed congressional Democrats to retain electoral strength in the South for decades after the region had become strongly Republican in presidential elections, and the recruitment of numerous moderate "Blue Dog" candidates to run for Republican-held seats in 2006 and 2008 helped the party capitalize on a temporarily favorable electoral environment caused by the declining popularity of Republican president George W. Bush. Yet the heavy losses suffered by Democratic incumbents representing normally Republican-leaning districts and states during the Obama years suggest that partisan heterodoxy is only a partial and weakening defense against the tides of regional polarization. The subtraction of numerous moderates from the

---

[22] Figure from 2012 Massachusetts exit poll as compiled by NBC News, elections.nbcnews.com/ns/politics/2012/massachusetts/senate/.

Democratic congressional caucus has increased its internal unity over time, but Democratic leaders face a serious challenge in winning and maintaining control of either chamber without finding a way to bolster the reputation of their party in what are now consistently unwelcoming sections of the nation.

The same set of regional party coalitions whose emergence has proved a boon to Democratic presidential fortunes over the past two decades thus simultaneously provides the congressional Republican Party with electoral advantages that are even more favorable. Upon winning reelection in 2012, Obama struggled to work productively with a House of Representatives controlled by Republicans who perceived no electoral incentive to engage in bipartisan compromise; the substantial acrimony between the parties even resulted in a two-week shutdown of the federal government within a year of the election. Whether or not the American people had intended to distribute institutional power in this fashion – Democratic House candidates had in fact received more total votes nationwide than Republicans in 2012 – divided government emerged from the electoral system all the same, with significant consequences for both the direction of federal policy and the functioning of public institutions. The persistence of frequent gridlock in an age of party-line voting reflects the ease with which midterm shifts in congressional party control can occur in an age of national partisan parity, as well as the ability of a single electoral map to simultaneously produce two separate partisan majorities under the American system of government.

RESURGENT REGIONALISM IN A NATIONALIZED PARTY SYSTEM

In the twenty-first century, often characterized as a time in which local and regional distinctiveness has largely given way to nationalizing, and even globalizing, trends in economics, information, and culture, the emergence of significant and consistent regional differences in the voting behavior of the American electorate has occurred somewhat unexpectedly. But there is a consistency underlying this apparent contradiction. The American parties were once noted for their internal heterogeneity, especially in comparison to the much more disciplined party system evident in the United Kingdom and other western democracies – a trait that allowed both Democratic and Republican politicians to adapt their policy positions and priorities to the specific local communities where they sought votes, which sometimes required separating themselves from their party's national reputation or leadership. "Variations – sometimes subtle, sometimes blatant – in the fifty political cultures of the states yield considerable differences overall in what it means to be, or to vote, Democratic or Republican," wrote Nelson W. Polsby two decades ago. "These differences suggest that one may be justified in referring to the American two-party system as masking something more like a hundred-party system."[23]

Although the variations described by Polsby have not entirely disappeared – California Democrats still tend to be more liberal than West Virginia Democrats, while Utah Republicans are usually more conservative than Massachusetts Republicans – the success of both parties in maintaining a competitive electoral standing in every state and region has markedly declined over the past several decades. Neither West Virginia Democrats nor Massachusetts Republicans are elected to office as frequently as they once were, while California Democrats and Utah Republicans have correspondingly multiplied in number. As activists and financial donors on both sides pressure the national parties to move away from the political center, the willingness of voters to split tickets or cross party lines to support maverick candidates nominated by the opposition has declined, thus creating a feedback loop of increasing polarization. Recent presidential nominees have concluded that few voters are now genuinely open to persuasion, prompting strategists to invest much of their campaign resources and strategy in efforts to mobilize the loyal base of their party to turn out at high rates – an approach that has often inspired candidates to emphasize controversial social and cultural issues that they believe will inspire particular enthusiasm among their own popular supporters. With public opinion on these matters remaining especially variable across geographic context, each party's campaign message finds a considerably warmer reception in some areas of the country than in others, further reinforcing the pattern of entrenched regional distinctiveness in federal elections.

The American party system has thus simultaneously become more nationalized and more regionalized. The parties are more nationally cohesive than ever, with the parochial interests of specific localities and the personal reputations of individual candidates counting for much less than they once did in the minds of voters while party labels and leaders have correspondingly increased in importance. Yet this national

[23] Nelson W. Polsby, "The American Party System," in Alan Brinkley, Nelson W. Polsby, and Kathleen M. Sullivan, eds., *New Federalist Papers: Essays in Defense of the Constitution* (New York: W. W. Norton, 1997), pp. 37–44, at 40.

standardization has caused the popular appeal of both parties to become more geographically constrained. Unable to adjust as they once did to the varying political contexts of every corner of America, Democrats and Republicans have retreated to an opposing set of regional bastions, producing a pronounced rise in the geographic variation of party strength. It should hardly be surprising that as each party broadcasts an increasingly clear and consistent signal across the entire nation, the friendliness of the response has come to differ significantly from place to place.

While many contemporary political analysts lament the rise of polarization, the increasing internal unity of the parties is not wholly bereft of positive consequences. In particular, strengthened bonds of partisanship can foster a productive relationship between the president and Congress during periods of unified party government; both George W. Bush and Barack Obama achieved substantial legislative accomplishments during the periods of their presidential administrations when Congress was in the sympathetic hands of their fellow co-partisans. However, the rise of comparably sized Democratic and Republican regional strongholds has not only contributed to deepening national conflict, but has also allowed the frequent incidence of divided government to persist in an era of strong and mutually antagonistic parties. This new continental divide has persisted across a lengthening sequence of elections, offering little reason to expect that the United States will soon emerge from an era in which the rising tide of partisanship strains visibly against a constitutional structure intentionally designed to frustrate the centralization of political power in order to combat what James Madison called the "mischiefs of faction." The regionally divided electoral map is not merely a metaphor for our partisan, polarized, and oft-deadlocked contemporary politics, but is in fact one of its most essential hallmarks.

OUTLINE OF THE BOOK

Chapter 2 proceeds to describe the growth of regional polarization in greater detail, placing this development in the larger context of the ongoing debate over the existence and nature of mass polarization that has emerged both inside and outside the academic community over the past two decades. Chapter 3 traces the intersection of geography, partisanship, and ideology through the electoral history of the twentieth century in order to illustrate the evolution of American party politics from an era of internal regional factionalism, through a transitional period of inconsistent national partisan majorities across branches of government, to the current partisan age of ideological and regional polarization. Chapter 4 examines the abrupt reappearance of regional variation in the 1990s after several decades in which both partisan and geographic divisions had appeared to recede within the American electorate – a development that also had significant (though opposite) implications for the relative balance between the parties in presidential and congressional elections. It proceeds to investigate the cause of these unanticipated shifts in partisan electoral coalitions within the mass public, concluding that the most central explanatory factor was the elevated salience of social and cultural issues in the American electorate beginning in the early 1990s. Chapter 5 describes the implications of resurgent regionalism for the composition of Congress, demonstrating that it has contributed to the 40-year trend of polarization between the congressional parties. Chapter 6 explores the trend of geographic polarization below the state level, illustrating how the red-versus-blue regional divide partially reflects a growing partisan divergence between large population centers and small-town or rural areas; it also examines the Midwest, the single geographic region that has remained evenly divided between the parties and thus become increasingly pivotal in national elections. Finally, Chapter 7 considers the implications of the findings presented in the previous chapters for the future trajectory of American politics.

CHAPTER APPENDIX: A NOTE ON REGIONAL DEFINITIONS

There are no consensus definitions of geographic regions in the United States. The website FiveThirtyEight cleverly illustrated this fact in April 2014 by conducting an opinion poll of Americans who personally identified as midwesterners, asking them to name the states that they considered to be part of their home region. The results revealed little agreement among respondents. Illinois, the most frequently named state, was cited by only 81 percent of surveyed midwestern residents, while less than 60 percent included Ohio or Missouri in their regional definition. At the same time, some respondents named states as far east as Pennsylvania and as far west as Montana (Wyoming alone received votes from 10 percent of those surveyed).[24]

Even the South, America's most consciously discrete region, is difficult to identify with precision. The 11 states that formed the Confederacy prior

[24] Walt Hickey, "Which States Are in the Midwest?" *FiveThirtyEight*, April 29, 2014, fivethirtyeight.com/datalab/what-states-are-in-the-midwest/.

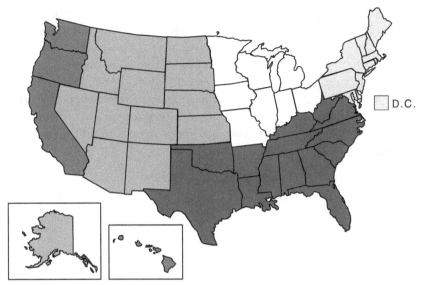

D.C.

FIGURE 1.4. The five political regions of the United States.

to the Civil War surely qualify as southern, even if more recent migration from outside the region has diluted the traditional cultural identity of the "New South" communities of South Florida, northern Virginia, and the Research Triangle of North Carolina. But restricting the South to ex-Confederate states omits West Virginia, Kentucky, and Oklahoma, which are sometimes ambiguously considered "border states," but can be viewed as culturally and politically southern. (Maryland and Delaware, also sometimes categorized as "border states," formerly shared some ideological similarities with the South proper, but today exhibit much more political affinity with the rest of the Northeast.)

Recognizing the impossibility of devising a classification system that reflects universal agreement, the analysis in this book assumes the presence of five distinct political regions in the United States, as denoted in Figure 1.4. The "interior West" refers to both the prairie states of the nation's midsection – Kansas, Nebraska, the Dakotas – and the Rocky Mountain states located between the Great Plains and the Pacific Coast; despite their topographical differences, these two areas exhibit a great deal of political coherence. The two noncontiguous American states are assigned to the continental region that they most closely resemble: the interior West for Alaska and the Pacific Coast for Hawaii.

Of course, more subtle political differences also exist inside these regions – such as those distinguishing the Deep South from the peripheral

South, New England from the Mid-Atlantic, and California from the Pacific Northwest – and even within individual states. But the large-scale changes in partisan geographic coalitions over the past several decades, during which the Northeast and Pacific Coast have become increasingly Democratic, the South and interior West have become increasingly Republican, and the Midwest has remained relatively competitive between the parties, are visible within nearly all of the individual states within each grouping, suggesting that the dynamics behind these shifts are fundamentally regional in nature.

2

Solid States: The Regional Bases
of the American Parties

DIVIDED CITIZENS OR DIVIDED ELECTIONS?

After the historically close and contested presidential election of 2000, a number of popular commentators interpreted visible regional differences in the electoral fortunes of the Democratic and Republican parties as representing direct proof of a deeply polarized citizenry torn in half by mutual cultural incompatibility – a claim that has been disputed by some academic studies. But as this chapter will show, the hardening partition of the American electoral map into corresponding regional zones of strong Democratic and Republican dominance is not simply a myth propagated by hyperbolic media pundits. In both presidential and congressional elections, voting patterns have become more sharply and consistently differentiated by region, separating the progressively Democratic-leaning Northeast and Pacific Coast from the increasingly Republican South and interior West. This trend has produced a historically unmatched degree of stability in electoral college results while reducing the proportion of actively contested battleground states to a small fraction of the nation.

Yet students of American politics should remain cautious about inferring the presence of widespread ideological extremity among individual voters from these broader collective outcomes. Relatively modest differences in the underlying distribution of voter preferences from one place to another can produce much larger effects in the results of winner-take-all elections, potentially leading observers to exaggerate the degree to which geographic subpopulations differ in their collective political views. While the partisan divergence on the electoral map has increased significantly since the 1980s, transforming states and even entire regions that were once open to persuasion by both parties into safe bastions for either Democratic or Republican candidates, this trend does not reflect the emergence of overwhelming political consensus within either Red or Blue America.

It is critical, therefore, to draw a distinction between the ideological polarization of individual voters and the regional polarization of aggregate partisan alignments. Analysts need not agree that the political preferences of citizens vary dramatically from one location to the next in order to acknowledge the emergence of significant and durable regional differences in electoral results – which in turn hold critical implications for the geographic coalitions and campaign strategies of the parties in both presidential and congressional elections. Regardless of whether American citizens have become sharply divided in their policy views, the outcomes visible on the electoral map have entered an era marked by unique stability and relative disparity, with a declining number of competitive states holding a narrow national balance of power between the two major parties.

THE COINING OF A COLORFUL VOCABULARY

Vice President Al Gore and Governor George W. Bush of Texas entered the presidential election of 2000 in a national dead heat, marking the first contest in 20 years in which prior public opinion surveys could not predict the winner with confidence. Because this uncertainty lent an unusually high level of interest and excitement to the reporting of vote returns on election night, producers for the multiple networks offering live television news coverage felt competitive pressure to announce projections of the results as quickly as possible, calculating that an aggressive approach to forecasting candidate victories in key states would attract considerable attention from viewers.[1] When the media-funded Voter News Service exit poll suggested the presence of a narrow Democratic lead in Florida, an outcome that would virtually clinch a national electoral college majority for the incumbent party, networks responded by hurriedly declaring that Gore had indeed carried the state, even though voting hours had yet to end in the portion of the Florida Panhandle that fell within the Central Time Zone. But Bush continued to outperform the exit poll results in the

[1] Joan Konner, "The Case for Caution: This System Is Dangerously Flawed," *Public Opinion Quarterly* 67 (Spring 2003), pp. 5–18.

actual Florida vote count as the night wore on, maintaining an unexpectedly steady lead that eventually convinced the news media first to retract predictions of a Gore victory and then, after it had become clear based on the closely divided outcome in other states that the allocation of Florida's 25 electoral votes would in fact decide the presidency, to pronounce Bush the winner instead. Gore had even telephoned his opponent to concede the election before a late-reporting set of heavily Democratic precincts in South Florida nearly erased Bush's statewide advantage, requiring another round of retractions in the early hours of the next morning as it became clear that the final result could not be determined at least until election officials in Florida counted any remaining absentee ballots and double-checked their initially reported vote returns.

The process of resolving the outcome in Florida, and thus determining the identity of the next president, ultimately stretched into a five-week ordeal of confusion and conflict over flawed ballot designs, error-prone voting technology, nonuniform standards for divining voter intent from ambiguous physical evidence, and multiple legal battles between the candidates in both state and federal courts. Florida officials ultimately awarded the state's 25 electors to Bush by a certified popular margin of 537 votes out of nearly 6 million cast, after the U.S. Supreme Court interceded on December 12 to prohibit the further reexamination of contested ballots based on the equal protection clause of the Fourteenth Amendment to the Constitution.[2] For many outraged Democrats, the Court's five-to-four ruling in the case of *Bush v. Gore* represented an unfounded judicial intervention in the election process. Their view of Bush as an illegitimate president was reinforced by Gore's first-place finish in the national popular vote, by a margin of 48.4 percent to 47.9 percent, even as Bush won 271 electoral votes to Gore's 266 – the first unambiguous split decision between the popular and electoral vote in the previous 112 years.[3] Republicans responded by characterizing their opponents as sore losers who refused to acknowledge Bush's officially declared victory and who had benefited from their own share of favorable decisions by a friendly Florida Supreme Court dominated by Democratic appointees.

[2] *Bush v. Gore*, 531 U.S. 98 (2000).
[3] Gore was entitled to 267 electoral votes based on his state-level victories, but one elector from the District of Columbia declined to cast a vote for him or any other candidate. Some scholars contend that the 1960 election should also be considered a historical case in which the winner of the national popular vote was denied the presidency, due to the complexity involved in counting popular votes cast for individual electors in the state of Alabama. See George C. Edwards III, *Why the Electoral College Is Bad for America*, 2nd edition (New Haven, CT: Yale University Press, 2011), pp. 67–70.

In this atmosphere of bitter partisan ill-feeling, many news media personalities seized on the visually arresting regional configuration of candidate support evident in the election returns as representing not only a manifestation of two distinct party coalitions but also a compelling symbol of a deeply divided America (see Figure 2.1). Referring to the colors used by television networks to denote the states' partisan alignments on what had become an oft-displayed map of the electoral college results, late-night comedian David Letterman joked several days after the election that the disputed outcome could be settled by means of a compromise that would "make George W. Bush president of the red states and Al Gore head of the blue ones."[4] The terms "red states" and "blue states" immediately entered the American political lexicon amid a growing belief that the nation had split into two mutually alienated halves, with conflict over the Florida recount and the *Bush v. Gore* decision seeming to represent merely the latest battle in an intensifying partisan war. Six years of frequent clashes between departing Democratic president Bill Clinton and a Republican-controlled Congress had reached a crescendo with Clinton's impeachment by the House of Representatives in late 1998 as a result of independent counsel Kenneth Starr's investigation of the Monica Lewinsky affair (Clinton remained in office after Republicans failed to muster the two-thirds vote necessary to convict him in the Senate). More broadly, the rising prominence of social and cultural issues as an additional dimension of partisan disagreement over the course of the 1990s added a particularly sharp edge to political rhetoric in America, with liberals and conservatives increasingly accusing each other of immorality or intolerance.

Once the widespread perceptions of an increasingly polarized nation were apparently confirmed by the geographic configuration of mass partisan preferences depicted in Figure 2.1, journalists began to produce an avalanche of think pieces attempting to identify the salient attributes supposedly distinguishing the inhabitants of red states from their blue-state counterparts. Much of this analysis took the form of amateur ethnography, typified by a 2001 *Atlantic Monthly* article by future *New York Times* columnist David Brooks entitled "One Nation, Slightly Divisible."[5] Brooks, a conservative residing in the mostly liberal enclave

[4] Paul Farhi, "Elephants Are Red, Donkeys Are Blue," *Washington Post*, November 2, 2004, p. Co1.
[5] David Brooks, "One Nation, Slightly Divisible," *Atlantic Monthly* 288 (December 2001), pp. 53–65.

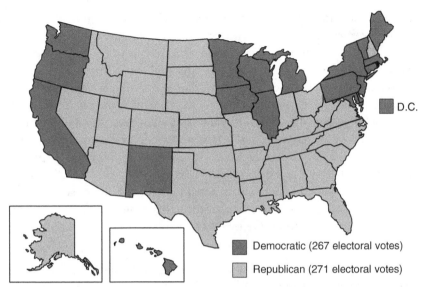

FIGURE 2.1. The 2000 presidential election (the original "red-versus-blue" map).

of Montgomery County, Maryland, characterized the apparent partisan divide between the Democratic-leaning coasts and the Republican-aligned heartland as predominantly reflecting different sensibilities, cultural tastes, and even recreational activities:

> Everything that people in my neighborhood do without motors, the people in Red America do with motors. We sail; they powerboat. We cross-country ski; they snowmobile. We hike; they drive ATVs. We have vineyard tours; they have tractor pulls …

> Different sorts of institutions dominate life in these two places. In Red America churches are everywhere. In Blue America Thai restaurants are everywhere. In Red America they have QVC, the Pro Bowlers Tour, and hunting. In Blue America we have NPR, Doris Kearns Goodwin, and socially conscious investing. In Red America the Walmarts are massive, with parking lots the size of state parks. In Blue America the stores are small but the markups are big.

Though largely anecdotal (and occasionally factually inaccurate),[6] Brooks's account of the red-versus-blue divide rang true with many readers. Fascination with the map's distinctively memorable chromatic pattern of partisan loyalties inspired commentators to draw similar conclusions about the dissimilar social identities and political concerns of

---

[6] See Sasha Issenberg, "Boo-Boos in Paradise," *Philadelphia*, May 15, 2006, www .phillymag.com/articles/booboos-in-paradise/.

Democratic and Republican identifiers by relying upon popular impressions of American regional cultures. Most commonly, these generalizations took the form of a perceived conflict pitting a North and urban West supposedly populated by highly educated and well-to-do social liberals, who voted Democratic to express their secular cosmopolitanism, against a South and rural West inhabited by salt-of-the-earth traditionalists who shared the God-and-country ethos of the Republican Party. As Paul Farhi of the *Washington Post* observed, "Red and blue ... have become more than just the conveniently contrasting colors of TV graphics. They've become shorthand for an entire sociopolitical worldview."[7]

Dante Chinni and James Gimpel noted journalists' widespread tendency after the 2000 election to suggest that the partisan and ideological orientations of regional electorates reflected an increasingly strong association in American life between political opinions and consumer preferences:

When we say "red" or "blue" in the context of American culture, it conjures up a set of stereotypes. Typical Red America makers might include watching [conservative television host] Glenn Beck, hating NPR, opposing gay marriage, getting coffee at the doughnut shop, drinking beer, eating hamburgers, living in the country, and standing up for tradition – most of the time. Typical Blue America markers might include watching [liberal comedian] Jon Stewart, hating Fox News, supporting gay marriage, getting coffee at the coffee shop, drinking wine, eating tofu burgers, living in the city, and standing up for change – most of the time.[8]

Brooks had similarly suggested the presence of a growing political clash between the hip and the square, though he ultimately concluded that Red America and Blue America shared important similarities as well as differences. Others perceived a more serious rift. Conservative journalist Michael Barone argued in a postelection essay that "the two Americas apparent in the ... 2000 election are two nations of different faiths. One is observant, tradition-minded, moralistic. The other is unobservant, liberation-minded, relativist ... In early 21st Century America the divide is not economic but cultural. But there are two nations, of almost equal size, between which there is little intercourse and sympathy, which are ignorant of each other's habits, thoughts, and feelings ... living together, uncomfortably."[9]

---

[7] Farhi, "Elephants Are Red, Donkeys Are Blue."

[8] Dante Chinni and James Gimpel, *Our Patchwork Nation* (New York: Gotham Books, 2010), p. 2.

[9] Michael Barone, "The 49% Nation," in Michael Barone and Richard E. Cohen, eds., *The Almanac of American Politics, 2002* (Washington, DC: National Journal, 2001), pp. 21–45, at 28, 29.

The belief that the United States had been irreconcilably torn by rising cultural disharmony into two mutually hostile segments of staunchly opposite partisanship thus found validity in the eyes of many prominent political commentators. As this view gained popularity in the news media, political scientists inevitably began to subject it to more systematic – and sometimes critical – examination. The conclusion that contemporary electoral outcomes have revealed the presence of deep ideological or moral divisions within the contemporary American electorate has not won the broad acceptance among academic scholars of public opinion that it has received from popular pundits in the years following the 2000 election. Instead, substantial disagreement remains over the nature and extent of polarization in the mass public, nearly two decades after the original "red-versus-blue" electoral map convinced many other observers that the American polity had become deeply fragmented along regional lines.

POLITICAL SCIENCE RESPONDS: IS AMERICA ACTUALLY "PURPLE"?

One frequent scholarly rejoinder to widespread popular claims of a severely divided America emphasized the narrow margins of victory in some states, which could thus be properly classified as neither solidly Democratic nor securely Republican. The simple binary categories of "red" and "blue" failed to distinguish states that overwhelmingly favored one party or the other from states in which the victorious candidate won by a nose, thus exaggerating the apparent magnitude of the geographic divide. Surely no unscalable wall of reciprocal cultural incompatibility separated Ohio (50 percent for Bush, 46 percent for Gore) from neighboring Pennsylvania (50 percent for Gore, 46 percent for Bush), while Florida had been so evenly split in 2000 that its status as a red or blue state fell within a margin of uncertainty that required weeks of further examination and ultimately invited controversial judicial intervention.

How many states were sufficiently competitive between the parties so as to be appropriately considered "purple" rather than fundamentally red or blue? According to some academics, most of the nation should be so classified. "The great divide across the American states is not really much of a divide at all," argued Stephen Ansolabehere, Jonathan Rodden, and James M. Snyder Jr. in their 2006 essay "Purple America."[10] The authors

[10] Stephen Ansolabehere, Jonathan Rodden, and James M. Snyder Jr., "Purple America," *Journal of Economic Perspectives* 20 (Spring 2006), pp. 97–118 (quote at 99).

constructed several measures of partisan balance at the state level and found a long-term decline in single-party dominance over the course of the twentieth century, concluding that "states do not sort cleanly into Democratic and Republican camps.... The quest to understand the differences between red and blue states, then, seems to us to be on the wrong track."[11]

A more prominent scholarly attack on popular claims of rampant polarization within the American public came from the pen of Morris P. Fiorina. In *Culture War? The Myth of a Polarized America*, written in collaboration with Samuel J. Abrams and Jeremy C. Pope and pointedly dedicated to the "tens of millions of mainstream Americans who have never heard of the culture war," Fiorina argued that the newly ubiquitous portrait of a national electorate riven by vicious political conflict, especially over social issues such as abortion and gay rights, was almost entirely mistaken.[12] Echoing the pioneering work of Philip E. Converse, who demonstrated in a well-known 1964 essay that ideology played a limited role in structuring the political preferences of most Americans, Fiorina described the mass public as mostly comprised of philosophically moderate and stylistically pragmatic citizens who had become alienated from a political elite class increasingly dominated by belligerent extremists on both sides.[13] He specifically disputed the popular red-versus-blue characterization of contemporary electoral politics, finding "numerous similarities between red and blue state voters, some differences, and a few notable differences, but little that calls to mind the portrait of a culture war between the states," and arguing that "many states are marginal and not securely in the camp of one party or the other."[14] Instead, Fiorina held the news media responsible for exaggerating the degree of political discord within the mass electorate in order to attract popular attention and market share.

To be sure, Fiorina's view has not remained unchallenged among scholars. In *The Disappearing Center* (2010), Alan I. Abramowitz argued that American voters have in fact become more ideologically polarized over time, especially within the most politically sophisticated and participatory stratum of the electorate: "engaged partisans now display more

[11] Ibid. at pp. 113, 114.
[12] Morris P. Fiorina, with Samuel J. Abrams and Jeremy C. Pope, *Culture War? The Myth of a Polarized America*, 3rd edition (New York: Pearson Longman, 2011).
[13] Philip E. Converse, "The Nature of Belief Systems in Mass Politics," in David E. Apter, ed., *Ideology and Discontent* (New York: Free Press, 1964), pp. 206–260.
[14] Fiorina, *Culture War?* pp. 17, 9.

consistent views across a range of issues than in the past, with Democratic identifiers increasingly clustered on the left side of the ideological spectrum and Republicans on the right."[15] In a related study, Abramowitz and Kyle L. Saunders also contended that mass polarization has become apparent in increasingly divergent voting patterns among state electorates. "Fiorina claims ... that the differences between red states and blue states have been greatly exaggerated," they wrote. "However, the evidence ... shows that states have become much more sharply divided along party lines since the 1960s: red states have been getting redder while blue states have been getting bluer."[16]

On the whole, however, political scientists as a group were less likely to embrace the chief tenets of the "polarized America" theme in news media analysis after 2000 than they were to assume the familiar role of skeptical academics debunking conventional wisdom propagated by the political press. Yet the unusual persistence of the red-versus-blue arrangement of regional partisanship in subsequent presidential elections – despite a steady parade of new events, issues, and candidates across the political stage over the succeeding years – seems to vindicate the belief that the outcome of the 2000 contest indeed reflected a notable and enduring evolution in the electoral constituencies of the two parties, even if declarations of an all-out "culture war" were arguable exaggerations. The apparent contraction of the campaign battleground to an ever-smaller share of the nation, in concert with an increasing convergence between presidential and congressional election outcomes, likewise challenges the assumptions of mass polarization skeptics that state-level partisan differences are largely insignificant and that the geographic divide in American politics is merely an invention of media talking heads prone to gratuitous overstatement. Evidence confirms that the vast majority of House districts, states, and even regions have settled firmly into the pattern of providing reliable support for either the Democratic or Republican Party in both presidential and congressional contests. Even if American citizens are not collectively polarized, American elections surely have become so – reflecting the critical importance of the institutional structure under which they are held.

---

[15] Alan I. Abramowitz, *The Disappearing Center: Engaged Citizens, Polarization, and American Democracy* (New Haven, CT: Yale University Press, 2010), p. 7.

[16] Alan I. Abramowitz and Kyle L. Saunders, "Is Polarization a Myth?" *Journal of Politics* 70 (April 2008), pp. 542–555, at 548.

HOW WINNER-TAKE-ALL ELECTIONS MAGNIFY GEOGRAPHIC POLARIZATION

Every democratic system must adopt rules governing the process by which the ballots cast by individual citizens determine the composition of elective institutions. For federal elections in the United States, the fundamental electoral unit is the geographically defined constituency: votes are aggregated at the level of the state or congressional district, and the distribution of popular support among candidates within these discrete boundaries determines the selection of senators, representatives, and members of the electoral college. Both presidential and congressional elections employ the winner-take-all principle (also known as "first-past-the-post"), with the candidate attracting the highest number of votes within a particular state or district deemed the sole winner of the seat (or, in the case of presidential elections, of all of the state's electoral votes) – even if he or she prevailed by the margin of a single ballot or failed to receive an overall majority of votes cast.[17]

The United States employs this system for two historical reasons: its colonial heritage (winner-take-all elections are a common legacy of British rule) and the presence of a constitutional framework in which states serve as the key constituent elements. The U.S. Constitution guarantees states equal representation in the Senate regardless of population, while state governments maintain the authority to draw the district boundaries used to elect the House of Representatives as long as they respect the federal requirements of equal population and racial fairness. Even the unitary national office of the presidency is filled via the electoral college, a federalist institution that awards victory to the candidate capturing a majority of state electors, whether or not he or she also receives a plurality of the national popular vote.

In American elections, therefore, the weight of a citizen's ballot varies by geographic context. (This attribute distinguishes single-member-district/winner-take-all rules from proportional representation systems, which – in their purest form – simply aggregate votes at the national level, rendering the specific locations of voters irrelevant to electoral outcomes.) Geography thus serves as a key component of the process of democratic representation, intermediating between the votes of individual Americans and the selection of congressional representatives and presidential electors.

---

[17] As noted in Chapter 1, Maine and Nebraska partially allocate electoral votes by congressional district.

The use of winner-take-all electoral rules within geographically defined constituencies fundamentally shapes the practice of democratic politics. For example, it reinforces the American two-party system by rendering minor parties vulnerable to the "spoiler effect" (which occurs when a third party disproportionately draws support from one of the major parties, thereby increasing the probability that the other major party will receive the most votes).[18] But one of the most distinctive consequences of winner-take-all systems is their tendency to magnify the victory margins of partisan majorities. Legislative elections held under winner-take-all rules normally reward the prevailing party with a disproportionately large share of seats compared to its proportion of the aggregate popular vote; under the "cube rule" of approximation, a legislative party receiving 55 percent of the total votes should normally expect to capture about 65 percent of the seats, depending on the specific distribution of votes across districts.[19]

Because a presidential candidate who carries a state even by a single ballot still receives all of the state's electoral votes, winning multiple states by slender popular margins can allow candidates to accumulate sizable majorities in the electoral college. For this reason, victorious presidential aspirants nearly always receive a much larger percentage of the total electoral vote than the national popular vote, as displayed in Figure 2.2. In 2012, for example, Barack Obama won the two-party popular vote by 4 percentage points over Mitt Romney (52 percent to 48 percent), but his narrow victories in nine of the election's ten battleground states allowed him to prevail in the electoral college by 24 points (62 percent to 38 percent). As the proportion of the popular vote received by the winning candidate increases, his or her share of the electoral vote rises by an even greater amount. Ronald Reagan's 1984 reelection campaign succeeded in translating 59 percent of the popular vote into a remarkable 98 percent of the electoral vote, thanks to the relatively even geographic distribution of his popular support across the nation.

Winner-take-all rules therefore reliably generate electoral outcomes that are much more decisive at the aggregate level of presidential electors and congressional seats than in the relative shares of the raw popular

[18] This relationship was famously identified by Maurice Duverger, *Political Parties: Their Organization and Activity in the Modern State*, 2nd revised edition (London: Methuen and Co., 1959).

[19] M. G. Kendall and A. Stuart, "The Law of Cubic Proportion in Elections Results," *British Journal of Sociology* 1 (1950), pp. 183–196.

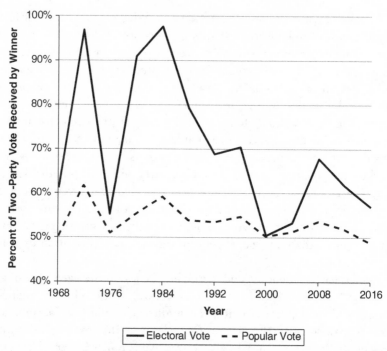

FIGURE 2.2. Popular and electoral vote winning percentages in U.S. presidential elections, 1968–2016.

vote. In the original "red-versus-blue" presidential election of 2000, George W. Bush received a full 44 percent of the popular vote in the 20 states that voted unanimously in the electoral college for Al Gore, while Gore attracted an identical 44 percent in the 30 states that awarded all of their electors to Bush – reflecting a significant degree of underlying political heterogeneity concealed by the traditional practice of allocating electoral votes to statewide winners in a unanimous bloc. Rather than assigning each geographic unit a single color representing the first-place candidate, some analysts generated alternative electoral maps in which states or counties were colored by mixing red and blue hues in proportion to the relative vote shares of the parties, arguing that this alternative depiction of the results – which produced large bands of subtly shaded purple – represented a more accurate depiction of the political preferences of the American electorate.[20] From this perspective, the winner-take-all

[20] For example, the election maps generated by Robert J. Vanderbei at www.princeton.edu/~rvdb/JAVA/election2012/; see also John Sides, "Most Americans Live in Purple America,

rules imposed by electoral institutions in the United States serve mainly to distort the true nature of mass partisan alignments, acting as a reality-distorting lens that systematically magnifies the geographic variation in citizens' political orientations. When even a modest difference in the relative popularity of the candidates from one state to another can produce diametrically opposite partisan outcomes, the presence of a deeply divided voting public cannot be confidently deduced merely from the fact that some states happen to land in the red column and others in the blue.

Such analyses provide a valuable corrective to popular accounts of electoral politics that risk overstating the severity of the partisan divide between the residents of Red and Blue America. However, the complexity of the relationship between individual behavior and aggregate results allows for congressional districts, states, and regions to produce strong dissimilarities in their collective partisan alignments even in the absence of correspondingly large differences among voters. Even scholars who argue that the American electorate fails to exhibit significant geographic variation in its collective political views occasionally concede that the nature of electoral institutions can still produce highly consequential differences in the likelihood of partisan victory from one district, state, or region to another. For example, while Matthew S. Levendusky and Jeremy C. Pope contended in 2011 that "there is a great deal of common ground" in the policy views of red- and blue-state residents, directly challenging Abramowitz's portrayal of an increasingly divided electorate, they also acknowledged that "single-member, simple-plurality [electoral constituencies] and the like mean that even small shifts in *opinion* can translate into large differences in *outcomes*."[21]

This distinction can be illustrated by comparing South Carolina, a representative red state, to Oregon, an equally typical blue state. Most political practitioners would characterize South Carolina as deeply conservative; it is widely known as the home of Bob Jones University, a fundamentalist Christian college that serves as a common stop on the campaign trail for Republican presidential candidates and famously forbids its students from dancing, holding hands, listening to popular music,

Not Red or Blue America," The Monkey Cage blog, *Washington Post* website, November 12, 2013, www.washingtonpost.com/blogs/monkey-cage/wp/2013/11/12/most-americans-live-in-purple-america-not-red-or-blue-america/.

21 Matthew S. Levendusky and Jeremy C. Pope, "Red States vs. Blue States: Going Beyond the Mean," *Public Opinion Quarterly* 75 (Summer 2011), pp. 227–248, at 243, 244 (emphasis in original).

or going to the movies. (An even more controversial rule banning inter-racial dating on campus was repealed in 2000.)[22] Oregon, in contrast, maintains a popular reputation as a haven of unchecked liberalism – a stereotype reinforced by the television comedy *Portlandia*, which por-trays the state as mostly populated by bohemian artists, radical femi-nists, animal rights activists, tree-hugging environmentalists, and other stridently leftist character types.

Yet neither state's electorate is politically homogeneous. Hillary Clinton received 43 percent of South Carolina's two-party popular vote in the 2016 presidential election, while Donald Trump won 44 percent of the two-party vote in Oregon. The simple assumption that a South Carolinian encountered at random was a staunch Republican, or that a representatively selected Oregonian was likewise a loyal Democrat, would result in an erroneous inference nearly nine times out of 20, and coloring each state in proportion to the relative popular vote shares received by the two parties produces two similar shades of purple rather than sharply contrasting hues of crimson and sapphire. Analysts who argue that the American public is not significantly polarized along geographic lines might point out that the partisan voting gap between these archetypical red and blue states amounted in 2016 to about 13 percentage points out of a possible 100, suggesting that the two statewide electorates overlap much more than they diverge.

But a difference of this magnitude, however modest it may seem in the abstract, still holds significant practical consequences for aggregate polit-ical outcomes. Oregon has allocated its electoral votes to the Democratic candidate in every presidential election since 1988, while South Carolina has voted Republican in every election since 1980. The partisan gap between the two states extends to other races as well. Oregon's con-gressional delegation has consistently contained more Democrats than Republicans since 1996, with Democrats holding both Senate seats and four of the state's five House seats after every election since 2008. South Carolina, in contrast, has elected a majority-Republican delegation to every Congress since 1994; both senators and six of its seven representa-tives are now affiliated with the GOP. Although the minority party in both states receives support from a substantial fraction of the voting public and can occasionally compete seriously for a few political offices, it is hardly an oversimplification to characterize Oregon as essentially

[22] Reg Henry, "Watch Out for a School Named Bob," *Pittsburgh Post-Gazette*, March 14, 2000, old.post-gazette.com/columnists/20000314reg.asp.

Democratic – a "blue state" – in electoral terms, and South Carolina as likewise fundamentally "red" and Republican. Were the dominant party in each state to instead receive 80, 90, or even 100 percent of the popular vote, the outcomes of state elections would not substantially differ from their current partisan alignment.

Neither presidential candidate in 2004, 2008, 2012, or 2016 viewed the outcome in Oregon or South Carolina as sufficiently uncertain to devote time or resources to building an active campaign in the state, suggesting that an expected popular victory margin within a particular geographic constituency on the order of 10 percentage points is more than large enough to render it politically secure for the prevailing party. Under winner-take-all rules, only a few percentage points in a candidate's expected share of the vote can separate hotly contested electoral battlegrounds such as Ohio and Florida from partisan strongholds openly conceded to one candidate or the other. Modern campaigns armed with sophisticated techniques for measuring and analyzing public opinion use these tools to estimate a state's potential competitiveness, directing their finite resources solely to the places where they believe an active mobilization effort might actually influence the order in which the candidates finish.

The divergent electoral outcomes in the two states routinely lead to the installation of officeholders with very different partisan affiliations, ideological positions, and styles of governing. Since 2009, Oregon has been represented in the U.S. Senate by two Democrats, Jeff Merkley and Ron Wyden, who ranked as the 12th and 24th most liberal members of the Senate in 2015–2016, according to the Poole-Rosenthal first-dimension common-space NOMINATE scores.[23] According to the same measure, South Carolina was represented by the nation's 7th and 33rd most conservative senators, Republicans Tim Scott and Lindsey Graham; Scott's predecessor Jim DeMint was also a prominent conservative purist who left the Senate in December 2012 to assume the presidency of the Heritage Foundation, an influential conservative think tank in Washington. Oregon's five-member delegation to the House of Representatives includes two members of the left-wing Congressional Progressive Caucus (Suzanne Bonamici of Beaverton and Peter DeFazio of Springfield) as well as a third leading liberal Democrat, Earl Blumenauer of Portland. In contrast, South Carolina's recent contingent of representatives has

[23] NOMINATE scores developed by Keith T. Poole and Howard Rosenthal; available at www.voteview.com. Wyden was tied with Chris Murphy of Connecticut.

been mostly comprised of Republicans sympathetic to the insurgent conservative Tea Party movement. Trey Gowdy of Spartanburg served as the aggressive chair of the select House committee that investigated the Obama administration's handling of the attack on the U.S. consulate in Benghazi, Libya; Mick Mulvaney of Indian Land was one of a handful of hard-line conservatives who refused to vote for fellow Republican John Boehner for speaker of the House in 2013 because they viewed Boehner as insufficiently loyal to party principles (Mulvaney left the House in early 2017 to become director of the Office of Management and Budget in the Trump administration); and Joe Wilson of Charleston is best known outside of his home district for shouting "You lie!" at Obama in the midst of a presidential address to a joint session of Congress in September 2009, causing a stir in the news media but winning Wilson widespread admiration from conservative activists. A few percentage points' worth of variation in the partisan alignment of a state can thus make the difference between electing a representative who provides a president with loyal support and one who subjects him to public heckling.

Since the 2000 presidential election, many political pundits have cited the perceived division of the American electoral map into sections of corresponding Democratic and Republican control as a highly visible indicator of a strongly and increasingly polarized voting public, while scholars who view mass polarization as a myth have likewise suggested that much of the nation is neither red nor blue but instead politically "purple." Yet these examples demonstrate the importance of conceptually and analytically distinguishing the ideological polarization of individual citizens from the partisan polarization of aggregate electoral outcomes. Due to the amplifying effects of winner-take-all rules, relatively minor differences in the preferences of voters can and do produce much larger effects on the macro-level partisan alignments of particular states or regions – with significant implications for electoral competition, party balance, and the behavior of public officeholders. Although Oregonians and South Carolinians may share considerable collective common ground, the two states are justifiably viewed by presidential candidates and congressional representatives alike as firmly attached to opposite parties with sharply contrasting ideological commitments.

A first-past-the-post electoral system in which votes are aggregated at the level of multiple separate geographic constituencies is thus fertile institutional ground for the emergence of polarized parties. Once a single party achieves a majority of sufficient size to render a particular state or district electorally predictable, there is little incentive for party leaders to encourage the nomination of moderate candidates for office or otherwise make concessions to the views of the remainder of the electorate. Winner-take-all rules are therefore especially insensitive to the preferences of popular minorities residing within the geographic boundaries where the election is held; even minority party blocs of significant size can be effectively deprived of electoral representation if the numerical advantage of the majority is sufficiently secure.

Because the numerical threshold for an electoral constituency to attain safe party status is as low as 55 percent of the popular vote, even seemingly minor increases over time in the popular margins separating victorious candidates from their unsuccessful opponents within particular states or districts can lead to a much larger rise in the proportion of the United States considered reliably Democratic or Republican, with a corresponding decline in the geographic scope of electoral competition. As the next section demonstrates, such a trend indeed has occurred over the past three decades of presidential elections. An increasingly entrenched geographic configuration of red and blue partisan alignments has emerged during this period, gaining ascendance at the expense of a shrinking span of "purple" territory that remains open to the entreaties of either party.

THE PARTISAN POLARIZATION OF STATES IN RECENT PRESIDENTIAL ELECTIONS

The validity of the red-versus-blue account of contemporary electoral politics rests upon the testable assumption that most American states have become more closely allied with a single party over time. One indicator of partisan dominance previously employed by analysts is the average state-level popular vote margin separating the two major-party presidential nominees. Figure 2.3 displays this measure for each of the 13 elections between 1968 and 2016. While the elections of the past two decades produced a clear upward trend, average state margins in recent elections still fell short of the peaks reached in the elections of 1972 (29 points) and 1984 (23 points). Some scholars have concluded from similar measures of electoral competitiveness that the United States has not, in fact, become more politically divided. For example, Edward L. Glaeser and Bryce A. Ward recently found "no evidence of a general downward trend in the number of swing states" (defined as states in which the electoral margin between the candidates failed to exceed 10 percentage points), proceeding to dismiss the claim that the nation is now split into

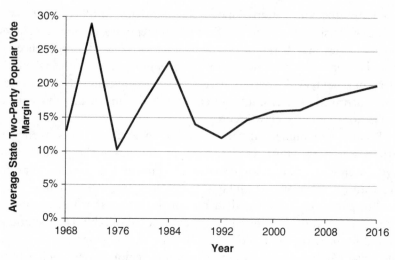

FIGURE 2.3. Average state popular vote margins in presidential elections, 1968–2016.

two politically homogeneous sections as a "myth of American political geography."[24]

Unfortunately, this indicator is a fundamentally flawed measure of geographic polarization because it fails to account for national as well as state-level popular margins. The 1972 and 1984 elections delivered unusually massive coast-to-coast victories to incumbent presidents Richard Nixon and Ronald Reagan, who each carried 49 of the nation's 50 states (only Massachusetts in 1972 and Minnesota in 1984, as well as the District of Columbia in both years, dissented from what was otherwise a clean national Republican sweep in each election). It is hardly surprising that the electoral margins in most states were particularly elevated in contests in which the victorious candidate prevailed in the national popular vote by 23 and 19 percentage points, respectively; even typically competitive states could be expected to vote overwhelmingly for the winning party under such circumstances. The mean state popular margin does not necessarily reveal the presence of state-level variation in electoral outcomes; when nearly every state in the union is temporarily colored a deep shade of partisan red, the result is geographic unity rather than divergence.

[24] Edward L. Glaeser and Bryce A. Ward, "Myths and Realities of American Political Geography," *Journal of Economic Perspectives* 20 (Spring 2006), pp. 119–144, at 121.

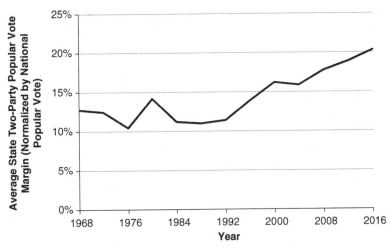

FIGURE 2.4. Average state popular vote deviation in presidential elections, 1968–2016.

Figure 2.4 introduces a superior indicator of electoral polarization that normalizes the previous measure by subtracting the national two-party popular vote margin from each state margin before calculating the mean value for each election. Employing the average state deviation from the national popular vote as a measure of electoral competition controls for the presence of short-term political tides that may push voters in a uniform partisan direction nationwide, thus isolating the degree of variation among state results in each presidential contest. (The figure can be interpreted as displaying the mean state-level popular margin assuming an even division of the national popular vote in each election.) With the normalization effectively smoothing out the temporary spikes in Figure 2.3 that simply reflected the massive scale of the Republican popular victories in 1972 and 1984, Figure 2.4 reveals a conspicuous trend of steadily increasing state-level partisan polarization that began in the 1990s. Between 1992 and 2016, the average normalized state popular margin increased from 11 to 20 percentage points – a near-doubling over the course of seven elections.

While the bitter conflict surrounding the disputed resolution of the 2000 presidential election surely helped to popularize the view that America had become divided into two hardening partisan factions, Figure 2.4 demonstrates that the contest that year between George W. Bush and Al Gore indeed represented a notable high water mark of state-level partisan variation compared to the previous several decades of presidential competition. The perception of most media pundits that the gap between Red America and Blue America has remained intact, and even deepened further, over subsequent elections is similarly confirmed by the additional growth in state electoral dispersion between 2004 and 2016. As illustrated by the examples of reliably blue Oregon and dependably red South Carolina, even an expected popular margin on the order of 10 percentage points between the candidates is more than sufficient to ensure an electoral victory for the majority party. By 2016, the normalized margin between the candidates equaled or exceeded 10 points in 36 states and the District of Columbia, with the average state producing a partisan gap of twice that amount.

THE DECLINING SHARE OF SWING STATES IN PRESIDENTIAL ELECTIONS

Though Ohio has been a reliable electoral bellwether for over a century (voting for every winning presidential candidate since 1964 and all but two since 1896),[25] its current well-publicized reputation as *the* archetypical swing state, capable of unilaterally selecting one president after another, has only been earned over the past few elections. In previous decades, Ohio shared the electoral spotlight with plenty of other politically competitive, vote-rich states that commanded a comparable volume of attention from candidates and reporters alike. For example, the state of New York was carried by the winning presidential candidate in 24 of the 27 elections between 1880 and 1984. Illinois backed the winner in each of the 20 elections between 1920 and 1996 except 1976, when Jimmy Carter lost the state by just 2 percentage points. California voted for the electoral college victor in 25 of the 28 elections between 1888 and 1996, Texas was a member of the electoral majority in 14 of the 15 elections between 1928 and 1988, and Kentucky supported the winning candidate in 19 of the 21 elections between 1924 and 2004.

By the early twenty-first century, however, this typicality had itself become increasingly atypical. The previously fluid partisan alignment of many states in federal elections has solidified over the past two decades into a significant and dependable advantage for either Democratic or Republican candidates, severely reducing the number of marginal states

---

[25] The exceptions were 1944 and 1960, when Republican presidential candidates carried Ohio but lost the election.

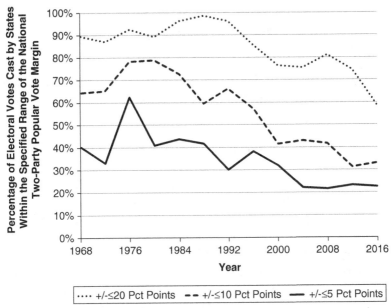

FIGURE 2.5. The decline of electorally representative states, 1968–2016.

that remain open to persuasion by either side. None of the formerly competitive states named above was actively contested by the two major presidential candidates in 2016: New York, Illinois, and California were each deemed safely Democratic and therefore forfeited outright to Hillary Clinton's campaign, while Texas and Kentucky were both considered solid Republican territory and likewise openly conceded to Donald Trump. Ohio's centrality to the electoral college strategies of contemporary presidential campaigns not only reflects its own persistently divided electorate, but also signifies the declining number of other states – especially other populous states casting large numbers of electoral votes – where the outcome also remains in doubt.

Figure 2.5 displays the proportion of electoral votes cast by states in which the two-party popular vote margin fell within 5, 10, and 20 percentage points of the national vote margin over the 13 elections between 1968 and 2016. As the figure reveals, it was once common for a large proportion of the electoral college to consist of states that were nationally representative and thus strategically pivotal. The share of total electoral votes cast by states remaining within 10 points of the national popular vote margin averaged 70 percent over the six elections between 1968 and 1988, while the share of electoral votes cast by states with margins that fell within 5 percentage points of the national vote division fell below 40 percent only once during this period, in the anomalous election of 1972.

Beginning in the 1990s, increasing state-level variation in popular vote margins sharply reduced the share of electoral votes cast by states that closely matched the national vote division between the presidential candidates. The proportion of electoral votes from states that fell within 10 percentage points of the national vote distribution declined by more than half between 1992 and 2012 (from 66 percent to 31 percent). Between 1968 and 1996, the average share of electoral votes cast by highly representative states (those that fell within 5 points of the national vote distribution) exceeded the share of votes cast by highly unrepresentative states (those that differed from the national vote by more than 20 points in either the Democratic or Republican direction) by a margin of 41 percent to 8 percent – a ratio of more than five to one. By the three elections between 2004 and 2012, however, the average share of electoral votes from the least representative states – such as the Democratic strongholds of Massachusetts, Vermont, and Maryland and the Republican bastions of Alabama, Oklahoma, and Nebraska – had increased to 23 percent of the electoral college, slightly exceeding the 22 percent average share of electoral votes cast by highly representative states that finished within 5 points of the national popular vote. In the 2016 election, more than 40 percent of the nation's electoral votes were cast by states where the two presidential candidates ran more than 20 percentage points better or worse than they did in the nation as a whole.

Because the winner-take-all state allocation of presidential electors renders the size of state popular vote margins irrelevant to electoral college outcomes, candidates face an incentive to concentrate their deployment of campaign resources within states where either party maintains a realistic chance of placing first. The decreasing share of nationally representative states over time has therefore been accompanied by a corresponding decline in the size of the campaign battleground. Figure 2.6 displays the share of electoral votes cast by states in which one or both candidates actively competed for support, based on measures of campaign activity in each election between 1976 and 2016. While two-thirds or more of the American electorate once routinely received attention from the presidential campaigns in the form of targeted advertising, public appearances by candidates and running mates, and get-out-the-vote initiatives, the geographic scope of voter persuasion and mobilization efforts led by

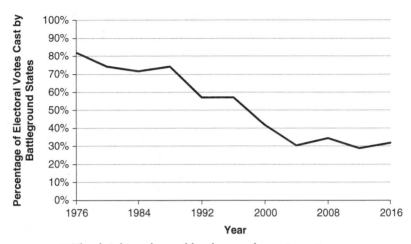

FIGURE 2.6. The shrinking electoral battleground, 1976–2016.
Source: Battleground state data derived from a variety of sources indicating campaign activity by one or both presidential candidates in particular states, including contemporaneous press accounts of candidate strategy, personal appearance schedules, and advertising expenditures, as well as the following: Darshan J. Goux, *The Battleground State: Conceptualizing Geographic Contestation in American Presidential Elections, 1960–2004* (Ph.D. dissertation, University of California, Berkeley, 2010); Daron R. Shaw, *The Race to 270: The Electoral College and the Campaign Strategies of 2000 and 2004* (Chicago: University of Chicago Press); Shaw, "The Methods Behind the Madness: Presidential Electoral College Strategies, 1988–1996," *Journal of Politics* 61 (1999), pp. 893–913; Larry M. Bartels, "Resource Allocation in a Presidential Campaign," *Journal of Politics* 47 (1985), pp. 928–936.

the candidates and parties has significantly contracted since the 1980s. The presidential election of 2000 was the first in decades to restrict this activity to less than half of the nation, accounting for the widespread perceptions that year of increasing geographic polarization between Red and Blue America among political commentators attuned to the details of candidate strategy. Since 2004, the share of electoral votes cast by states actively contested by the presidential candidates has held steady at about 30 percent of the national total.

The influence of the electoral college on the strategic behavior of presidential campaigns is therefore much more apparent – and consequential – under conditions of geographic polarization. In past decades, when most states were potentially open to aligning with either party, candidates ran broadly targeted campaigns. Richard Nixon even fulfilled a public pledge to visit all 50 states as the Republican presidential nominee

in 1960 – a campaign stunt that would be unthinkable today, given the
rigidity of the contemporary electoral map. Nixon's Democratic opponent John F. Kennedy declined to match this uniquely ambitious itiner-
ary, but still managed to campaign in 44 different states over the final
67 days of the 1960 campaign.[26] As late as the 1980s, presidential candidates still devoted a substantial proportion of their budgets to purchas-
ing national television airtime, rather than adopting the now-universal
practice of restricting nearly all campaign advertising to a relative handful of strategically critical states; as journalist Sasha Issenberg explained,
"until 1988, basically, campaigns would cut three checks – one to each
of the [major] television networks – and communicate with the electorate
through national ads."[27]

Before the advent of geographic polarization in the 1990s, populous
states in particular were nearly always both politically competitive and
aggressively contested by both parties. Theodore H. White reported that
the Kennedy and Nixon campaigns identified each of the seven largest
states in 1960 – New York, California, Pennsylvania, Illinois, Ohio, Texas,
and Michigan – as electorally critical, with Nixon advisors dubbing them
the "Big Seven"; the final popular margin between the candidates fell
within 2 percentage points in five of these states and within 6 points
in all seven.[28] In the 1968 election, Nixon (once again the Republican
nominee) and Democratic opponent Hubert Humphrey finished within 7
points of each other in each of the nation's eight largest states (and within
5 points in seven of the eight). In 1976, the popular margins separating
Republican incumbent Gerald Ford and Democratic challenger Jimmy
Carter did not exceed 5 percentage points in each of the nine largest
states (representing a collective 241 electoral votes, or 45 percent of the
national total).

---

[26] Charles Kenney, *John F. Kennedy: The Presidential Portfolio* (New York: PublicAffairs, 2000), p. 51.

[27] Jim Tankersley, "Why Donald Trump's 1980s-Style Campaign Is Struggling in 2016," *Washington Post*, August 20, 2016, www.washingtonpost.com/news/wonk/wp/2016/08/20/why-donald-trumps-1980s-style-campaign-is-struggling-in-2016/. The first modern presidential candidate to adopt a targeted advertising approach concentrated within bat-tleground states was George H. W. Bush in 1988; his opponent Michael Dukakis mostly followed the traditional practice of buying commercial time on national television net-works. See Lloyd Grove, "Bush to Spend at Least $32 Million on TV Ads," *Washington Post*, September 22, 1988, p. A27. By 1992, both parties had largely abandoned national advertising purchases in favor of a state-based approach.

[28] Theodore H. White, *The Making of the President, 1960* (New York: Atheneum, 1961), p. 325.

Although the electoral college is often described as providing small states with a systematic advantage due to the modest numerical overrepresentation that they receive from the inclusion of senators in the constitutional formula allocating state electors, Nelson W. Polsby and Aaron Wildavsky observed in 1971 that because populous states still cast more electoral votes in an absolute sense, "it is primarily the larger states, through the [winner-take-all] principle, who benefit from the Electoral College ... a Presidential candidate [should therefore] spend his energy in the larger states and tailor his programs to appeal to their voters, provided that energy expended there is nearly as likely to yield results."[29] As long as the large states remained electorally uncertain, presidential nominees were likely to campaign where the voters were, behaving much as they would if the office were instead filled via a simple national popular election and thus somewhat obscuring the mechanics of the electoral college from public visibility.

But the trend of increasing geographic polarization has transformed many formerly competitive states into single-party bastions, including several of the nation's largest population centers. In particular, former perennial battlegrounds California, Texas, and New York – three of the four biggest numerical prizes in the electoral college – have all evolved into Democratic (California and New York) or Republican (Texas) strongholds over the course of the last three decades: New York was last actively contested by the presidential nominees in the 1988 election, Texas in 1992, and California in 1996. The nearly 82 million Americans who reside in these states as of the 2010 census, representing more than one-quarter of the total national population, now attract minimal notice from candidates, parties, and interest groups once the general election campaign begins, even as the much smaller but more closely divided electorates of Iowa, Nevada, and New Hampshire (collectively home to about 7 million residents as of 2010) receive ample attention from both sides every fourth autumn. Due to the combined strategic effect of winner-take-all electoral allocation rules, the uneven distribution of partisan strength across state boundaries, and the unique institutional structure created by the constitutional framers, the road to the White House in the twenty-first century bypasses New York City, Los Angeles, and Houston in favor of Nashua, Reno, and Dubuque.

---

[29] Nelson W. Polsby and Aaron B. Wildavsky, *Presidential Elections: Strategies of American Electoral Politics*, 3rd edition (New York: Charles Scribner's Sons, 1971), pp. 260–261.

The role of winner-take-all elections in sharply reducing the scope of the active campaign battleground under conditions of increasing state-level partisan disparity has particularly dismayed critics of the electoral college. While the institution has long been faulted by advocates of pure majoritarian principles for allowing a candidate to achieve the presidency despite losing the national popular vote, detractors increasingly accuse the electoral college of violating democratic values even in contests in which the popular and electoral winners coincide, blaming it for compelling presidential nominees on the campaign trail to pay little heed to a majority of the American electorate. "Instead of encouraging candidates to take their cases to the entire country," wrote George C. Edwards in one critical appraisal, the electoral college "distort[s] the electoral process and [gives] the candidates strong incentives to ignore most of the country."[30] As a result, argued Robert W. Bennett in another book-length critique, "a voter in a state that is closely divided among presidential candidates effectively casts a weightier vote than does one in a similarly populous but electorally lopsided state."[31] This objection has become more frequent in recent years as the proportion of safe states has increased relative to the size of the electoral battleground, leaving the inhabitants of predictably red or blue geographic territory to watch the presidential competition from afar as the residents of the remaining purple states are smothered with candidate attention.

The progression of geographic polarization has also produced a historically unmatched degree of state-level partisan stability. The configuration of red and blue states that attracted extensive notice in 2000 remained almost entirely intact when George W. Bush won a second presidential term four years later; only three small states – Iowa, New Hampshire, and New Mexico – switched partisan sides between the two elections. Even Barack Obama's 2008 victory, frequently portrayed in the moment as a revolutionary event in American politics, failed to fundamentally transform the geographic coalitions of the parties. Obama won all 21 states (plus the District of Columbia) that had voted Democratic at least once in 2000 and 2004, adding just 7 of the 29 states that had been carried twice by Bush. "If you paid even the slightest attention to the news media in the hours and days following the election of Barack Obama as president, one idea was unavoidable: that America was a profoundly

---

[30] Edwards, *Why the Electoral College Is Bad for America*, pp. 10, 132.
[31] Robert W. Bennett, *Taming the Electoral College* (Stanford, CA: Stanford University Press, 2006), p. 163.

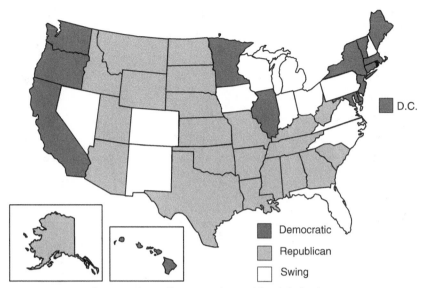

FIGURE 2.7. State partisan alignments in presidential elections, 2000–2016.

changed place," observed Dante Chinni and James Gimpel, "... [but] the fact is, the long-term voting patterns of most communities in the United States are pretty predictable."[32] Donald Trump's upset victory in 2016 was similarly treated by the news media like a political earthquake that fundamentally redefined the popular coalitions of the parties, but Trump achieved his electoral majority by adding six perennial swing states to the 24 states carried by fellow Republican Mitt Romney four years before. In total, 37 of the nation's 50 states (plus the District of Columbia) supported the same party in each of the five elections between 2000 and 2016 (see Figure 2.7), confirming the widespread perception that the vast majority of states have become dependably red or blue in their presidential voting habits.

As Figure 2.8 reveals, this 75 percent rate of partisan consistency represents the highest level of state-level stability across any set of five consecutive presidential elections since the South returned to presidential voting at the end of Reconstruction, further demonstrating that electoral politics has evolved from the instability of the mid-twentieth century to an era distinguished by historically durable geographic coalitions. While a small group of "purple" states remains open to capture by either side

[32] Chinni and Gimpel, *Our Patchwork Nation*, pp. 159, 162.

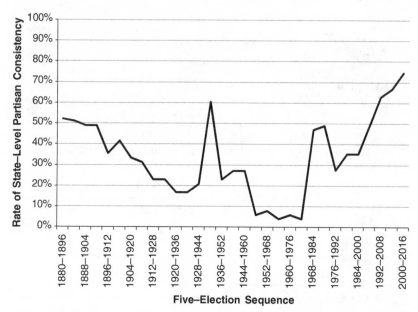

FIGURE 2.8. State-level partisan consistency across five consecutive presidential elections, 1880–2016.
Note: Third-party candidates Strom Thurmond (1948) and George Wallace (1968) are counted as Democrats for purposes of measuring state-level partisan consistency; Theodore Roosevelt (1912) is counted as a Republican.

(and therefore occupies a decisive strategic position in the electoral college), the popular contemporary practice of characterizing the vast majority of states as dependably allied with a single party in presidential voting thus reflects a fundamentally accurate perception of electoral reality. Even if the electorates of most states are neither politically homogeneous nor ideologically extreme, their prevailing partisanship has become sufficiently entrenched to assure the dominant party of victory regardless of the short-term factors present in any particular election year – such as specific candidates, issues, or events – that push the few remaining swing states in one partisan direction or the other and thus determine the national outcome.

Because change, however modest in scope, tends to attract more interest than does stasis, the existence or prospect of even modest partisan shifts in a few individual states sometimes receives considerable notice from media analysts. For example, several states (including Virginia and Colorado) have moved in a measurably Democratic direction since the 1990s, while others (such as Arkansas and Missouri) have become increasingly Republican. These trends frequently attract plentiful news media coverage and can be critical to the national outcome in an era in which close elections are the norm. Yet they have occurred against a much wider background of exceptional geographic stability in presidential voting, with relatively few states now exhibiting partisan ambivalence or inconsistency. Neither party's candidates have found much success over the intervening years in dislodging a significant section of the nation from its existing political orientation; as a result, the 2000-vintage partisan geographic configuration remains intact nearly two decades after it first captured public attention.

THE NEW REGIONAL DIVIDE

While the results of the Bush–Gore presidential election famously inspired pundits to coin the terms "red states" and "blue states" in order to signify a newfound durability in geographic alignments, the electoral college map that year received an unusual degree of notice from journalists, commentators, and citizens alike because these relatively firm state-level affiliations were arranged in a much broader and more conspicuous regional pattern. Rather than being distributed at random across the continent, blue states were tightly clustered in the urban North and Far West while red states were likewise concentrated in a single bloc across the South and interior West – forming a memorable visual representation of a country that seemed to be literally splitting itself in two. As Figure 2.7 illustrates, these regional groupings remained in place over subsequent presidential contests, further validating the widespread perception of an inexhaustible conflict between Red and Blue America. Each party has achieved electoral dominance not just over collections of isolated individual states, but across wide, contiguous sections of the nation.

With congressional election results increasingly conforming to presidential outcomes within individual constituencies over the same period in which the latter have become geographically polarized, House and Senate elections now also exhibit the same red-versus-blue regional pattern that has become famously characteristic of presidential contests. Figure 2.9 displays the aggregate share of both the two-party popular vote and the House seats won by congressional Democrats in each national election between 1968 and 2016; both the vote and seat proportions are separated into sets of red (South and interior West) and blue (Northeast and Pacific Coast) regions. Prior to the 1994 midterm elections, blue-region

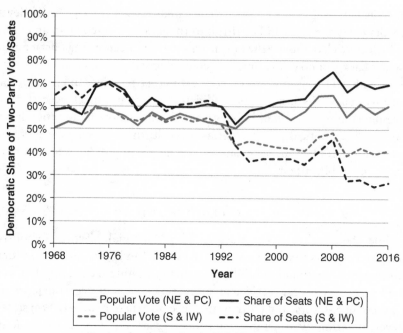

FIGURE 2.9. Regional polarization in U.S. House elections, 1968–2016.

residents were no more likely than their red-region counterparts to vote Democratic in House elections; until 1974, in fact, Democratic candidates achieved more electoral success in what is now Red America than they did in today's Blue America.

But the "Republican Revolution" of 1994, notable for ending 40 consecutive years of Democratic rule over the House, marked a historical turning point in regional politics as well. House Republicans won a majority of both popular votes and congressional seats across the South and interior West for the first time since the end of Reconstruction – and have repeated this success in every subsequent congressional election. In Blue America, by contrast, House Democrats quickly rebounded after their 1994 losses to build an increasingly secure popular and electoral advantage that by 2006 consistently met or exceeded the margins achieved by the party in the previous 40 years, including the national Democratic landslide of 1974 that occurred in the wake of the Watergate scandal and subsequent resignation of Richard Nixon from the presidency.

The partisan divergence in the popular preferences of red- and blue-region electorates after 1994 produced a substantial numerical divide in regional House delegations due to the intensifying effects of winner-take-all electoral rules. As late as the 1992 election, House Democrats received an identical 52 percent of the two-party popular vote and held 60 percent of the total seats within the two sets of regions. Over the succeeding eight years, the difference in the collective popular vote between Red and Blue America widened to 16 percentage points, producing a 26-point difference in seat share in the 107th Congress of 2001–2002 (Democrats captured 63 percent of the districts in Blue America and just 37 percent of those in Red America). The regional gap in the popular vote remained relatively stable thereafter, varying between 16 and 19 points in each election between 2004 and 2016, but the divergence in partisan seat share continued to grow. By the 115th Congress of 2017–2018, Democrats held more than two-thirds (69 percent) of the House seats from the Northeast and Pacific Coast, while Republicans held nearly three-quarters (73 percent) of the seats from the South and interior West.

Regional differences in Senate elections followed a very similar trajectory, as demonstrated by Figure 2.10 – although the aggregation of votes for Senate candidates at the state level predictably ensures an even greater variation in seat share between regions than occurs among the smaller districts used to elect the House. Before the 1980s, the partisan alignments of what later became Red America and Blue America were reversed in Senate elections due to residual Democratic strength in the South; after about 15 years of regional convergence, the 1994 election marked the advent of the now-familiar contemporary pattern of red-versus-blue partisan geography. By 2000, the popular gap between red-region and blue-region voters had reached 10 percentage points, corresponding to a 35-point difference in the relative seat share of the two parties. The trend of regional divergence progressed further in succeeding years; by 2016, the partisan preferences of blue-region residents differed from those of red-region voters by 22 points, while the gap in seat share had widened dramatically to a full 74 points (Democrats held 93 percent of the Senate seats in the Northeast and Pacific Coast during the 2017–2018 Congress, while Republicans held 81 percent of the seats elected in the South and interior West).

The rapid transformation of the geographic bases of the congressional parties after 1994 has thus brought elections for the legislative branch into close congruence with presidential outcomes at the level of congressional districts, states, and even entire regions. As a result, the solidification of respective Republican and Democratic electoral dominance

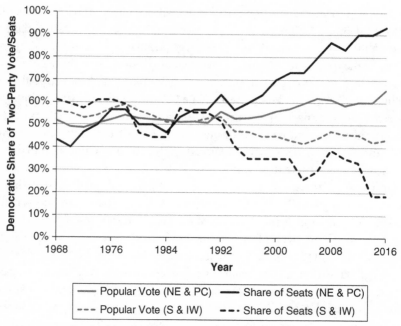

FIGURE 2.10. Regional polarization in U.S. Senate elections, 1968–2016.
Note: Both seat shares and popular votes are aggregated across the three Senate
elections ending in the year denoted in the figure, in order to account for the
Senate's staggered six-year terms.

in the red and blue sections of the nation since the 1990s now extends
beyond presidential contests to encompass House and Senate races
as well. A substantial minority of voters in Red America still support
Democratic candidates for both the presidency and Congress, while a
similar fraction of Blue America residents likewise continues to prefer
Republican nominees for federal office. These voters are systematically
underrepresented among the ranks of elective officeholders due to the
role of winner-take-all rules in producing a much larger – and widening –
divergence in party control of presidential electors and congressional
seats across geographic constituencies. Though inferences from these
aggregate results can dramatically overstate the magnitude of regional
differences in the preferences of *voters*, the fundamental validity of the
"red" and "blue" nomenclature as applied to electoral *outcomes* has only
been further enhanced in the years since its initial appearance, confirming the view that national elections in the twenty-first century are indeed
dominated by a formidable and consequential regional divide.

CONCLUSION: THE UNFULFILLED PURSUIT
OF NATIONAL UNITY

The heated aftermath of the controversial 2000 presidential election was far from an ideal environment to foster measured, objective, and well-reasoned political analysis. As the Florida recount dragged on, fueling a partisan battle over the fairness of George W. Bush's victory over Al Gore that was left unresolved by a Supreme Court ruling narrowly decided along ideological lines and the subsequent certification of the state's official results by Florida's Republican secretary of state (and Democratic nemesis) Katherine Harris, any scrap of evidence – however ambiguous or anecdotal – that could be used to substantiate the widespread perception of a bitterly divided America would have received substantial attention from news media personalities preoccupied, as ever, with the theater of political conflict. Under such conditions, the instantly memorable regional configuration of partisan preferences produced by the 2000 election was guaranteed to inspire passionate and enduring interest among the political commentariat, not least because its suggestion of a deep-seated cultural conflict in which brainy but snobbish coastal Democrats faced off against unsophisticated but authentic heartland Republicans neatly matched the respective simplistic personal caricatures of Gore and Bush that journalists and pundits had repeatedly sketched over the course of the campaign.

Drawing confident conclusions about the state of American politics from the results of a single election is a risky endeavor even in the best of circumstances, and the atmosphere of unrestrained partisan discord that had set in by the end of 2000 readily encouraged the proliferation of hyperbolic pronouncements at the expense of empirically grounded evaluations. Naturally, many scholars reacted with skepticism to claims of a raging ideological war fought along geographic lines, especially when the evidence cited to corroborate such assertions often amounted to little more than a regurgitation of well-worn regional stereotypes. Plenty of loyal Democratic voters continued to reside in Republican-leaning states and vice versa, seriously complicating the popular portrait of a mass public segregated into two politically homogeneous regional halves.

Similar objections have been voiced by politicians who either sincerely or tactically wished to express a preference for cooperation and common ground. Bush, for example, had often described himself as a "uniter, not a divider" during the 2000 campaign; he promised in his first inaugural address to "advance my convictions with civility" while calling for a spirit of "shared accomplishment" among politicians of both parties. Barack Obama, Bush's successor in the White House, was even more specific, repeatedly employing the familiar regional divide in the American electorate as an explicit rhetorical foil. In his keynote address at the 2004 Democratic national convention – a speech that served as his debut on the national political stage – then-Senate candidate Obama criticized "the pundits [who] like to slice and dice our country into red states and blue states," and thus emphasize division and dissent. "I've got news for them," he announced, "… we are one people, all of us pledging allegiance to the Stars and Stripes, all of us defending the *United* States of America." This idea became a signature oratorical theme for Obama, who returned to it on several prominent occasions thereafter, including his 2008 and 2012 election night victory speeches and his final State of the Union address in 2015, in which he reiterated his vow that the nation was "more than a collection of red states and blue states, [but] the *United* States of America."

Despite these sentiments, the elections that installed Bush and Obama in the White House for two terms apiece were distinguished by historically elevated and increasing levels of geographic polarization – a trend that remained intact during the election of the less rhetorically inclusive Donald Trump as Obama's successor in 2016. The tendency of some commentators to wildly overstate the extent of the political differences separating the individual citizens of various states or regions should not obscure the presence of this trend at the level of aggregate constituencies, which has caused a significant expansion of safe partisan territory at the expense of the electoral battleground. While it was common not long ago for a strong majority of states to be closely divided between the parties and thus actively contested in national elections, nearly three-quarters of American voters now indeed reside within either a redoubt of red or a bastion of blue.

The color-war account of mass partisan politics that was initially inspired by the results of the 2000 presidential election has thus revealed itself to be essentially sound when applied to the collective alignments of American electoral constituencies. In fact, its fundamental aptness has only strengthened over the succeeding decades. The previously unmatched consistency of state-level outcomes over the five presidential elections since 2000 has been accompanied by a growing convergence between presidential and congressional results within districts, states, and regions that has transformed the familiar red-versus-blue electoral map into an increasingly accurate representation of the two parties' popular coalitions in House and Senate contests as well. While individual citizens may not always be cleanly sorted into politically homogeneous locations, the interaction of aggregate voting preferences with long-standing rules and institutions has nevertheless produced a rapidly hardening divide separating the deepening blues of the metropolitan coasts from the brightening reds of the nation's interior. Even when they publicly proclaim their intent to do so, none of today's political leaders has yet managed to transcend this enduring national rift.

3

The Geographic Roots of Party Strength
and Cohesion

A DECLINE AND RESURGENCE OF
REGIONALIZED PARTIES

Polarization of the parties in government, accompanied by the increasing frequency of party-loyal voting in the mass electorate, has become both a familiar attribute of contemporary American politics and the subject of widespread concern among intellectuals, journalists, and citizens. According to one perspective, habitual party-line voting – whether at the ballot box or on the floor of Congress – is politically detrimental because it risks blinding voters and policymakers to factual realities or potential solutions to national problems. A different view holds that the existence of strong and philosophically divergent parties is not inherently troublesome, but often creates procedural gridlock and other practical difficulties when situated amid an American constitutional framework allowing for divided partisan control of elective institutions.

Accounts that lament the growth of polarization at least implicitly – and often openly – compare today's political climate unfavorably to that of previous decades, when Democratic and Republican politicians were more mutually cooperative and party mavericks were more plentiful on both sides. Both the ideological division between party elites and the electoral loyalty of party voters declined significantly from previous historical peaks during the mid-twentieth century, only to return unexpectedly over the past generation to levels that exceed those within living memory. As this trend continues to progress despite the arrival and departure of specific political events, issues, and leaders, it has become increasingly clear that the resurgent partisanship of the present day rests upon sturdy electoral foundations – including, importantly, the distinctive and stable contemporary regional coalitions of the Democrats and Republicans.

This chapter surveys more than half a century of American history in order to illustrate the central role of political geography in determining the relative strength and cohesion of the two major parties. The severe economic shock of the Great Depression replaced the entrenched regional alignments of the early 1900s with a national Democratic majority that stretched across sectional boundaries but contained substantial internal disunity. As this New Deal coalition began to disperse in the 1960s, American politics entered a long transitional period in which a succession of Republican presidents faced a Congress that remained almost entirely under Democratic control; each party achieved a persistent cross-regional majority within a single branch of government and therefore shared an overlapping set of electoral constituencies, encouraging regular occasions of bipartisan compromise. This intermediate era lasted until the 1990s, when improving Democratic fortunes in presidential elections coincided with newfound Republican success in congressional contests, while the reappearance of sharp regional differences after 60 years of increasingly nationalized electoral majorities coincided with the growing ideological polarization of the parties in government.

At each stage of this historical evolution, political experts regularly expressed significant dissatisfaction with the state of the American parties. The post-1932 party system was dominated by an electorally formidable but ideologically divided Democratic majority, whose disparate factions represented a serious obstacle to the enactment of a policy agenda favored by liberal leaders – prompting many scholars to advocate reform measures designed to improve internal party discipline. When the Democratic Party lost its advantage in presidential elections after 1968 to the Republican opposition but continued to maintain a durable majority in Congress, political scientists voiced apprehension over the increasing tendency of voters to divide federal power between the parties, warning that the erosion of party loyalty among citizens – for which the parties themselves received substantial blame – endangered democratic representation and governmental accountability.

Today, previous concerns over the declining strength, excessive factionalization, and insufficient substantive distinctiveness of the parties have been eclipsed by equally urgent warnings deploring the negative consequences of ideological polarization and incessant partisan conflict. While many critics, as ever, propose to solve the perceived flaws of the party system by implementing further modifications to election law or internal party operations, the extent to which the behavior of the parties in government has been shaped historically by the nature of their electoral coalitions – especially their regional constituencies – suggests that the current polarized party system is deeply rooted in the political geography of the nation. If history is a proper guide, any future large-scale change in the strength and cohesion of the parties is unlikely to proceed from the successful enactment of minor procedural reforms. It will instead require a more fundamental transformation of the two parties' popular bases of support.

HISTORICAL REGIONALISM AND PARTY REALIGNMENT THEORY

In a democratic electorate, political coalitions are almost always geographic coalitions. The characteristics that shape the partisan, ideological, and policy preferences of individual citizens are inevitably distributed unevenly across the territory of a nation; geographic differences in electoral outcomes often illustrate spatial patterns of settlement, conquest, immigration, religious conversion, economic specialization, and other phenomena for decades or even centuries after the historical circumstances in which they first appeared. Yet political geography can reflect change as well as continuity. As voters migrate from place to place, as different leaders and issues arise and recede, and as the social constituencies of the parties evolve due to the ongoing march of political events, one set of regional alignments may give way to an alternate configuration – gradually in some cases, very abruptly in others.

The sheer size and diversity of the American population ensures that the prevailing political orientation of the electorate will vary from one place to another; the magnitude of these differences is multiplied further as raw votes are converted by winner-take-all electoral rules into the distribution of congressional seats and presidential electors. Indeed, the political history of the United States over its first 140 years was largely defined by regional conflict. The two-party system that emerged in the early years of the nation placed a Federalist Party based principally in the coastal towns of New England and the Mid-Atlantic in opposition to a Republican (later Democratic) Party preferred by the inhabitants of the agricultural South. Four decades of growing regional tension over the expansion, and later the permissibility, of slavery erupted during the 1860s into civil war between the North and the South that left more than half a million Americans dead. After Reconstruction, the South returned political power to a single-party Democratic regime that symbolized its white citizens' regional identity and collective resistance to northern rule and racial integration, even as Republicans in the North continued for decades to benefit from residual loyalty among their own constituents to the party of Abraham Lincoln and U. S. Grant. Toward the end of the 1800s, political divisions emerged along a second regional axis as well, due to the rise of a Populist movement based in the agrarian West that sought to combat perceived economic exploitation by northeastern financial interests.

Prior to the 1930s, highly regionalized partisan competition appeared to be a constant, and perhaps inescapable, element of American politics. The reemergence of this pattern in recent elections tends to strike political observers who came of age in the two generations after World War II as historically exceptional, yet it would seem quite familiar to a time-traveling politician from the nineteenth century – as would the routinely slender electoral margins separating the two parties at the national level. As Frances E. Lee notes, today's era "stands out as the longest sustained period of competitive balance between the parties since the Civil War ... Looking back, the period most similar to the present was the Gilded Age (1876–96), another era of close and alternating party majorities, as well as of ferocious party conflict ... raising the political stakes of every policy dispute."[1] The late 1800s produced a series of narrowly decided presidential elections (and alternating partisan control of Congress), relatively sharp collective differences in the voting habits of the congressional parties, and a largely stable regional alignment in which a Republican majority in the Northeast and Midwest was balanced by a safely Democratic South.

Sectional tensions endured even after the Republican Party managed to gain a consistent national partisan advantage in the early twentieth century (Republican candidates won six of the eight presidential elections between 1896 and 1928, with Democratic nominees failing to win a national popular majority in all eight). In fact, the solidification of Republican electoral supremacy in the North and West after World War I merely increased the partisan gap between the stubbornly Democratic "Solid South" and the rest of the nation. Democratic nominee John W. Davis carried 12 southern states in the 1924 presidential election by

---

[1] Frances E. Lee, "American Politics Is More Competitive Than Ever, and That Is Making Partisanship Worse," in John Sides and Daniel J. Hopkins, eds., *Political Polarization in American Politics* (New York: Bloomsbury, 2015), pp. 76–79, at 76–77.

a collective popular margin of 64 percent to 31 percent over Republican incumbent Calvin Coolidge, even as Coolidge swept the remaining 36 states (with the lone exception of Wisconsin, which opted for favorite-son third-party candidate Robert M. La Follette) by an equally lopsided advantage of 57 percent to 25 percent. The association between regional identity and party membership had reached a historical apex, and there would have been little reason at the time to anticipate an imminent reordering of the social coalitions or relative popular strength of the two parties. As David R. Mayhew observes, "We have good reason to believe that, absent the abrupt economic downturn in 1929, voters would have kept on electing [Republican] presidents like Coolidge and [Herbert] Hoover for quite a while."[2]

The stock market crash that year and ensuing Great Depression caused arguably the most dramatic reversal of partisan fortune in American history, sufficiently discrediting the ruling Republicans that most voters in the North, East, and West alike promptly joined the South under the Democratic banner. The strong sectional partisan alignments that had dominated American electoral politics since the early years of the republic abruptly receded in the face of universal economic crisis, inaugurating a new era in which a single party predominated across regional lines for more than a generation. After 1968, Republicans regained an advantage in presidential (though not congressional) elections, reflecting elevated rates of ticket-splitting among American voters that produced routinely inconsistent partisan outcomes at the national, regional, state, and district levels. The election of Bill Clinton to the presidency in 1992, followed immediately by the Republican congressional victories of 1994, signaled the onset of yet another new era in American electoral politics distinguished by resurgent party loyalty in the mass public, rapidly polarizing congressional parties, a series of close presidential elections and slim legislative majorities, and a significant and expanding gap separating the Democratic-leaning Northeast and Pacific Coast from the increasingly Republican South and interior West. For the first time since the 1920s, the two major parties have returned to the habit of maintaining distinct and solid regional bases from which they battle each other for national victory.

Dividing nearly a century of political history into three distinct periods necessarily requires a degree of simplification that risks overstating

[2] David R. Mayhew, *Electoral Realignments: A Critique of an American Genre* (New Haven, CT: Yale University Press, 2002), p. 63.

both the amount of stability within each era and the magnitude of the differences between them, yet it also allows for the identification of larger patterns amidst the transient noise of individual electoral outcomes. The best-known and most intellectually influential analysis of partisan periodization in the United States is party realignment theory, principally developed in works by Walter Dean Burnham, E. E. Schattschneider, and James L. Sundquist that built on ideas first proposed by V. O. Key Jr. in his influential 1955 essay "A Theory of Critical Elections."[3] Realignment theory posits that the electoral coalitions of the American parties have rearranged themselves at periodic intervals around a new set of salient issue cleavages and social groupings, with one party gaining a natural majority in the electorate until the next critical election produces what Key characterized as a "sharp and durable" revision of the existing party structure.[4] The lack of a widely acknowledged critical election in the years since the New Deal realignment of 1932 has long represented a challenge for scholars seeking to apply the theory to the party politics of the past several decades, and recent critiques by Mayhew and Larry M. Bartels have even questioned its validity as a tool for analyzing the first 150 years of American history.[5] Yet one need not accept all or even most of the ambitious empirical claims associated with realignment theory (Mayhew identified 15 such claims in his survey of previous studies) in order to acknowledge the value of Key's initial observation that significant short-term shifts in the electoral coalitions of the parties can be separated by longer periods of relative stability – a pattern that Edward G. Carmines and James A. Stimson, borrowing a concept from evolutionary biology, have dubbed "punctuated equilibrium."[6]

---

[3] Walter Dean Burnham, *Critical Elections and the Mainsprings of American Politics* (New York: W. W. Norton, 1970); E. E. Schattschneider, *The Semi-Sovereign People: A Realist's View of Democracy in America* (New York: Holt, Rinehart and Winston, 1960); James L. Sundquist, *Dynamics of the Party System: Alignment and Realignment of Political Parties in the United States*, revised edition (Washington, DC: Brookings Institution, 1983); V. O. Key Jr., "A Theory of Critical Elections," *Journal of Politics* 17 (1955), pp. 3–18.

[4] Quote from Key, "Theory of Critical Elections," p. 4.

[5] Mayhew, *Electoral Realignments*; Larry M. Bartels, "Electoral Continuity and Change, 1868–1996," *Electoral Studies* 17 (1998), pp. 301–326. On the problem of identifying a post-1932 critical election, see Everett Carll Ladd, "Like Waiting for Godot: The Uselessness of 'Realignment' for Understanding Change in Contemporary American Politics," in Byron E. Shafer, ed., *The End of Realignment? Interpreting American Electoral Eras* (Madison: University of Wisconsin Press, 1991), pp. 24–36.

[6] Edward G. Carmines and James A. Stimson, *Issue Evolution: Race and the Transformation of American Politics* (Princeton, NJ: Princeton University Press, 1989).

While this definition of political eras is thus consistent with some previous accounts of party realignment – in particular, it mirrors the research of John H. Aldrich, who identified the 1930s, 1960s, and 1990s as moments of transition between distinct party systems – the analysis presented here is not intended to test or defend existing theories of electoral periodicity.[7] Instead, it endeavors to demonstrate how the relative popularity and internal unity of the two parties has reflected the nature of their respective geographic constituencies, which evolved markedly during the twentieth century. The decline of traditional regional differences in partisanship after 1932 corresponded to the emergence of strongly factionalized parties, while the onset of frequent ticket-splitting after 1968 created two parallel national partisan majorities. Each of these conditions fostered a degree of bipartisan cooperation. In the first era, the parties' internal divisions allowed for the formation of cross-partisan coalitions based on ideological affinity (especially between Republicans and conservative Democrats); in the second, the substantial overlap of geographic constituencies between Republican presidents and Democratic members of Congress provided party leaders on both sides with strategic incentives to seek compromise. By the 1990s, however, the reemergence of distinct regional coalitions in both presidential and congressional elections discouraged the pursuit of bipartisan policy agreement even under conditions of divided party government, as partisan strength increased abruptly in elite and mass politics alike. The key characteristics of these three partisan eras are summarized in Table 3.1.

Importantly, the three eras of post-1932 party politics identified in Table 3.1 also correspond to distinct phases of empirical and normative analysis by American party scholars. The existence of regional party factions with distinct ideological colorations during the 1932–1968 period prompted a number of political experts to lament the weakness of the parties in government and to propose reform measures designed to fortify the power of national party officials to enforce discipline on their membership; party identification among the mass electorate, in contrast, was generally held to be highly robust during this era. After 1968, the uncoupling of congressional election results from presidential outcomes prompted scholars and practitioners alike to turn their attention from the limited power of national party leaders over congressional committee

---

[7] John H. Aldrich, "Political Parties in a Critical Era," *American Politics Research* 27 (January 1999), pp. 9–32.

TABLE 3.1. *The three eras of modern party politics*

	1932–1968	1968–1992	1992–present
Presidential majority party	Democratic	Republican	Closely divided
Congressional majority party	Democratic	Democratic	Closely divided (Republican lean)
Party strength in government	Weak	Moderate	Strong
Party strength in electorate	Strong	Weak	Strong
Partisan regional divisions	Weak	Weak	Strong
Regional factionalism within parties	Strong	Moderate	Weak

chairs and party organizations to the declining centrality of partisanship in the minds of voters.

Today, resurgent party loyalty among politicians and citizens alike has prompted a new round of critical analyses examining the effects of highly conflictual and polarized party competition. The reappearance of significant and consistent regional partisan differences across both presidential and congressional elections after more than half a century of absence represents a highly visible indicator of political change. It is hardly surprising that the emergence of the red-versus-blue map in the current era appears to represent a new and important development in American politics, even if the lack of an obvious recent "critical election" or a consistent national partisan majority continues to undermine the applicability of traditional realignment theory to the contemporary party system.

FACTIONALIZED PARTIES AND THE POLITICAL GEOGRAPHY OF THE NEW DEAL ERA

The "New Deal coalition" that assembled under the big tent of an ascendant Democratic Party in 1932, electing Franklin D. Roosevelt to the presidency four times and simultaneously gaining long-term control of Congress, is most commonly described as an alliance of discrete social groups – the urban poor and working class, union members, Roman Catholics and Jews, agricultural workers, northern blacks, and southern whites – united by a common interest in an activist federal government during a time of economic catastrophe. But the breadth of these groups' collective geographic distribution also rendered the coalition an unusually potent electoral force, building on the existing Democratic base in the Solid South to form a sizable national partisan majority. Urban

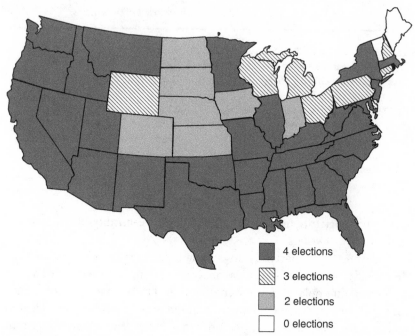

FIGURE 3.1. Total number of presidential victories per state by Franklin D. Roosevelt (D), 1932–1944.

melting-pot electorates delivered sufficiently overwhelming popular margins to Roosevelt and his fellow partisans in Congress to tip formerly Republican-leaning states across the Northeast and industrial Midwest into the Democratic electoral column over the dissenting votes of small-town Protestants and the business class, while the support of farmers, ranchers, and miners for New Deal policies likewise proved sufficient to give the Democrats a newfound strength in the rural West. As Figure 3.1 illustrates, 32 of the nation's 48 states voted Democratic in all four of Roosevelt's victories between 1932 and 1944; at the zenith of his popularity in 1936, FDR carried 46 states in his bid for a second presidential term, losing only Maine and Vermont to Republican challenger Alfred M. Landon. Just three states (the two Landon states and North Dakota) did not send at least one Democratic senator to the 75th Congress of 1937–1938.

The extent of the Democratic Party's electoral hegemony during this period might initially suggest that the national crisis of the Great Depression and the Roosevelt administration's ambitious series of policy responses (including federal jobs programs, assistance to the poor, unemployment insurance, the Social Security Act, economic development initiatives, pro-labor regulations, crop supports, and rural electrification, among other measures) had largely quelled previously salient geographic differences in the prevailing political views of the American voting public. However, the apparent national unity suggested by the electoral results of the New Deal era concealed the persistence of a significant ideological rift that soon divided the new partisan majority along regional lines. The political shock caused by the Depression threw most northern city dwellers and most rural southerners into the same political party for the first extended period since the 1820s (when viable two-party competition had temporarily ceased in American elections), but was not sufficiently strong to compel the various Democratic constituencies to suppress or resolve their considerable policy-related differences. Instead, the persistent regional factionalism of the Democratic Party became a defining characteristic of American politics in the New Deal era.

Like Roosevelt himself, most northern and western Democrats were devoted from the 1930s forward to an extensive policy program of federal activity that came to face regular resistance from a dissenting minority faction led by more conservative southern officeholders. Race was a natural subject of regional tension, after the African Americans and northern racial liberals attracted to the Democratic cause by New Deal economic policies began to pressure party leaders to support civil rights measures over the opposition of southern segregationists.[8] But internal Democratic divisions extended to many other issue domains as well; in comparison to fellow Democrats elsewhere, for example, southern conservatives tended to be less supportive of strong intervention by the federal government in economic redistribution, business regulation, and public education; more hostile to labor unions; and more hawkish in foreign affairs.[9]

While they lacked the capacity to exert direct control over the nomination of Democratic presidential candidates and the leadership of the House and Senate, conservative southern Democrats still retained a great deal of institutional power. The seniority system in Congress provided Dixiecrats with a disproportionate share of committee chairs and guarded their autonomy from infringement by more liberal fellow partisans. As Julian E. Zelizer notes, "toward the end of the Great Depression …

---

[8] Brian D. Feinstein and Eric Schickler, "Platforms and Partners: The Civil Rights Realignment Reconsidered," *Studies in American Political Development* 22 (2008), pp. 1–31.

[9] V. O. Key Jr., *Southern Politics in State and Nation* (New York: Alfred A. Knopf, 1949).

southern Democrats began to stake their political fortunes on the committee process, when a coalition of urban and labor liberals attempted to move Democrats into new areas of labor policy and even civil rights (by WWII). When this happened, southerners turned to the committee process in order to defend their particular vision of the American state."[10]

Southern Democrats also represented a pivotal voting bloc on the House and Senate floor. When issues arose that split the Democratic majority, an alliance between Dixiecrats and conservative Republicans could usually outvote regular Democrats. Such divisions were rare in the early years of FDR's presidency, but by 1937 a significant bloc of southerners had become increasingly wary of the liberal direction taken by the Second New Deal. "When the Conservative Coalition [of Republicans and southern Democrats] joins the issue," observed John F. Manley, "it wins far more than it loses."[11] The alliance was most influential in exerting negative power by defending the policy status quo against the perennially ambitious agenda of northern and western Democrats; Nelson W. Polsby described it in retrospect as "mostly obstructionist in character, preventing action on a variety of issues."[12]

From the mid-1930s forward, the institutional clout of the Dixiecrats in Congress increasingly frustrated party regulars. Roosevelt himself attempted to roll back the power of the southern conservative faction in 1938, embarking on a barnstorming tour to leverage his personal popularity in support of allied congressional candidates who were challenging New Deal opponents in Democratic primary elections. (This "purge campaign" proved famously unsuccessful.)[13] In an angry 1939 floor speech, liberal Senator Claude Pepper of Florida referred to a "scheming alliance" arrayed against the New Deal, causing several of his southern colleagues to respond with umbrage. Several years later, Senator Joseph Guffey of Pennsylvania similarly charged that an "unpatriotic and unholy alliance" had opposed strong voting rights for (presumably pro-Roosevelt) World War II servicemen in the 1944 election, which inspired Senator Josiah Bailey of North Carolina to warn publicly that southern conservatives could respond to such "insults" by forming their own separate party that

---

[10] Julian E. Zelizer, *On Capitol Hill: The Struggle to Reform Congress and Its Consequences, 1948–2000* (New York: Cambridge University Press, 2004), p. 14.

[11] John F. Manley, "The Conservative Coalition in Congress," *American Behavioral Scientist* 17 (November/December 1973), pp. 223–247, at 223.

[12] Polsby, "American Party System," p. 14.

[13] For more on the 1938 purge campaign, see Susan Dunn, *Roosevelt's Purge: How FDR Fought to Change the Democratic Party* (Cambridge, MA: Belknap Press, 2010).

would "hold the balance of power in this country."[14] Four years later, South Carolina governor Strom Thurmond attempted to make good on this threat by breaking with the national Democratic Party over civil rights, carrying four southern states as the presidential candidate of the States' Rights Party but failing in his aim to force the selection of the president by the House of Representatives – as the Constitution provides when no candidate receives a majority of electoral votes – where southern members might play a decisive role in the outcome.

Roosevelt and other exasperated party regulars may have entertained the notion that the conservative Dixiecrats who dominated southern delegations in Congress did not reflect the true policy preferences of their constituents. Indeed, the system of popular representation in the South was fundamentally distorted during this era by the intentional exclusion of many potential voters from participation via poll taxes, literacy requirements, and other antidemocratic measures. But little evidence exists to suggest that those southerners who did retain access to the ballot box were dissatisfied with the substantive positions taken by their region's elected officials. Not only did Roosevelt's purge campaign fail to convince Democratic voters in the South to replace their sitting representatives with new officeholders who would vote more loyally with the national party, but even Democratic congressional incumbents who acquired a liberal reputation during this period could also find themselves vulnerable to defeat by a more conservative primary opponent when seeking reelection – such as Pepper, the outspoken critic of the conservative coalition, who notably lost the Florida primary in 1950.[15] According to Devin Caughey, "Democratic primaries in the one-party South created a qualified but real electoral connection between voters and politicians ... Southern Democrats in Congress were roughly in step with the Southern white public on economic issues[.]"[16]

While Democratic regional divisions were both more dramatic and, due to the party's dominance of American politics after 1932, more consequential for policymaking, factionalism existed in a slightly more muted form within the Republican Party as well during this period. Ideological

[14] Quotes from Manley, "Conservative Coalition."
[15] Pepper's career in Congress did not end with his primary defeat. He was elected to the U.S. House of Representatives in 1962 from a Miami-based district populated mostly by liberal transplants from the North, serving until his death in 1989.
[16] Devin Caughey, "Representation Without Parties: Reconsidering the One-Party South, 1930–62," paper delivered at the Annual Meetings of the American Political Science Association, Washington, DC, August 28–31, 2014, pp. 1, 26.

differences among Republican party leaders, elected officials, and voters likewise tended to follow geographic boundaries. Senator Robert Taft of Ohio unofficially led a midwestern faction that favored small-government conservatism and isolationist or unilateralist foreign policy. His main rivals within Republican ranks were more moderate party members – especially New York governor Thomas E. Dewey and two-term president Dwight D. Eisenhower – who were reconciled to varying degrees with the New Deal at home and internationalism abroad; most of these "modern Republicans" represented East or West Coast constituencies.[17]

THE CALL FOR PARTY "RESPONSIBILITY"

The internal factionalization of both Democrats and Republicans during the New Deal era encouraged many experts to conclude that American parties inevitably consisted of loose, diverse coalitions of discrete interests and social groups strewn across the continent. While *The American Voter* and other foundational studies of the behavior of the American mass electorate portrayed party identification as a stable and fundamental attribute of the individual citizen that normally outweighed all other considerations when making decisions in the voting booth, neither the ties binding voters to parties nor those connecting party elites to each other were necessarily formed from a common ideology or issue agenda, frustrating efforts by political leaders to galvanize popular or legislative support for specific policy programs.[18] Nowhere was this more apparent than in the South, where voters overwhelmingly supported Roosevelt in four consecutive elections (and, to a lesser degree, Harry Truman in 1948) while simultaneously electing many of both presidents' most powerful congressional antagonists to office by equally decisive margins.

The national parties' attempts to function effectively while simultaneously holding together geographically diverse internal coalitions informed normative debates of the era over the proper role of parties within the political system as a whole. To some scholars, the decentralized character of American parties was a constitutional necessity, if not an active good. They pointed out that an institutional structure based on

---

[17] Nicol C. Rae, *The Decline and Fall of the Liberal Republicans* (New York: Oxford University Press, 1989), p. 6. See also Geoffrey Kabaservice, *Rule and Ruin: The Downfall of Moderation and the Destruction of the Republican Party, from Eisenhower to the Tea Party* (New York: Oxford University Press, 2012).

[18] Angus Campbell, Philip E. Converse, Warren E. Miller, and Donald E. Stokes, *The American Voter* (New York: John Wiley and Sons, 1960).

separation-of-powers principles necessarily (and, indeed, intentionally) tended to frustrate the efforts of a single political majority to gain complete control of the levers of federal power, requiring leaders to accommodate multiple interests in order to realize their policy goals and preventing the implementation of disciplined "party government" in the style of the British Parliament. "Most present-day students of the American party system believe that the primary determinant of its [factionalized] nature is the fact that it must operate within a constitutional system that sets up too many and too effective barriers to the development of unified and responsible parties," observed Austin Ranney in 1951.[19] "The Constitution of the United States has been much admired, and certainly in many respects it is admirable," wrote Dayton David McKean in 1949. "But it was not intended to provide for party government, and it does not; rather it makes responsible party government often impossible and always difficult."[20]

According to this view, the internal incoherence of the American parties not only derived from the electoral independence of the executive and legislative branches, but also reflected underlying regional variation in the political preferences of the electorate. National Democratic and Republican leaders tolerated substantial internal disunity as a necessary cost of maintaining popular support across sectional lines. The American electoral system "assure[s] a dispersion or decentralization of power within the party structures," concluded V. O. Key Jr. "In the dominant party of the moment [i.e., the Democrats] the standpat districts [of the South] provide foundations for party factions not beholden to the national leadership and immune to the depredations of the opposition. The resultant cleavages within the majority are duly recorded on the front pages every day."[21]

Pendleton Herring similarly argued in 1940 that "Our [American] party structure is one product of our system of geographic representation. At best it is broadly sectional, at worst narrowly parochial."[22] To Herring, writing at a time when the Union contained 48 states, the

[19] Austin Ranney, "Toward a More Responsible Two-Party System: A Commentary," *American Political Science Review* 45 (June 1951), pp. 488–499, quote at 492.

[20] Dayton David McKean, *Party and Pressure Politics* (Boston: Houghton Mifflin, 1949), p. 49.

[21] V. O. Key Jr., *Politics, Parties, and Pressure Groups*, 5th edition (New York: Thomas Y. Crowell, 1965), pp. 572–573.

[22] Pendleton Herring, *The Politics of Democracy: American Parties in Action* (New York: W. W. Norton, 1940), p. 211.

parties' factional character represented a consequence of American federalism: "Public policy in the United States is divided between at least forty-nine different governments. Hence, each of the major parties may have forty-nine different platforms."[23] This freedom to adapt readily to the distinctive political conditions of different regions, states, and localities thus demonstrated the critical role of the parties in reflecting and channeling a multiplicity of social divisions within the political system of a diverse and sprawling nation.

Yet other scholars of the era came to view the parties' ideological disunity as far from inevitable – and manifestly undesirable. In 1950, the Committee on Political Parties of the American Political Science Association (APSA) released a report entitled "Toward a More Responsible Two-Party System" under the leadership of Professor E. E. Schattschneider of Wesleyan University. Though the report ostensibly applied to both parties, the authors' dissatisfaction with the status of American politics at the time of publication primarily reflected their observation of the governing Democratic Party, which had controlled both houses of Congress for 16 of the preceding 18 years and had held the White House for all 18. Its central claim that "[a]n effective party system requires, first, that the parties are able to bring forth programs to which they commit themselves and, second, that the parties possess sufficient internal cohesion to carry out those programs" expressed frustration with the oft-demonstrated power of the Dixiecrat bloc to block elements of its own party's national platform from legislative enactment.[24]

The Schattschneider report advocated a series of specific reforms intended to enhance the capacity of the national party leadership to enforce programmatic discipline on individual candidates and office-holders. Among other initiatives, the authors recommended a central role for national party organizations in developing party policies, changes to the process of candidate nominations in order to allow more influence by national party leaders in choosing nominees for the House and Senate, and repeal of the Senate filibuster and the automatic seniority rule for congressional committee chairs. It is hardly a coincidence that these and other measures proposed by the APSA committee as a means of

---

[23] Herring, *Politics of Democracy*, p. 210. He was writing before Alaska and Hawaii achieved statehood.

[24] American Political Science Association, "Toward a More Responsible Party System: A Report of the Committee on Political Parties," *American Political Science Review* 44, part 2 (supplement), p. 18.

strengthening the "internal democracy" of the parties would have had the practical effect of shifting power within the Democratic Party in favor of northern and western party regulars at the expense of southern conservatives. For example, the report's suggestion that the authority of the House Rules Committee – an institutional power center due to its ability to regulate legislative access to the House floor that was mostly ruled by the conservative coalition during the 1940s and 1950s – be curtailed in favor of "open party control" of legislative traffic echoed the wishes of many House liberals, who founded the Democratic Study Group in 1959 as an organizational base to push for such reforms from within Congress itself.

The central importance of sectional factionalism in the party politics of the New Deal era illustrates the critical role played by geographically defined electoral institutions in intermediating between citizens and officeholders. The lack of regional convergence between voters' prevailing partisan and ideological preferences exerted demonstrable effects on the relative electoral strength and internal discipline of the two major parties. In particular, American politics was fundamentally influenced during this period by the existence of an entire region of the country dominated by voters who usually insisted on nominating conservatives over liberals in Democratic congressional primaries and electing them over Republicans of any type in general elections. The role of politically diverse constituencies in limiting the extent of party unity from the late New Deal forward suggests more generally that partisan-ideological configurations at the elite level tend to reflect the nature of geographic alignments out in the wider electorate; if the latter evolve over time, the former will likely be transformed as well.

In time, the parties indeed achieved a greater degree of "responsibility" – not because political leaders enthusiastically embraced the recommendations of a committee of academic experts (though a few of the reforms endorsed by the Schattschneider report were eventually implemented), but instead due to important changes in the composition of the Democratic and Republican mass coalitions. This process, however, took decades to reach completion. The 1930s-era party system had arisen as an instantaneous popular response to the unique national crisis of the Great Depression – an event of sufficient enormity to inspire a partisan revolution that simultaneously extinguished the Republican electoral dominance of the 1920s and replaced the regional divisions that had traditionally defined party conflict in the United States with a national majority that was much more uniform in partisan, if not policy, terms. But no equally dramatic historical development marked the end of the

New Deal era and the immediate advent of increased party responsibility. The path from the internally divided and externally indistinct parties of the 1940s and 1950s to the ideologically and regionally polarized parties of today wound through a quarter-century of transition, during which the emergence of two mutually inconsistent national partisan majorities in presidential and congressional politics appeared to signal a pronounced – and, for many scholars, worrisome – decline in the importance of party affiliation in the minds of American voters.

THE 1964 ELECTION AND THE REPUBLICAN PRESIDENTIAL RESURGENCE

In some respects, the election of 1964 represents the culmination of the era of liberal predominance that began with the New Deal: a national Democratic landslide victory followed by a burst of activist policymaking during the subsequent session of Congress combining FDR-style economic populism – the war on poverty, national education initiatives, the creation of Medicare and Medicaid – with a newly aggressive federal commitment to combating racial inequality. Attempts by the conservative coalition to obstruct this bold legislative program were thwarted by the sheer number of regular Democrats from the North and West who rode into office on the electoral coattails of Lyndon B. Johnson. Johnson, who had succeeded to the presidency upon the assassination of John F. Kennedy on November 22, 1963, carried 44 states and the District of Columbia in his only campaign atop the Democratic ticket, winning 61.1 percent of the national popular vote – still the highest share received by any presidential candidate since James Monroe ran unopposed in the election of 1820. In the 89th Congress of 1965–1966, Democrats representing constituencies outside the 11 former Confederate states constituted 47 percent of the total membership of the House and 48 percent of the Senate; with the additional presence of southern liberals and northern Republicans who supported individual pieces of his agenda, Johnson had the benefit of a working majority in both chambers that, when combined with his considerable personal skill at persuasion and deal making, resulted in the legislative achievements known collectively as the Great Society.

At the same time, other results of the 1964 election pointed toward a different partisan future. Johnson's opponent, Senator Barry Goldwater of Arizona, was a purist Sun Belt conservative whose successful campaign for the Republican presidential nomination represented an unexpected defeat for both the party's ideologically moderate northeastern faction and its traditionally pragmatic midwestern wing. Goldwater was routed across most of the country in the November election – in particular, his remark that "the country would be better off if we could just saw off the Eastern Seaboard and let it float out to sea" did nothing to help his standing in that region – but five of the six states that he carried were located in the Deep South, no doubt reflecting his vote in the Senate against the Civil Rights Act of 1964 just weeks before his nomination.[25] Southern dissatisfaction with the policy trajectory of the national Democratic Party had long predated Goldwater, and Democratic presidential candidates had ceased to enjoy automatic support across the South after the Thurmond-led defection of 1948. Even so, 1964 was the first presidential election since the founding of the Republican Party in which the Republican candidate received a greater share of the popular and electoral vote within the South than outside the region (even though his Democratic opponent was a born-and-bred southerner) – a pattern that has persisted in every subsequent presidential contest except the Jimmy Carter elections of 1976 and 1980.

In his best-selling book *The Emerging Republican Majority* (1969), former Nixon aide Kevin Phillips drew upon the Republican victory in the 1968 presidential election to predict the emergence of a new stable regional configuration.[26] "The upcoming cycle of American politics is likely to match a dominant Republican Party based in the Heartland, South and California against a minority Democratic Party based in the Northeast and the Pacific Northwest," he concluded, perceiving "a populist revolt of the American masses who have been elevated by prosperity to middle-class status and conservatism ... against the caste, policies and taxation of the mandarins of Establishment liberalism."[27] This was indeed a plausible scenario; southern whites had demonstrated a willingness after 1964 to abandon their hereditary identification with a national Democratic Party that took increasingly left-of-center positions on racial as well as economic issues, while the rising appeal of conservative Republicanism in the increasingly populous West was illustrated by the election of Goldwater ally Ronald Reagan to the governorship of California in 1966 and 1970.

While Phillips correctly noted that Nixon's victory in 1968 marked the decline of the New Deal coalition, thus concluding a three-decade period

[25] Carmines and Stimson, *Issue Evolution*, pp. 44–47.
[26] Kevin P. Phillips, *The Emerging Republican Majority* (New Rochelle, NY: Arlington House, 1969).
[27] Phillips, *Emerging Republican Majority*, pp. 544–545, 550.

of Democratic primacy in presidential elections, the strong sectional alignment anticipated by his analysis never formed. Instead, American politics entered a disorienting era in which the political behavior of the electorate remained regionally indistinct while becoming less reliably partisan. The Republican Party indeed achieved a popular resurgence in presidential elections from 1968 forward, but its gains occurred across the electoral map and were not limited to, or even strongly concentrated in, the band of states from Virginia to California that Phillips had identified as the geographic base of the emerging Republican majority. At the congressional level, by contrast, Republicans made notable but initially limited inroads in southern constituencies, introducing two-party competition to the region's House and Senate elections by the 1970s but failing to win a majority of southern seats in either chamber until the 1994 midterm election – fully 30 years after Johnson supposedly remarked, upon signing the Civil Rights Act of 1964, that he was handing the South to the Republican Party for a generation.[28] The electoral record of the 1970s and 1980s does not support the conclusion that Republican inroads in the South decisively influenced the overall balance between the parties; instead, the period produced two parallel majorities – routine Republican victories in presidential elections balanced by consistent Democratic control of Congress – that were both primarily national rather than regional in character.

Nixon's defeat of Hubert Humphrey in 1968 signaled the end of an extended phase of Democratic presidential supremacy (seven victories in the nine elections between 1932 and 1964) and inaugurated what turned out to be a historically exceptional period of electoral success for his own party. Republican nominees received, on average, 55 percent of the national two-party popular vote and 78 percent of the two-party electoral vote between 1968 and 1988 – in both cases, the most dominant partisan advantage in any sequence of six consecutive presidential elections since the advent of American mass parties in the 1820s. The Republican margin of victory exceeded 300 electoral votes in four of these elections and topped 500 electoral votes twice (1972 and 1984) – a feat achieved

[28] Like many well-known quotations, there appears to be no contemporaneous evidence that the credited source actually said it. In his 2004 memoir, aide Bill Moyers recalled Johnson remarking to him several hours after signing the Civil Rights Act that "I think we just delivered the South to the Republican Party for a long time to come," but by that point the anecdote had already been told many times over by political journalists (often qualified with words such as "reportedly" or "legend has it"). See Bill Moyers, *Moyers on America: A Journalist and His Times* (New York: New Press, 2004), p. 167.

only one other time in American history (by Franklin D. Roosevelt in 1936). The lone Democratic triumph during this period, Jimmy Carter's 1976 defeat of Gerald Ford, was both numerically slender (Carter won just 51 percent of the two-party popular vote and 55 percent of the electoral vote) and perhaps a short-term consequence of the Watergate scandal; Ford's unpopular pardon of Nixon after his predecessor's resignation in 1974 may have sealed his narrow defeat. "In short, with respect to presidential voting," concludes James E. Campbell, "1968 was the onset of the post-New Deal party system."[29]

Most Republican presidential victories during this era extended across the American continent, producing decisive national outcomes without major regional variation. While a great deal of popular attention focused on Republican presidential candidates' newfound success across the South, Democratic candidates would have been able to survive the loss of that region if they had been able to maintain the support received by FDR, Truman, and Johnson in the Northeast, Midwest, and West. Instead, Democratic popular margins collapsed everywhere. All 50 states were carried by a Republican presidential candidate at least once between 1968 and 1980, with 21 states voting Republican in all six contests between 1968 and 1988 – including the future Democratic bastions of Vermont, New Jersey, Illinois, and California – and another 17 states voting Democratic only once during this period (see Figure 3.2).[30] Even Carter's aberrant victory in 1976 reflected his identity as an ideologically moderate, peanut-farming Baptist from Georgia, which allowed him to bring all but two southern states back into the Democratic fold for one final presidential election (with Virginia and Oklahoma remaining in Republican hands) – though his opponent Ford received a plurality of popular votes outside the South and won 57 percent of the nonsouthern electoral vote.

In a break with the usual pattern of American history, however, the sustained electoral success of Republican presidential candidates between 1968 and 1988 was not accompanied by comparable gains for the party in House and Senate contests. Richard Nixon became the first new president since Zachary Taylor in 1848 to take office with both houses of Congress controlled by the opposition party; even his landslide 1972

---

[29] James E. Campbell, "Party Systems and Realignments in the United States, 1868–2004," *Social Science History* 30 (2006), pp. 359–386, quote on p. 378.

[30] Four of the states that voted only once for the national Democratic presidential nominee between 1968 and 1988 – Alabama, Arkansas, Louisiana, and Mississippi – were carried in the 1968 election by the third-party sectional candidate George Wallace.

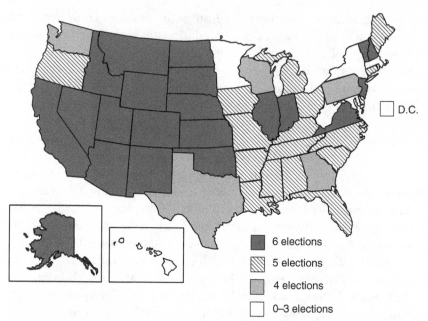

FIGURE 3.2. Total number of presidential victories per state by Republican or independent candidates, 1968–1988.

reelection victory (in which he won 49 states and prevailed in the national popular vote by 23 percentage points over Democratic challenger George McGovern) failed to dislodge Democratic majorities in either chamber. Ronald Reagan managed to carry a Republican-controlled Senate into office with him in 1980 (though the House still remained under Democratic rule), but heavy Republican losses in the 1986 midterm elections returned the Democratic Party to unified control of Congress once again, which endured through the single-term presidency of George H. W. Bush. The lonely landslides of Republican presidential nominees between 1968 and 1988 prompted a scholarly reevaluation of the role of party identification in motivating the electoral behavior of voters, inspiring a new round of normative concerns about the vitality of the American party system.

NATIONALIZED POLITICS AND PARTY DECLINE
IN THE MASS PUBLIC

The American electorate's newfound penchant after 1968 for dividing control of the federal government between a Republican president and a

Democratic Congress presented political scientists, journalists, and politicians alike with a puzzling phenomenon demanding further explanation. These results seemed to contradict traditional theories of voting behavior that emphasized the salience of party identification in guiding the electoral choices made by citizens. Short-term circumstances, such as a particularly unpopular incumbent administration or an especially attractive opposition candidate, might cause a significant minority of voters to temporarily defect from their home party at the ballot box – such as the Democrats who crossed party lines to support Eisenhower for president in 1952 and 1956 – but voters who consistently supported the opposite party's nominees in a long series of elections, or who regularly split their ticket by voting for one party for president and the other for Congress, seemed to have become unmoored from the party system itself, producing aggregate election results that defied easy interpretation and failed to send a clear message to policy-makers about the collective political will of the public.

It is hardly a coincidence that a revisionist school of thought began to question whether party identification was as stable and central an attribute in the minds of voters as the authors of *The American Voter* had believed. Several new studies portrayed party identification not as an "unmoved mover" of political attitudes and candidate preferences, but rather as frequently sensitive to short-term considerations such as the performance of incumbent officeholders, the popularity of individual party candidates, and the emergence of political issues that cut across traditional party lines.[31] In addition, the proportion of American citizens who identified with neither major party increased after the mid-1960s (rising from 28 percent to 37 percent between 1966 and 1976, according to the American National Election Studies), suggesting a decline in the importance of party affiliation as a force structuring the political orientations of individuals.[32]

The persistence of durable national Democratic congressional majorities built on a popular partisan advantage that stretched across regional boundaries, even as Republican presidential candidates repeatedly

[31] For example, Morris P. Fiorina, *Retrospective Voting in American National Elections* (New Haven, CT: Yale University Press, 1981); Charles H. Franklin and John E. Jackson, "The Dynamics of Party Identification," *American Political Science Review* 77 (1983), pp. 957–973; Benjamin I. Page and Calvin C. Jones, "Reciprocal Effects of Policy Preferences, Party Loyalties, and the Vote," *American Political Science Review* 73 (1979), pp. 1071–1089.

[32] Harold D. Clarke and Motoshi Suzuki, "Partisan Dealignment and the Dynamics of Independence in the American Electorate, 1953–88," *British Journal of Political Science* 24 (January 1994), pp. 57–77.

achieved popular victories that were equally decisive and geographically broad, directed the attention of electoral scholars during the 1970s and 1980s toward the means by which congressional candidates had apparently managed to insulate themselves from the partisan tides that determined presidential outcomes, thus producing the first sustained period of divided government in American history. The rise of television was frequently credited for bolstering the electoral fortunes of incumbent members of Congress, who exploited the individual attention provided by the new medium as a means of cultivating a strong personal following in their home states and districts that could transcend party affiliation. Sitting senators and representatives also enjoyed an inherent advantage in raising the rapidly increasing amount of money required to wage an effective congressional campaign once costly television advertising became the primary means of communicating with voters, and in exploiting their offices to provide popular benefits and services to their constituents. Scholars also emphasized the effects of candidate quality, demonstrating that political experience and skill (as well as fundraising success) tended to provide candidates with significantly more support from voters than they could expect based on party affiliation alone.[33] The consistent Democratic advantage in congressional races during this period partly reflected the party's superior recruitment of quality candidates – especially in southern constituencies, where the traditional Democratic affiliation of state and local elected officials provided the party with a larger supply of strong potential congressional nominees.[34]

Two landmark studies of the era, David R. Mayhew's *Congress: The Electoral Connection* (1974) and Richard F. Fenno Jr.'s *Home Style* (1978), examined the efforts of congressional representatives to maintain a positive reputation among their constituents during a time of decaying popular trust in Congress, the party system, and the entire public sector.[35] Mayhew noted the ways in which the organization of Congress worked

[33] Thomas E. Mann, *Unsafe at Any Margin: Interpreting Congressional Elections* (Washington, DC: American Enterprise Institute, 1978); Bruce Cain, John Ferejohn, and Morris Fiorina, *The Personal Vote: Constituency Service and Electoral Independence* (Cambridge, MA: Harvard University Press, 1987).

[34] Gary C. Jacobson, *The Electoral Origins of Divided Government: Competition in U.S. House Elections, 1946–1988* (Boulder, CO: Westview Press, 1990); James E. Campbell, *The Presidential Pulse of Congressional Elections*, 2nd edition (Lexington: University Press of Kentucky, 1997).

[35] David R. Mayhew, *Congress: The Electoral Connection* (New Haven, CT: Yale University Press, 1974); Richard F. Fenno Jr., *Home Style: House Members in Their Districts* (Boston: Little, Brown, 1978).

to the advantage of individual members seeking to maintain a strong personal appeal among the voters who had elected them. Such familiar institutional features as the committee system, roll-call voting, and bill sponsorship provided opportunities for incumbents to attract politically valuable publicity, whether for staking out popular issue positions or for delivering particularized benefits to their constituencies such as federally funded infrastructure projects. Fenno accompanied members of the House of Representatives as they traveled within their home districts, finding that the officeholders whom he observed strategically presented themselves as sympathetic and relatable personalities who shared more in common with their constituents than they did with their congressional colleagues: "one of you" rather than "one of them." As he memorably observed, "members of Congress run *for* Congress by running *against* Congress."[36]

The repeated success of Republican presidential nominees from the late 1960s onward signaled an end to the era in which the New Deal coalition routinely carried the Democratic Party to electoral victory. Yet the inability of Republican candidates to achieve broader success in down-ballot races, as well as the persistence of the Democratic numerical edge in the aggregate party identification of the American public, dissuaded many scholars from classifying 1968 as a critical election establishing a new Republican majority nationwide. Instead of a standard party *realignment*, some observers concluded that Nixon's election alongside a securely Democratic Congress marked the beginning of a period of *dealignment* in the American electorate, characterized by elevated rates of split-ticket voting, declining levels of party loyalty, rising proportions of citizens who identified as independents or weakly attached partisans, and decreasing rates of electoral participation (which occurred in tandem with growing disaffection from the political system in general and political parties in particular).[37] Fewer voters, it appeared, oriented themselves within the political arena by means of a strong Democratic or Republican identity, opening up a vacuum of influence that was instead filled by "candidate-centered" campaigns that deemphasized party affiliation in favor of personality, incumbency, or other alternative bases of appeal.[38]

---

[36] Fenno, *Home Style*, p. 168.
[37] Walter Dean Burnham, "The Reagan Heritage," in Gerald Pomper et al., eds., *The Elections of 1988: Reports and Interpretations* (Chatham, NJ: Chatham House), pp. 1–32; Paul Allen Beck, "The Dealignment Era in America," in Russell J. Dalton, Scott C. Flanagan, and Paul Allen Beck, eds., *Electoral Change in Advanced Industrial Democracies* (Princeton, NJ: Princeton University Press, 1984), pp. 240–266.
[38] Martin P. Wattenberg, *The Decline of American Political Parties, 1952–1984* (Cambridge, MA: Harvard University Press, 1986).

Political scientists often touted strong and effective parties as essential components of a healthy democracy, and the "party decline" thesis of the 1970s and 1980s often engendered a distinctly pessimistic tone in the analyses of party scholars. Academics and popular commentators alike held the parties themselves largely responsible for their flagging ability to inspire devotion and enthusiasm in the hearts of the American citizenry. "The picture of political parties [today] is not a pleasant one," wrote William Crotty in 1984. "The biggest difficulty will be in the absence of the bonds that held party coalitions together and that allowed for some coherence among different levels of party concerns (the president, Congress, and the voter)."[39] With the deterioration of party strength, argued Martin P. Wattenberg in 1986, "many citizens have been set adrift without an anchor in a political world full of strong eddies and currents."[40] David H. Everson explained in 1982 why political experts viewed the apparent fraying of partisan ties in the electorate as a deeply concerning development:

[M]any analysts ... argue that policymaking has become too fragmented to respond adequately to complex issues, such as energy and the economy. The result is that many policies are incoherent and government is often immobilized. At the heart of the problem, according to many writers, is the decline of parties, because parties have historically been the essential elements of the coalitions necessary for making coherent policies. Some suspect that the collapse of parties is virtually irreversible and therefore regard the future of American politics as bleak ...

The decline of party loyalty means that presidential elections involve fewer voters, many of whom base their choice on the personal characteristics of the candidates as communicated via the mass media ... The links between the winners of presidential elections and their fellow partisans in Congress have diminished, making it increasingly hard for presidents to govern effectively ... A new code of American politics is necessary – one that sees political accountability in party rather than in individual terms.[41]

From our current vantage point in an era of revived partisanship that many critics now view as alarmingly excessive, such anxieties seem quaint – even humorously so. But the decline of party-line voting and apparent rise of candidate-centered elections after 1968 not only appeared to jeopardize the connection between the policy preferences of voters and

---

[39] William Crotty, *American Parties in Decline*, 2nd edition (Boston: Little, Brown, 1984), pp. 275, 280.
[40] Wattenberg, *Decline of American Political Parties*, p. 130.
[41] David H. Everson, "The Decline of Political Parties," *Proceedings of the Academy of Political Science* 34 (1982), pp. 49–60, at 49, 52, 59.

the actions of elected officials, but also threatened to produce habitual legislative stalemate at the federal level by frequently dividing institutional control between the parties. If the barrier to realizing the ideal of efficient, responsive "party government" in the 1940s and 1950s had chiefly resided in the national majority party's lack of sufficient internal unity around a common substantive platform, this objective was now also frustrated by the insistence of many American voters in each region of the nation on repeatedly splitting their partisan tickets between Republican presidents and Democratic members of Congress.

The prospect of citizens increasingly choosing candidates on the basis of the appeal of their individual personalities, their ability to bestow government largesse on their constituents, and the cleverness (or ruthlessness) of their television advertising campaigns understandably worried political analysts who viewed electoral outcomes as ideally signaling the preferred policy direction of the American public. Elections such as 1972 or 1984, when coast-to-coast Republican presidential landslides were balanced by the preservation of geographically broad Democratic congressional majorities, were difficult to interpret as conferring a coherent mandate on national leaders to enact a specific legislative program. For advocates of vigorous, responsible parties, this was a disconcerting development. Despite numerous contemporary complaints of habitual "deadlock" and "stalemate," however, this historical period was not bereft of bipartisan compromise – an observation that is more apparent in retrospect, looking back from a later age in which cooperation across party lines has become an even less common occurrence.

BIPARTISANSHIP IN DIVIDED GOVERNMENT, 1968–1992

If the majority of congressional Democrats from the South had remained conservatives in the Dixiecrat tradition during the post-1968 era of Republican presidential dominance, the new norm of divided government would have been easier to reconcile as ideologically consistent – and potentially auspicious for the passage of a sweeping right-of-center policy agenda – even if it remained stubbornly contradictory in partisan terms. But the proportion of Dixiecrats in both houses of Congress declined after the 1960s, due in part to the rise of an organized Republican Party in the South over the course of the 1960s and early 1970s. Newly successful Republican candidates were more likely to defeat or succeed right-leaning Dixiecrats than mainstream Democrats – presumably because

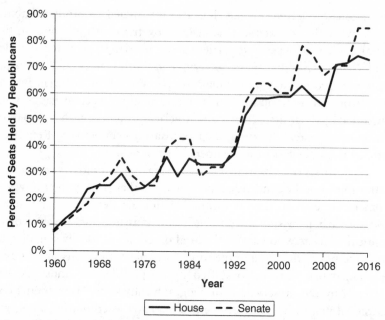

FIGURE 3.3. Share of southern congressional seats held by Republicans, 1960–2016.

the most conservative constituencies in the region were initially the most receptive to the Republican cause – while a few conservative Democratic incumbents, such as South Carolina senator and ex-Dixiecrat presidential candidate Strom Thurmond, reinforced this trend by switching parties themselves.[42]

Congressional Republicans established electoral viability in isolated southern outposts as early as the 1950s, but the party's progress in House and Senate elections significantly lagged its surging regional popularity in presidential voting. The share of southern seats held by Republicans rose from 8 percent in the House and 7 percent in the Senate as of the 1960 election to 25 percent and 29 percent, respectively, ten years later (see Figure 3.3). But this rate of growth slowed in the 1970s and 1980s; with the exception of the Senate in 1982 and 1984, the proportion of Republicans in the southern delegation of either chamber never exceeded 40 percent. Democrats continued to

[42] Polsby, "American Party System"; David Lublin, *The Republican South: Democratization and Partisan Change* (Princeton, NJ: Princeton University Press, 2004); Seth C. McKee, *Republican Ascendancy in U.S. House Elections* (Boulder, CO: Westview Press, 2010).

hold two out of every three House and Senate seats from the South as late as the early 1990s.

Dixiecrats in Congress also faced a new threat from the left after the mid-1960s due to a changing southern electorate. The passage of the federal Voting Rights Act in 1965 granted millions of black southerners (and a significant number of previously disenfranchised whites) fair access to the ballot box for the first time, which exerted a collectively liberalizing effect on the politics of the region and transformed Democratic primary elections into treacherous ground for old-line conservative candidates, especially those opposed to civil rights. While only 15 percent of Senate Democrats and 27 percent of House Democrats from the eleven ex-Confederate states voted in favor of the Voting Rights Act as originally enacted in 1965, amendments and extensions to the law introduced ten years later gained support from 64 percent of southern Democratic senators and 75 percent of southern Democratic House members, demonstrating the speed with which racial politics changed within the southern Democratic Party after the enfranchisement of African Americans. By 1982, when Congress approved an additional round of Voting Rights Act revisions, no southern Democrat in either chamber voted in opposition. As *Congressional Quarterly* observed, "The steady upward trend in Southern support for the Voting Rights Act reflected not only changing social and political mores but – more directly – a dramatic increase since 1965 in the number of blacks registered to vote in the South and their growing clout at the polls."[43]

Regional factionalism within the congressional Democratic Party did not disappear entirely, however. As the Dixiecrat old guard thinned out after the mid-1960s, many were replaced by a different breed of politician: the moderate southern Democrat. Often elected by successfully appealing to biracial voting coalitions in their home constituencies, these members were not the outright ideological misfits within their party that their more conservative predecessors had been. Yet the need to win support from a less liberal general electorate than their Democratic colleagues from northern states provided an incentive to regularly stake out positions to the right of the party median on certain salient issues, giving the southern bloc of congressional Democrats a distinctively centrist tinge. This generation of moderate Democrats dominated southern politics between the enactment of the Voting Rights Act in 1965 and the

---

[43] "Voting Rights Act Extended, Strengthened," *CQ Almanac 1982* (Washington, DC: Congressional Quarterly, 1983), pp. 373–377.

Republican congressional victories of the 1990s. Prominent members of Congress who fit this political profile included senators Ernest "Fritz" Hollings of South Carolina, Dale Bumpers of Arkansas, Lawton Chiles of Florida, Sam Nunn of Georgia, Chuck Robb of Virginia, Lloyd Bentsen of Texas, John Breaux of Louisiana, and Wendell Ford of Kentucky; and House members Wilbur Mills of Arkansas, Ed Jenkins of Georgia, Tom Bevill of Alabama, and Jake Pickle of Texas.

The Republican Party of the 1970s and 1980s contained its own smaller moderate faction. Most Republican moderates represented constituencies located in the Northeast, urban Midwest, or West Coast. Prominent moderate figures of the era included senators Jacob Javits of New York, Lowell Weicker of Connecticut, John Chafee of Rhode Island, Clifford Case of New Jersey, Charles Percy of Illinois, and Mark Hatfield of Oregon; and House members Silvio Conte of Massachusetts, Bill Green of New York, Carl Pursell of Michigan, and Pete McCloskey of California.

In retrospect, this period of congressional history seems to represent a happy medium between the weak-party era of the mid-twentieth century and the bitter polarization of recent years. The parties in government had become more ideologically distinct by the early 1970s than they had been in the 1940s and 1950s, yet each still retained a sizable centrist bloc that helped to facilitate regular occasions of bipartisan lawmaking. Especially in the House, the apparent inevitability of perpetual Democratic control reduced the partisan stakes of congressional elections and discouraged party leaders from engaging in unfettered procedural warfare.

The temporary eclipse of strong regional differences in the partisan preferences of the electorate during this period thus played a significant role in shaping the character of the congressional parties. The existence of large numbers of Democrats representing what are now known as the red states, as well as a smaller but still significant bloc of blue-state Republicans, exerted a collectively moderating effect on national politics. The substantial proportion of Americans whose policy views fell between doctrinaire liberalism and dogmatic conservatism were therefore well represented among the ranks of federal officeholders, due in large part to the ability of both parties to attract popular support across geographic lines.

In addition, ticket-splitting voters generated a plethora of divided partisan constituencies – states and congressional districts that were carried by Republican presidential nominees yet elected Democratic candidates to Congress – that similarly encouraged party leaders on both sides to seek political common ground. Because Democratic identifiers and Democratic-leaning independents still collectively constituted a majority of the national electorate, Republican presidents understood that their political success depended upon winning crucial support from voters who did not consider themselves Republicans, such as the "Nixon Democrats" and "Reagan Democrats" who regularly defected from their own party's presidential nominees during this period while continuing to support Democratic candidates for congressional office. At the same time, Democratic senators and House members, equally aware that the Republican presidents with whom they served had often carried their home states or districts by comfortable margins, were reluctant to flatly obstruct the policy agenda of the White House. "The presence of these 'cross-pressured' legislators," notes David Karol, "often allowed chief executives to find allies across party lines."[44] Presidents of the era often attempted to mobilize citizen support by "going public" with their legislative demands, using the modern electronic media as a tool to exert political leverage over members of Congress.[45]

Many observers expressed concerns about the capacity of divided party control to reduce democratic responsiveness and encourage institutional gridlock. For example, Randall Ripley wrote in 1983 that "In general, not much legislation is produced in [conditions of divided government], particularly on domestic matters. What domestic legislation does pass is likely to be bland and inconsequential."[46] David H. Everson concluded in 1982 that "Once the election is over, the coalition that produced victory in the presidential election is often unable to produce an effective and durable governing coalition ... The final costs of party decline are to be found in the diminished effectiveness and legitimacy of government action."[47]

Yet a retrospective assessment of the 1968–1992 period finds considerable bipartisan policy-making activity. Republican presidents from Richard Nixon through George H. W. Bush succeeded in cooperating with Democratic leaders in the House and Senate to pass a series of major laws across a variety of issue domains: the Occupational Health

[44] David Karol, *Party Position Change in American Politics: Coalition Management* (New York: Cambridge University Press, 2009), p. 210.

[45] Samuel Kernell, *Going Public: New Strategies of Presidential Leadership* (Washington, DC: CQ Press, 1986).

[46] Randall B. Ripley, *Congress: Process and Policy* (New York: W. W. Norton, 1983), p. 355.

[47] Everson, "Decline of Political Parties," pp. 53–54, 59.

and Safety Act, Clean Air Act, Endangered Species Act, and Title IX education amendments (all during the Nixon presidency); Social Security reform, tax reform, and immigration reform (during the administration of Ronald Reagan); and the Americans with Disabilities Act, an expanded Clean Air Act, and the deficit reduction agreement of 1990 (during the presidency of the elder Bush). In several other cases, most notably Reagan's 1981 budget and tax proposals, moderate congressional Democrats (especially from the South) crossed party lines to help enact popular Republican initiatives over the objections of Democratic leaders. If anything, the single term of united Democratic control during the presidency of Jimmy Carter (1977–1981) marked a low point in presidential relations with Congress during this period, due to recurrent conflict between the Carter White House and Democratic leaders in the House and Senate. A comprehensive 1991 study by David R. Mayhew challenged the conventional wisdom of the time by concluding that legislative productivity did not in fact suffer under conditions of divided government.[48]

In summary, the simultaneous preference of voters in the North, South, East, and West alike for both Republican presidents and Democratic members of Congress produced election results from the late 1960s until the early 1990s that were as nationally uniform in character as they were inconsistent in partisan direction. While both parties retained identifiable ideological factions with discrete geographic bases, internal party cohesion steadily increased beginning in the 1970s, resulting in the empowerment of party leaders at the expense of cross-partisan coalitions in Congress. Divisions within the congressional Democratic Party became more manageable, as the rise of a viable southern Republican party organization and the liberalization of the southern Democratic electorate after the passage of the Voting Rights Act cooperated to reduce the numbers of conservative Dixiecrats. With the question of federally enforced formal racial equality largely settled after 1968, and the South undergoing rapid processes of population growth, urbanization, and economic development, some analysts suggested that the region might become fully integrated into the national party system and therefore shed much of its distinctive political culture.[49]

---

[48] David R. Mayhew, *Divided We Govern* (New Haven, CT: Yale University Press, 1991).

[49] Byron E. Shafer and Richard Johnston, *The End of Southern Exceptionalism: Class, Race, and Partisan Change in the Postwar South* (Cambridge, MA: Harvard University Press, 2006).

The relatively national character of party coalitions during the 1968–1992 period also reflected the lack of a highly salient policy domain that split the electorate along regional boundaries. The issue positions that separated Democratic from Republican voters, primarily the long-standing conflict over economic interests and domestic policy preferences that characterized post–New Deal partisan competition, did not strongly divide the North from the South, or the interior West from the Pacific Coast. Each party's ability to hold a broad geographic constituency together over several decades of elections – in presidential contests for Republicans, in congressional voting for Democrats – suggested to some observers that American politics had entered an age of permanently muted regional differences. After decades of nationalized elections, few analysts anticipated the abrupt return of geographically polarized outcomes in the 1990s – a development that, as Chapter 4 describes, signified the rising electoral importance of a new set of issues and coincided with an unexpected resurgence of partisan strength in both mass and elite politics.

CONCLUSION: A RETURN TO NORMAL POLITICS

From the perspective of the mid- to late twentieth century, many analysts understandably regarded the waning of partisan regionalism in the New Deal era and thereafter as the virtually inevitable product of a political environment that had been fundamentally transformed by the growth of federal power. According to this viewpoint, the sectional alignments that had dominated American electoral politics from the nation's founding through the 1920s mostly reflected competition over parochial issues and interests during a historical period when the national government was relatively small in size and limited in authority. The building of a modern state with dramatically expanded responsibilities both at home and abroad, prompting broad philosophical conflict within the country's political leadership over the appropriate scope and role of government activity and America's proper place in the world, could therefore be expected to stimulate the replacement of regionally based parties with geographically uniform partisan competitiveness – thus signaling a logical progressive evolution from archaic provincialism to national integration.

Several of their generation's most distinguished party scholars endorsed this view. V. O. Key Jr. predicted an "erosion of sectionalism" as early as 1955 – nearly a decade before the Civil Rights Act – while

E. E. Schattschneider devoted a passage of his landmark 1960 study *The Semisovereign People* to what he called the "nationalization" of American politics.[50] "The elections since 1932 have substituted a national political alignment for an extreme sectional alignment," Schattschneider wrote. "[T]here has been a sharp decline in the number of one-party states ... [and] elections are now dominated by factors that work on a national scale ... We are, for the first time in American history, within striking distance of a competitive two-party system throughout the country, and the nationalizing tendency has continued regardless of which of the parties is successful."[51]

The much-lamented decline of party affiliation as a voting cue after the 1960s could likewise be plausibly explained as reflecting the march of a certain kind of progress – in particular, as representing a consequence of modern technological innovations such as television. While many analysts who viewed robust parties as necessary attributes of a well-functioning democracy expressed serious concerns that the rise of candidate-centered campaigns threatened the strength of the political system, they acknowledged an apparent connection between the popular adoption of new forms of mass communication and the decline of traditional party ties. As Martin P. Wattenberg argued in 1986:

The tremendous growth of the media has undoubtedly been one of the most important factors in reshaping the American electoral scene in recent years. Where once candidates for public office had to rely on mustering organizational strength to communicate with voters, it is now increasingly possible for them to establish direct contact through the media ... Such a style of media campaigning reinforces attitudes about candidates but does little to reinforce partisan attitudes.[52]

Frank J. Sorauf agreed, writing in 1980 that "It is the candidate, not the party, who is 'sold.' The image transmitted by TV and the other media is of a person, not of the abstraction known as a political party."[53]

For decades, scholars maintained the view that regionally indistinct and electorally weakened parties reflected the arrival of political

[50] V. O. Key Jr., "The Erosion of Sectionalism," *Virginia Quarterly Review* 31 (Spring 1955), pp. 161–179.

[51] E. E. Schattschneider, *The Semisovereign People: A Realist's View of Democracy in America* (Hinsdale, IL: Dryden Press, 1960), pp. 89, 90 (italics in original omitted).

[52] Wattenberg, *Decline of American Political Parties*, pp. 90–91.

[53] Frank J. Sorauf, *Party Politics in America*, 4th edition (Boston: Little, Brown, 1980), p. 255.

modernity. "The 1928–1936 election sequence," Harvey L. Schantz concluded in a 1992 retrospective study, "marks the transition from an era of sectional politics to one with more nationally uniform voting patterns ... [and] without large regional bases safe for each of the parties."[54] Larry M. Bartels noted as late as 2000 that the declining popular strength of partisanship "is one of the most familiar themes in popular and scholarly discourse about contemporary American politics."[55] But recent empirical research by Bartels and other analysts has established that "the American political system has slipped ... into an era of increasingly vibrant partisanship in the electorate" since the 1970s and 1980s, while the findings presented in Chapter 2 demonstrate the reappearance of regional divisions in presidential and congressional elections over the same period.[56] While scholars once commonly concluded otherwise, it is now clear that neither the development of the modern American state nor the advent of electronic media necessarily precludes the existence of strong and heavily regionalized parties, forcing an overdue reappraisal of the conventional wisdom of an earlier era.

With the contemporary period of resurgent mass and elite partisanship now extending well into its third decade of existence, there is little reason to assume that the current state of ideological and geographic polarization represents a temporary or easily reversed departure from an assumed historical norm of bipartisan compromise and philosophical moderation. As the years pass, both the internally divided parties of the New Deal system and the candidate-centered elections of the "dealignment" era increasingly appear in retrospect to have been the products of unique and impermanent circumstances – such as the crisis of the Great Depression, the fervent Democratic loyalty of the conservative white South in the period between Reconstruction and the civil rights movement, and the formerly limited association between partisanship and ideology in the mass electorate. Yet the reemergence of significant regional differences in electoral outcomes from the early 1990s forward was not itself an

---

[54] Harvey L. Schantz, "The Erosion of Sectionalism in Presidential Elections," *Polity* 24 (Spring 1992), pp. 355–377, at 375.

[55] Larry M. Bartels, "Partisanship and Voting Behavior, 1952–1996," *American Journal of Political Science* 44 (2000), pp. 35–50, at 35.

[56] Quote from Bartels, "Partisanship and Voting Behavior," p. 44; see also Marc J. Hetherington, "Resurgent Mass Partisanship: The Role of Elite Polarization," *American Political Science Review* 95 (September 2001), pp. 619–631.

inevitable development. As the next chapter explains, it reflected the return of evenly matched partisan competition at the national level in both presidential and congressional elections, coupled with the simultaneous extension of party conflict into an issue domain that drove a new political wedge between the denizens of the coasts and their cousins in the heartland.

4

Mapping the Cultural Battlefield: How Social Issues Fuel the Regional Divide

A REGIONAL RESPONSE TO NATIONALIZED POLITICS

The events of the 1970s and 1980s encouraged scholars to conclude that American politics had abandoned its long tradition of entrenched sectional conflict in order to enter a new "modern" era of national integration. But each party's ability to maintain electoral popularity across regional boundaries – especially Republicans in presidential elections and Democrats in congressional contests – depended upon the existence of a national issue agenda that did not produce substantial geographic variation in the views of citizens. Once an alternative set of policy questions arose that split northerners from southerners and urbanites from rural inhabitants, and once voters began to support one party or the other on the basis of these issues while exhibiting a diminishing tendency to reward incumbency or other personal characteristics of candidates regardless of their party label, a significant regional schism immediately reemerged in American elections. Parties that could no longer easily win votes by adapting to the local prevailing political culture each sank into permanent minority status across large sections of the nation, allowing the dominant opposition to achieve a prohibitive popular advantage that reduced the incentive for elected officials to adopt moderate policy positions.

It is no accident that the emergence of today's familiar set of regional divisions in presidential and congressional elections occurred alongside the expansion of partisan conflict to a new array of issues. As this chapter demonstrates, the newfound salience of social and cultural concerns during the 1990s was the driving force behind the divergence of the blue Northeast and Pacific Coast from the red South and interior West. These developments simultaneously bolstered the electoral fortunes of Democratic presidential nominees and Republican congressional candidates, breaking the existing respective partisan "locks" on the two elective branches of government and inaugurating a new era of nationally competitive – but regionally divisive – contests for control of both the White House and Capitol Hill.

Some pundits have claimed that these newer cultural battles signal the declining importance in the minds of voters of older partisan disagreements over economic issues and interests. However, quantitative analyses indicate that Democratic and Republican supporters remain strongly divided over economic matters – in fact, they are more so today than in years past. There is little evidence that cultural issues, though a significant secondary axis of partisan conflict, weigh more heavily than economic concerns in guiding the candidate choices of individual Americans.

Yet social issues are more important than economic issues in accounting for aggregate differences in electoral outcomes across regional boundaries. The significant divide between the residents of Red and Blue America in collective religiosity and adherence to cultural traditionalism has gained a newfound political importance over the past three decades that is particularly powerful in shaping the geographic coalitions of the parties. The conflict over culture may not serve as the primary factor producing partisan differences between individual voters, but it has come to define the national electoral map.

WANDERING IN THE WILDERNESS

At the end of 1991, the Democratic congressional majority stood at 271–164 in the House of Representatives and 57–43 in the Senate. Democrats held 28 of the nation's 50 governorships (compared to 20 Republicans and 2 independents) and controlled a remarkable 72 of 99 state legislative chambers nationwide (with just 23 led by Republicans, 3 divided evenly between the two parties, and one formally nonpartisan unicameral legislature in Nebraska). The party was entering its seventh consecutive decade of holding a numerical advantage among the American public; according to the 1990 American National Election Studies, 39 percent of respondents considered themselves Democrats (while another 12 percent were independents who leaned Democratic), compared to just 25 percent reporting Republican identification. By every measure except control of the presidency, the Democratic Party enjoyed a durable majority status in American politics that prevailed across geographic regions and levels of government.

Yet the party's frequent victories in races for Congress and state office during this period merely directed further attention to what had become a 20-year record of futility in presidential elections. Republican candidates not only won five of the six contests between 1968 and 1988 – excepting only a very narrow loss in 1976 – but repeatedly achieved victories that were historic in scale, amassing overwhelming electoral margins in 1972 (carrying 97 percent of the national electoral vote), 1980 (91 percent), 1984 (98 percent), and 1988 (79 percent). Due to the unique visibility and power of the presidency, this departure from the broader pattern of Democratic popular success in the 1970s and 1980s was more than sufficient to mark the era as one of Republican dominance: the age of Richard Nixon and Ronald Reagan.

Electoral defeat inspires second-guessing and assignment of blame both within and outside the campaign that suffers it, reinforced by the common assumption that the outcome would have been favorable had different tactics been employed, a more appealing message conveyed, or embarrassing gaffes avoided. When a party loses multiple elections, either for a single office in succession or simultaneously across an array of seats, these analyses inevitably supplement their rehearsal of the various perceived blunders committed by individual candidates with a broader indictment of the substantive direction and strategic competence of the party itself. Democratic leaders suffered such a fate during the Nixon and Reagan years. By the early 1990s, the party's repeated defeats in presidential elections had set off political alarms that blared from all directions.

Many pundits concluded that Democratic presidential ambitions had been taken captive by the inflexible programmatic demands of a cadre of activists and interest groups, which invariably led to electoral misfortune once the party's nominee advanced to face the politically savvy Republican opposition. These supposed obstacles to political pragmatism included big-city mayors, who seemed to represent a bygone era of public-sector expansion; labor unions, whose membership ranks and clout in general elections had declined considerably over the previous three decades; and, perhaps above all, representatives of various disadvantaged social groups – racial minorities, feminists, the poor – whose ceaseless clamor for special attention from the government was allegedly indulged to excess by Democratic politicians, thereby alienating many self-identified "regular"

Americans from the party that claimed to be their most loyal champion.[1]
This view won widespread acceptance from triumphant Republicans and
nonpartisan media commentators but was also shared by a number of
frustrated Democratic politicians, consultants, and policy specialists who
argued that the party needed to adapt to changing times in order to win
back the White House. Democratic-aligned intellectuals William Galston
and Elaine Ciulla Kamarck of the Progressive Policy Institute warned
in 1989 that "contemporary liberals have lost touch with the American
people ... During its heyday, the liberal governing coalition brought
together white working-class voters and minorities with a smattering of
professionals and reformers. Over the past two decades, however, liberal
fundamentalism has meant a coalition increasingly dominated by minority groups and white elites – a coalition viewed by the middle class as
unsympathetic to its interests and its values."[2]

Attempts to identify the cause of the Democratic Party's presidential
difficulties after the 1960s often turned to an examination of Democratic
identifiers who defected to vote Republican for president but returned
to the partisan fold in down-ballot races. Analysts failed to settle on a
consensus demographic profile of these Nixon and Reagan Democrats
– in some accounts, they were mostly middle-class professionals alienated by the party's tolerance of high taxes and crime rates, while other
descriptions portrayed them as largely consisting of white Catholics and
blue-collar southerners dissatisfied with Democratic leaders' cultural per-
missiveness and dovish approach to foreign policy. However, commentators largely agreed that a serious gap had emerged between a stubbornly
liberal national party leadership and an increasingly conservative electorate, allowing Republican candidates to capture the support of enough
independents and disaffected Democratic identifiers to repeatedly win the
presidency by comfortable margins despite their own party's smaller proportion of adherents in the mass public.

These pundits found abundant evidence to substantiate their conclusions in the state-by-state results of national elections. Southern voters'
collective abandonment of the Democratic ticket in years when the party
nominated liberals, Yankees, or liberal Yankees – Democratic candidates
Hubert Humphrey (1968), George McGovern (1972), Walter Mondale

---

[1] William Schneider, "The Suburban Century Begins," *Atlantic Monthly*, July 1992,
pp. 33–44.

[2] William Galston and Elaine Ciulla Kamarck, "The Politics of Evasion: Democrats and the
Presidency," Progressive Policy Institute report, September 1989.

99 - 145

46 pgs

(1988) carried a total of one ex-Confederate
as they continued to elect more moderate
wn-ballot offices suggested that excessively
played a large role in explaining the party's
ting for the presidency. But the South was
untry where Democratic strength eroded in
pr~~esiden~~ mid-1960s, or where nominal Democratic
majorities in the mass electorate failed to produce actual Democratic victories at the ballot box. How had Republicans succeeded in achieving
electoral dominance on a national scale?

Some experts looked beneath the state level in order to more precisely
identify the source of all these new Republican votes in the North and
West. They concluded that the growth of presidential Republicanism
reflected the transformation of the United States into "a nation of suburbs" (in the words of political scientist and election analyst William
Schneider).[3] Steady, and in some cases explosive, population growth in
suburban areas beginning after World War II soon tipped the electoral
balance in many states decisively in favor of voters who resided outside traditionally Democratic central cities. No longer within the reach of
urban party organizations, and perhaps intent on establishing a separate
political identity, suburbanites provided Republican presidential candidates Nixon (1968 and 1972), Reagan (1980 and 1984), and George
H. W. Bush (1988) with large popular margins. The old big-city vote that
had carried Democrats to victory in the era of Franklin D. Roosevelt and
Harry Truman was no longer large enough to deliver key states such as
New Jersey, Pennsylvania, Ohio, Illinois, and California, accounting for
Democratic presidential candidates' declining popularity in the former
party strongholds of the metropolitan North and coastal West.

Critics on the ideological center and right interpreted suburbaniza-
tion as a telling rejection by middle-class Americans of urban life and
the liberal politics with which it was associated. "To many new suburbanites," wrote Kevin Phillips, "their relocation represented a conscious
effort to drop a crabgrass curtain between themselves and the ... central
cities ... psychologically, the suburban boom is an anti-urban phenomenon – an attempt to escape crime, slums and slumdwellers."[4] Echoing
Phillips's conclusion that "suburbia and Great Society social programs

[3] Schneider, "The Suburban Century Begins."
[4] Kevin P. Phillips, *The Emerging Republican Majority* (New Rochelle, NY: Arlington
House, 1969), p. 193.

were essentially incompatible,"[5] Schneider argued after the Republican presidential successes of the 1980s that suburbanites "resent it when politicians take their money and use it to solve other people's problems, especially when they don't believe that government can actually solve those problems" – rendering them natural supporters of Reagan-style conservatism.[6] In a retrospective account of the 1988 presidential election, Rhodes Cook of *Congressional Quarterly* wrote that "Republicans were able to identify the national Democratic Party as beholden to minorities and the poor, and the GOP painted [Democratic nominee Michael] Dukakis into a corner on hot suburban issues such as crime. As a result, Dukakis was unable to make the inroads in the suburbs that he needed" to win the presidency.[7]

Any party that found itself unable to attract a majority of presidential votes in either the South or the suburban North and West faced a serious threat to its political health regardless of its success in competing for lower offices. By the 1980s, claims that the Republican Party had fastened an "electoral lock" on the White House – a term first coined by Horace W. Busby Jr., a former aide to Lyndon B. Johnson – had, in the words of I. M. Destler, become "conventional wisdom among political gurus."[8] Articulating a view that was increasingly shared by frustrated Democrats as well as triumphant Republicans, Galston, a political scientist who had served as issues director for Walter Mondale's 1984 presidential campaign, wrote after Mondale's 49-state loss to Reagan of a "new Democratic minority" whose "current weakness ... is not temporary, but fundamental," and whose "road to renewed strength is obscured."[9] Schneider argued in a July 1988 analysis that "the national Democratic Party has no [geographic] base ... [Between 1968 and 1984] only the District of Columbia, with three electoral votes, has voted for the Democratic ticket every time," while "twenty-three states with a total of 202 electoral votes have voted Republican every time."[10] Later that year, an item in the column of Godfrey Sperling Jr., veteran Washington

[5] Phillips, *Emerging Republican Majority*, p. 194.
[6] Schneider, "The Suburban Century Begins."
[7] Rhodes Cook, "Bush Victory Fits 20-Year Presidential Pattern," *CQ Weekly*, November 12, 1988, pp. 3241–3244.
[8] I. M. Destler, "The Myth of the 'Electoral Lock,'" *PS: Political Science and Politics* 29 (September 1996), pp. 491–494, at 491.
[9] William A. Galston, "The Future of the Democratic Party," *Brookings Review* 3 (Winter 1985), pp. 16–24, at 16, 20.
[10] William Schneider, "An Insider's View of the Election," *Atlantic Monthly*, July 1988, pp. 29–54.

correspondent for the *Christian Science Monitor*, noted that Democratic pollster Paul Maslin "told reporters the other morning that he saw the Democratic Party wandering in the wilderness for the next 10 or 15 years before it finds a formula for recapturing the presidency."[11]

Elections are a game of numbers, and the simple arithmetic of demography seemed to give Republicans a prohibitive advantage. Suburbanites outnumbered city dwellers; whites outnumbered racial minorities; the nonpoor outnumbered the poor. The Democrats' electoral difficulties only promised to worsen in the future as a "Reagan generation" of young conservatives inspired by the popular president seemingly stood ready to cement Republican rule for years after his administration left office. (In *Family Ties*, one of the most popular television comedies of the 1980s and a declared favorite of Reagan himself, actor Michael J. Fox played a teenage Republican named Alex P. Keaton whose conservative political views baffled his hippie-generation parents.) Galston and Kamarck quoted Republican pollster Bob Teeter as quipping that "the bad news is that there are still more Democrats in the electorate, the good news is that they're dying off," adding that "among those young people who are involved in politics and from whose ranks future talented candidates are likely to arise ... it is clear that there has been a resurgence of political activism among Republicans while Democrats have been all but moribund."[12] Reflecting a common view among the political prognosticators of the decade, Michael Barone and Grant Ujifusa observed after the 1988 election that "[t]he young voters of the 1980s, Republican strategists hope, and Democratic strategists fear, will carry their sunny Republicanism into the 2030s and 2040s," producing a near-permanent conservative majority.[13]

According to most of these experts, any potential road back to the White House for the Democratic Party inevitably ran in a southerly direction. "Like professionals in both parties, [an advisor to Democratic presidential candidate Richard Gephardt] contends that 'there is no way to put together 270 electoral votes without getting some from the South,'" reported the *New York Times* in 1987.[14] Lee Atwater, a South

[11] Godfrey Sperling Jr., "The Republicans' 'Lock' on the Presidency," *Christian Science Monitor*, November 15, 1988, p. 13.

[12] Galston and Kamarck, "Politics of Evasion," p. 14.

[13] Michael Barone and Grant Ujifusa, "The American Half Century," in *The Almanac of American Politics, 1990* (Washington, DC: National Journal, 1989), pp. xxiii–xxxi, at xxx.

[14] Phil Gailey, "Taking a Stand for Dixie's 1988 Vote," *New York Times*, February 15, 1987, sec. 4, p. 4.

Carolina political consultant who managed the Bush presidential campaign in 1988, claimed that "the Democrats ... are not going to crack the presidency again in this century unless they carry the South," while Democratic pollster Keith Frederick agreed that "we can't rack up the electoral votes anywhere else [because] the West is solidly Republican."[15] These strategists continued to treat Jimmy Carter's narrow 1976 victory as the model for Democratic presidential victory; Carter cobbled together a slim majority in the electoral college by achieving a near-sweep of the South while picking off a few key states in the Northeast and Midwest (such as New York, Ohio, Pennsylvania, and Wisconsin), even as he lost every state west of Missouri except Texas and Hawaii.

A near-consensus thus formed in Washington around two related axioms: that the Democratic Party could broaden its appeal in presidential elections only by repositioning itself closer to the ideological center, and that the reassembly of a national electoral majority required rebuilding the popularity of Democratic presidential nominees in the South. The natural leaders of any collective internal party "reinvention" were therefore the members of the party's southern moderate bloc, who still constituted a significant proportion of Democratic officeholders due to the party's continued success at winning congressional seats and governorships in the region during the 1970s and 1980s. These elected officials perceived that the successful nomination of a relatively moderate candidate for the White House would serve their own political interests (especially since some of them nurtured presidential ambitions themselves), but they could also claim personal experience in gaining votes from large numbers of Nixon and Reagan supporters. Aside from the potential electoral advantages, moderate Democrats also argued that the march of time required the party to rethink its New Deal– and Great Society–era policy commitments in order to offer effective solutions to a new set of challenges facing the nation – including growing budget deficits, a rising violent crime rate, and increased economic competition from overseas.

From these objectives sprang institutional initiatives designed to bolster the influence of moderate policies and politicians within the Democratic Party as a whole. The Democratic Leadership Council, founded in 1985, provided intellectual support, model legislation, and public visibility for these "New Democrats" as they attempted to gain a stronger voice in national party affairs. Less successfully, the coordinated effort in 1988

---

[15] Evans Witt, "South Shaping Up as Battleground for '88 Election," Associated Press, February 14, 1987.

of 12 southern states to hold their presidential primaries on the same date, dubbed "Super Tuesday," near the start of the primary calendar was intended to assist "ideally an electable Democrat, but at least a candidate southern Democrats could politically afford to be seen with in public," win the nomination, as described by Charles D. Hadley and Harold W. Stanley;[16] it backfired when civil rights leader Jesse Jackson won five southern states due to overwhelming support from black voters, while Michael Dukakis, the liberal governor of Massachusetts and eventual 1988 nominee, carried the large delegate prizes of Texas and Florida on the basis of his popularity among Latinos and transplanted northerners.[17] After Dukakis was decisively defeated in the November election after a campaign in which he failed to effectively counter Republican attacks questioning his foreign policy credentials, toughness on crime, and patriotic fervor, moderate Democrats interpreted the electoral outcome as further vindication of their belief that any future presidential victory would require a fundamentally new approach.

THE PICKING OF TWO ELECTORAL LOCKS

Efforts to steer the national Democratic Party in a new ideological direction found more success in 1992 with the presidential nomination of Governor Bill Clinton of Arkansas. Clinton had been identified with the New Democratic movement from its inception, serving as an official cofounder of the Democratic Leadership Council and its president in 1990 and 1991. His campaign took a series of measures to differentiate itself from that of previous Democratic presidential nominees, going out of its way to avoid the perceived strategic mistakes of the past that had encouraged Republican opponents to portray those candidates as hapless liberals. In contrast to Walter Mondale in 1984, who acknowledged that he would raise taxes if elected, Clinton promised a middle-class tax cut. Dukakis had been attacked for opposing the death penalty; Clinton returned to Arkansas during the campaign to oversee an execution. To combat the assumption that Democratic politicians supported excessively generous public assistance programs, Clinton vowed to "end welfare as we know it" by imposing time limits and work requirements

[16] Charles D. Hadley and Harold W. Stanley, "Super Tuesday 1988: Regional Results and National Implications," *Publius* 19 (Summer 1989), pp. 19–37.

[17] E. J. Dionne Jr., "Bush Routs Dole in Primaries as Dukakis, Jackson and Gore Move Far Ahead of Gephardt," *New York Times*, March 9, 1988, p. A01.

on beneficiaries. Rather than balancing the national ticket by choosing a more liberal officeholder from another region of the nation as his vice presidential running mate, Clinton selected Senator Al Gore of Tennessee, another southerner of moderate reputation who was also associated with the Democratic Leadership Council.

Some of these actions irked liberal activists, but it was difficult for victory-starved Democrats to deny the pragmatic rationale that seemed to justify them. In addition to Clinton's careful issue positioning, his southern drawl, extraverted style, and modest economic background collectively suggested to political analysts that he could single-handedly revive the South's ancestral Democratic alignment, which could ensure the electoral college victory that had repeatedly eluded the party for nearly a generation. The *New York Times* claimed several weeks before the 1992 election that "enough voters have come back to the Democrats that virtually every Southern state is up for grabs for the first time since the last Democrat, Jimmy Carter, won the White House in 1976 ... Mr. Clinton and Mr. Gore have run close to a perfect race for the South, blunting social issues ... and hitting hard on economic ones."[18]

Clinton was elected comfortably, winning the national popular vote over incumbent president George H. W. Bush by a margin of 43 percent to 37 percent (independent candidate H. Ross Perot received 19 percent) and easily prevailing in the electoral college with 370 electoral votes to 168 for Bush and none for Perot. Commentators across the political spectrum interpreted the election results as a vindication of Clinton's moderate persona and southern identity. Democrats were happy to take credit for an effective political strategy, centrists cheered the election of a president who seemed to be one of their own, and Republicans consoled themselves in defeat that a Democratic presidential candidate seemingly needed to distance himself from his own party's liberal base in order to win.

Despite this broadly popular conclusion, not much direct evidence existed that Clinton's ideological maneuvering was decisive to the outcome. The elder Bush was an unpopular president at the time of his reelection campaign, with a job approval rating measured at only 34 percent in a Gallup poll taken in mid-October 1992.[19] Americans were particularly

---

[18] Peter Applebome, "Loss of Democratic Vote Imperils Bush in South," *New York Times*, October 18, 1992, sec. 1, p. 28.

[19] Figure from Gallup Presidential Job Approval Center, www.gallup.com/poll/124922/presidential-approval-center.aspx.

dissatisfied with the state of the national economy, which had entered a recession in late 1991 and remained unacceptably weak in the eyes of the voting public; under the circumstances, any competent Democratic challenger would have stood a strong chance of defeating the incumbent. In addition, the tactics deployed by the Clinton campaign to reinforce their candidate's persona as a New Democrat received substantially more notice from the press corps and other elites than the less attentive mass public. The National Election Studies found that when respondents were asked to place Clinton's ideological position on a scale from 1 (extreme liberal) to 7 (extreme conservative), their average answer was 3.1 – only slightly less liberal than the mean placement of Michael Dukakis in 1988 at 3.0. (When Clinton ran successfully for reelection in 1996, his mean placement on this scale was 2.9 – to the liberal side of Dukakis and roughly equal to Walter Mondale's perceived position in 1984.)[20]

Crucially, though it was not widely noted at the time, Clinton also did not fulfill expectations that he would firmly return the South to the Democratic camp. Clinton and Gore carried their home states of Arkansas and Tennessee but won just four other states in the region, in comparison to eight southern states won by the Bush campaign. Bush defeated Clinton in the South narrowly in the popular vote (42 percent to 41 percent) but by a much wider margin in the electoral vote (69 percent to 31 percent). A comparison of Clinton's geographic coalition with that of Jimmy Carter in 1976 is instructive; though he won a larger national margin than Carter in both the popular and electoral vote, Clinton ran well behind his predecessor in the South, losing six states that Carter had carried 16 years before (see Figure 4.1).

It was the suburban problem, not the southern problem, that Bill Clinton solved for the Democratic Party in 1992. As Figure 4.1 illustrates, his electoral college majority was built on a near-sweep of the North (carrying every state in the Northeast and Midwest except Indiana) and the Pacific Coast, where California – the biggest prize by far in the electoral college with 54 electoral votes – swung decisively into the Democratic column for the first time in 28 years and only the second time since the Truman presidency. These state-level victories reflected significant pro-Democratic shifts in populous suburban areas that had previously delivered wide electoral margins to Republican presidential candidates. For example, Clinton carried Middlesex County, New Jersey (suburban

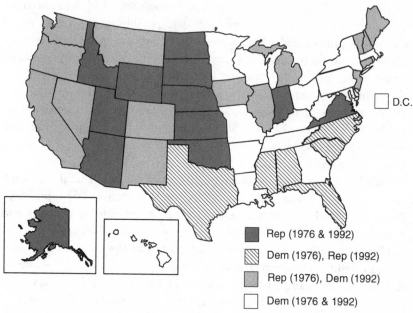

FIGURE 4.1. Comparison of the 1976 and 1992 presidential elections by state.

New York) by 7 percentage points (Dukakis had lost it by 10 points in 1988); Baltimore County, Maryland (suburban Baltimore) by 5 points (Dukakis lost by 15); Montgomery County, Pennsylvania (suburban Philadelphia) by 3 points (Dukakis lost by 22); Will County, Illinois (suburban Chicago) by 1 point (Dukakis lost by 19); and Ventura County, California (suburban Los Angeles) by 2 points (Dukakis lost by 24).

Though the terms had yet to be coined, it is clear in retrospect that the 1992 presidential election began to signal the emerging configuration of "red" and "blue" geographic coalitions that came to define contemporary partisan competition after they were further solidified in the election of 2000. The presence of some residual Democratic loyalty in the upland South states of West Virginia, Kentucky, Arkansas, and Tennessee that was destined to dissipate by the end of the decade, as well as a few narrow Clinton victories in Mountain West states such as Montana and Colorado that were likely aided by Perot's presence on the ballot, prevented the 1992 electoral map from producing the visually stark regional divisions that attracted such widespread fascination when they ultimately appeared eight years later, but these exceptions were not decisive to the outcome. In fact, Clinton would have prevailed without receiving a single electoral vote from the South or interior West due to his success in what is now known as Blue America. Rather than return his party to its traditional geographic base, the New Democrat from Arkansas unexpectedly forged a new alignment altogether.

The 1992 election represented a milestone marking the reemergence, after more than 20 years' absence, of a sizable bloc of states that could be relied upon thereafter for automatic support of Democratic presidential nominees. For the first time in the history of the Democratic Party, its strongest electoral territory was located exclusively outside the South, including Massachusetts, New York, New Jersey, and Maryland in the Northeast; Illinois in the metropolitan Midwest; and the Pacific Coast states of Washington, Oregon, and California – all of which have supported the Democratic candidate in every subsequent presidential election. A solitary but prescient article by C. B. Holman had foreshadowed this development in 1989, concluding from an analysis of public opinion data that the Democratic Party would in fact find more fertile electoral territory along the Pacific Coast than by revisiting the sites of faded past glory in the South; "Go west, young Democrat," Holman had urged.[21]

While few other analysts had foreseen the establishment of a new national Democratic presidential majority that did not rely upon a revival of the party's historical southern bulwark, the next congressional election two years later produced an even more unexpected partisan outcome. Democrats entered the 1994 midterms having controlled the Senate for 34 of the previous 40 years and the House of Representatives for all 40; if Republicans indeed held an electoral lock on the presidency, surely Democrats appeared to maintain an even firmer grip on Congress.[22] However, Republicans gained a net 52 seats in the House of Representatives and 8 seats in the Senate to win a majority in both chambers, representing a bracing popular judgment on the first two years of Clinton's job performance as president. Although a strong pro-Republican popular trend was evident from coast to coast, electoral change was particularly concentrated in regions that already leaned Republican in presidential elections.[23] Republican candidates defeated 14 incumbent House Democrats in the South and interior West while capturing 13 of the 18 seats left open by Democratic retirees. Senate Republicans won all three

---

[21] C. B. Holman, "Go West, Young Democrat," *Polity* 22 (Winter 1989), pp. 323–339.

[22] See William F. Connelly Jr. and John J. Pitney Jr., *Congress' Permanent Minority? Republicans in the U.S. House* (Lanham, MD: Rowman & Littlefield, 1994).

[23] Gary C. Jacobson, "The 1994 House Elections in Perspective," *Political Science Quarterly* 111 (Summer 1996), pp. 203–223.

GOP
take
over?
1994

open Democratic seats in the two regions, defeated incumbent Democrat Jim Sasser of Tennessee, and convinced former Democrats Richard Shelby of Alabama and Ben Nighthorse Campbell of Colorado to switch parties soon after the election. After years of relative stagnation, the congressional realignment of the South advanced dramatically in a single leap, leaving Republicans with what has proven to be an enduring majority of southern seats in both chambers. As it happened, Clinton had not only proved unable to coax most of the South back to the Democrats in presidential elections, but less than two years of his presidency were sufficient to precipitate a lasting Republican takeover of the region in Congress as well.

For the first time in American history, the Republican Party's political center of gravity now lay firmly below the Mason-Dixon line. The incoming Republican majority in the House of Representatives chose southerners for each of the party's three top leadership positions: Newt Gingrich of Georgia as speaker; Dick Armey of Texas (suburban Dallas) as majority leader; and Tom DeLay, also of Texas (suburban Houston), as majority whip. Leadership of the Senate passed to sitting minority leader Bob Dole of Kansas, though Trent Lott, a Mississippian who had just been elected to his second six-year term, successfully challenged incumbent whip and 16-year Senate veteran Alan Simpson of Wyoming to become Dole's top lieutenant. Lott's triumph over the more pragmatic and socially moderate Simpson represented a victory for the rising southern contingent within his party, as well as for a cadre of younger and more ideologically purist Republican senators who viewed the existing leadership as insufficiently loyal to conservative principles.[24] When Dole left the Senate in the spring of 1996 to devote full attention to his campaign for the presidency, Lott ascended to majority leader, becoming the first in a succession of southerners at the helm of the Senate Republican Party (Lott was replaced in 2002 by Bill Frist of Tennessee, who was himself succeeded by Mitch McConnell of Kentucky in 2006).

In retrospect, the 1992 and 1994 elections stand out as a collective turning point in both the relative balance and the comparative constituencies of the two parties. John H. Aldrich observed in 1999 that over a few years "the greatest electoral lock in American history, that of the congressional Democrats over the last 40 years, and the less certain lock of the GOP over the presidency over the last 20 years ... have exactly reversed," while "the rise of the South in Republican politics" was demonstrated

---

[24] Sean Theriault, *The Gingrich Senators: The Roots of Partisan Warfare in Congress* (New York: Oxford University Press, 2013).

by the growing representation of southerners within the ranks of congressional Republicans and in the ways in which "southern GOP sensibilities have also taken over leadership in the party's agenda setting and policy making."[25] For Aldrich, these developments represented clear signs of a new "critical era" in American elections, perhaps marking the inauguration of a seventh party system. In any event, the 1990s marked a relatively sharp and durable break with the previous pattern of partisan outcomes and geographic coalitions – a shift that endured, and even intensified, in the first two decades of the following century.

What factor or factors precipitated this change? During the long electoral drought suffered by Democratic presidential nominees in the 1970s and 1980s, conventional wisdom held that the party needed to become more moderate on taxes, welfare, and crime in order to lure both southerners and suburbanites away from the Republican Party of Nixon and Reagan – a conclusion that clearly influenced the strategies adopted by Bill Clinton in his 1992 campaign. But if the cross-regional pro-Republican trend in presidential elections after 1968 indeed represented the common resistance of citizens both within and outside the South to the out-of-date big-government liberalism advocated by Democratic candidates, as many pundits argued, one might expect the public repositioning of the party in the Clinton era to prove equally successful in attracting new electoral majorities across regional lines.

Instead, the Democratic Party principally owed its renewed presidential success in 1992 and thereafter to a boost in voter support within the metropolitan North and coastal West – especially California, New Jersey, Maryland, Connecticut, and the rest of what are now known as the blue states – while the rural West and Clinton's home region of the South remained mostly Republican. Clinton's careful efforts to maintain ideological distance from the liberal wing of his party as well as the Republican opposition on his right – an approach that advisors dubbed "Third Way" or "triangulation" – similarly cannot account for the declining electoral success of moderate congressional Democrats in the South and interior West after 1992. Nor, in retrospect, can it explain the ability of subsequent Democratic presidential nominees, who expended rather less effort than Clinton did to separate themselves from the policies and public figures of the Democratic left, to nonetheless retain his popular strength within the party's new geographic base on the East and West coasts.

---

[25] John H. Aldrich, "Political Parties in a Critical Era," *American Politics Quarterly* 27 (January 1999), pp. 9–32; quotes on pp. 14, 16.

It is quite possible that the breaking of the Republican lock on the White House in the 1990s represented a simple shift in fundamental electoral forces more than the consequence of strategic ideological positioning. Clinton's relative success compared to his Democratic presidential predecessors may have reflected the weakness of the national economy and resulting unpopularity of the Republican incumbent president, which rendered the political environment much more favorable to his party than it had been in 1972, 1980, 1984, or 1988. But while this "nature of the times" interpretation of the outcome can account for the Democratic ticket's national victory in 1992 after three consecutive Republican presidential landslides, it cannot explain the significant changes in the geographic location of the party's popular base. Clinton's electoral strength was much more concentrated in the North and coastal West than was the support in 1976 for Jimmy Carter, the previous Democratic president, who in turn had run much better in the South; in fact, as Figure 4.1 shows, 21 of the nation's 50 states, casting nearly half of the total number of electoral votes (268 of 538 under the state electoral vote allocation figures in place in 1992), voted for opposite parties in the 1976 and 1992 elections, despite only 16 years of intervening history. By the 1990s, even a presidential ticket comprising two southern candidates running as ideological moderates could no longer count on winning the South in an otherwise friendly electoral context.

It is hardly a coincidence that the advent of regional polarization in both presidential and congressional elections occurred just as the two parties were increasingly differentiating themselves on social issues such as abortion, gay rights, and moral traditionalism. Public opinion on these matters tends to be particularly divided along geographic lines, separating the culturally conservative Bible Belt and rural West from the more progressive Northeast and Pacific Coast. The growing visibility of partisan conflict over social issues after the 1980s can simultaneously account for the Democratic Party's resurgence in large metropolitan areas outside the South, the significant growth of the Republican congressional vote in Red America, and the formation of the unusually stable and electorally secure regional bases now maintained by both parties across the two elective branches of government.

FROM CULTURAL CONFLICT TO PARTISAN DIVIDE

The U.S. Supreme Court delivered its judgment in the case of *Roe v. Wade* on January 22, 1973, finding that the Constitution contained a right to privacy that prohibited legal bans on abortion during the first stages of pregnancy. Few could foresee that the Court's ruling would only deepen a political conflict that remains fully intact more than four decades later; a *New York Times* editorial published two days after the decision even expressed hope that it would provide "a strong foundation for final and reasonable resolution of a debate that has divided America too long."[26] Moreover, it was far from clear in 1973 that abortion would ultimately become a decidedly partisan issue; at the time of *Roe v. Wade*, each party contained substantial pro-choice and pro-life sentiment at both the mass and elite levels. Over time, most national Democratic figures came to support the pro-choice position, responding to the influence of liberal activists and the feminist movement, while the increasing political mobilization of evangelical Christians – particularly numerous in the South – encouraged Republican politicians to adopt the pro-life view.[27] Related policy disputes over gay rights, the permissibility of prayer in public schools, and the role of government in promoting moral traditionalism more broadly also grew in partisan salience over the course of the 1970s and 1980s, likewise distinguishing socially liberal Democratic party leaders from their conservative Republican counterparts.[28]

One might well expect the increasingly distinctive positions taken by Democratic and Republican officeholders on these issues to provoke a corresponding separation of party identifiers in the electorate, given the central role of elite messages and behavior in shaping mass opinion.[29] The debate over legalized abortion, arguably the most prominent of the social issues, illustrates this influence. As Figure 4.2 demonstrates, pro-choice voters were no more likely to support Democratic candidates for president and Congress in the 1980 election than were pro-life voters, according to data from the American National Election Studies (ANES). By 1988, a modest partisan gap had emerged on the issue: 55 percent of pro-choice respondents voted Democratic for president, as compared to 41 percent of pro-life voters. (This divide also appeared, though with a narrower margin, in congressional voting: 63 percent of pro-choice

[26] "Respect for Privacy," unsigned editorial, *New York Times*, January 24, 1973, p. 40.
[27] David Karol, *Party Position Change in American Politics: Coalition Management* (New York: Cambridge University Press, 2009).
[28] Bruce Nesmith, *The New Republican Coalition: The Reagan Campaigns and White Evangelicals* (New York: Peter Lang, 1994).
[29] John R. Zaller, *The Nature and Origins of Mass Opinion* (New York: Cambridge University Press, 1992).

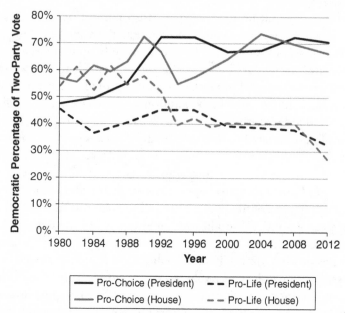

FIGURE 4.2. The increasing partisan divide over abortion, 1980–2012.
Note: ANES respondents who agree that "by law, a woman should always be able to obtain an abortion as a matter of personal choice" are classified as pro-choice. Respondents who agree that "by law, abortion should never be permitted" or that "the law should permit abortion only in cases of rape, incest, or when the woman's life is in danger" are classified as pro-life.
Source: Data from the American National Election Studies.

voters and 55 percent of pro-life voters supported Democratic candidates for the House of Representatives that year.)[30]

The relationship between citizens' positions on abortion and their choices in the voting booth strengthened rapidly after 1988. The difference in partisan preferences between pro-choice and pro-life voters nearly doubled in size – from 14 to 27 percentage points – in the four years between the 1988 and 1992 presidential elections alone, with nearly all of Bill Clinton's gains over the electoral performance of previous Democratic nominee Michael Dukakis occurring among voters with left-leaning abortion views. This gap increased further in subsequent elections; by 2012, 71 percent of pro-choice voters supported Democrat Barack Obama for president, compared to just 32 percent of pro-life

[30] See Greg D. Adams, "Abortion: Evidence of an Issue Evolution," *American Journal of Political Science* 41 (1997), pp. 718–737.

voters – a gap of 39 points. In congressional elections, an 8-point partisan gap between pro-choice and pro-life voters in 1988 similarly increased to 15 points by 1992, 24 points by 2000, and 40 points by 2012.[31]

Other measures similarly indicate that partisan supporters in the electorate became abruptly divided on social and cultural matters between the 1980s and the 1990s, with further intensification in subsequent elections. The difference in partisan alignment between highly devout voters and those with less religious attachment – sometimes referred to colloquially as the "God gap" – also emerged suddenly between 1988 and 1992. Prior to the early 1990s, voters who reported attending religious services on at least a weekly basis voted much like those who rarely or never participated, as indicated by Figure 4.3. But nonchurchgoers swung decisively toward the Democrats in the 1992 presidential election, opening up a significant partisan divide in religiosity that has endured in subsequent elections for both the presidency and Congress. Because devoted practitioners collectively maintain more conservative views on social issues than nominal adherents within virtually all major religious dominations, the rise of the "God gap" in the 1990s reflects the cultural separation of the parties in the electorate.[32]

The growing association between religious practice and party affiliation in American politics is most visibly represented by the rise of socially conservative Protestants as key components of the Republican electoral coalition, especially in the South. Democrats and Republicans have responded by adopting increasingly distinct views of this religious community. Figure 4.4 shows that while Democratic and Republican voters did not differ significantly in their collective evaluation of "fundamentalist Christians" (the phrase used by the American National Election Studies) in the 1988 election, four years later a partisan gap had emerged on this measure that widened further after 2000 in both presidential and congressional elections.

In summary, a variety of evidence indicates that partisan differences in the mass electorate over social issues and religiosity appeared rather suddenly in the early 1990s, enduring – and even widening further – in both presidential and congressional elections during the succeeding decades. Several scholars of American public opinion noted this development in the wake of the 1992 election, finding a newfound partisan salience to

[31] Data from the 2016 American National Election Studies was not available at press time.
[32] Laura Olson and John C. Green, "The Religion Gap," *PS: Political Science and Politics* 39 (2006), pp. 455–459.

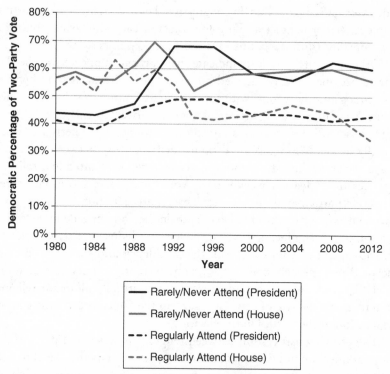

FIGURE 4.3. The emergence of the "God gap," 1980–2012.
Note: "Regularly attend" refers to respondents who report attending church every week or more. "Rarely/never attend" refers to respondents who attend church a few times a year or less.
Source: Data from the American National Election Studies.

cultural and moral issues that had not previously been strongly associated with vote choice. Alan I. Abramowitz concluded that "attitudes toward abortion had a strong influence on candidate choice in the overall electorate [in 1992]. Furthermore, approximately one fourth of all major-party voters were aware of the candidates' positions on abortion and mentioned abortion at least once in response to the open-ended questions dealing with national problems, party differences, and likes and dislikes about the parties and candidates. Among these aware and concerned voters, abortion had a much stronger influence on candidate choice than any other issue, including the state of the economy."[33]

---

[33] Alan I. Abramowitz, "It's Abortion, Stupid: Policy Voting in the 1992 Presidential Election," *Journal of Politics* 57 (February 1995), pp. 176–186, quote on p. 185.

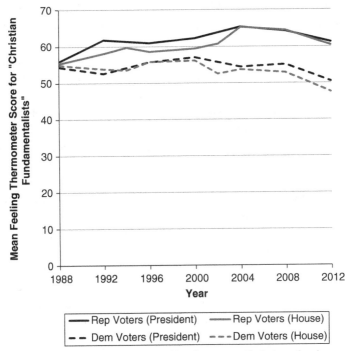

FIGURE 4.4. The growing partisan divide over Christian fundamentalism, 1988–2012.
Note: Feeling thermometer measures ask respondents to rate political figures or groups on a scale from 0 ("cold") to 100 ("hot").
Source: Data from the American National Election Studies.

Likewise, Warren E. Miller and J. Merrill Shanks determined after the 1992 election that "voters' positions concerning traditional morality had a substantial impact on vote choice in 1992 that must be distinguished from liberal or conservative positions in other areas," while Geoffrey C. Layman and Thomas M. Carsey agreed that "party polarization on cultural issues increased sharply after 1988" in the mass electorate.[34] According to an analysis conducted by Donald M. Gooch, citizens surveyed by the American National Election Studies became much more likely in the 1990s to mention social issues in their responses

[34] Warren E. Miller and J. Merrill Shanks, *The New American Voter* (Cambridge, MA: Harvard University Press, 1996), p. 305; Geoffrey C. Layman and Thomas M. Carsey, "Party Polarization and 'Conflict Extension' in the Mass Electorate," *American Journal of Political Science* 46 (October 2002), pp. 786–802, quote on p. 794.

to open-ended questions asking what they liked and disliked about the parties; the proportion of social-issue mentions rose from 12 percent in 1988 to 16 percent in 1992 and 23 percent in 1996. This doubling of the citation rate for cultural issues over just eight years was driven in particular by a significant rise in voters' citations of legalized abortion as an important matter on which the parties differed.[35]

Why did the division between Democratic and Republican supporters over social issues and relative religiosity arise suddenly in the early 1990s? Several plausible explanations could account for this development. First, the U.S. Supreme Court handed down two key decisions on the subject of legalized abortion between the 1988 and 1992 elections that attracted a significant amount of news media attention and controversy, heightening the issue's public visibility and giving party leaders the opportunity to communicate their opposing viewpoints to the electorate. In *Webster v. Reproductive Health Services* (decided July 3, 1989), a divided Supreme Court upheld several restrictions on abortion enacted by the Missouri legislature, including a ban on the use of state facilities to perform abortion procedures and a requirement that physicians perform viability tests after 20 weeks of pregnancy. After the *Webster* decision was announced, legal experts suggested that a future case might reverse the central holding of *Roe v. Wade* itself; while an otherwise splintered Court upheld additional state-imposed regulations of abortion access in *Planned Parenthood of Southeastern Pennsylvania v. Casey* (decided June 29, 1992), a majority of justices affirmed the constitutional prohibition on outright bans established in *Roe*.

Second, the political activism of social conservatives similarly intensified during this era, which may well have caused the American electorate to take increasing notice of cultural issues. Pat Robertson, a former Southern Baptist minister who rose to national prominence as the cohost of the syndicated television program *The 700 Club*, founded the Christian Coalition after his unsuccessful candidacy for the 1988 Republican presidential nomination, which soon became one of the most visible mass-membership interest groups in American electoral politics under the leadership of executive director Ralph Reed. At the peak of its influence, Robertson's organization was credited with mobilizing evangelical congregations – especially in the South – to support Republican

---

[35] Donald M. Gooch, "It's the Culture War, Stupid: The Increasing Role Social Issues Play in Public Perceptions of the Parties, 1972–2004," paper presented at the Annual Meeting of the Midwest Political Science Association, Chicago, IL, April 11–14, 2013.

candidates via such measures as church-distributed preelection voter guides. The Christian Coalition, along with other interest group organizations identified with the religious right such as Focus on the Family and the antiabortion Operation Rescue, attracted a great deal of news media attention in the early 1990s, which itself may have encouraged socially conservative voters to view the Republican Party as their natural political home while simultaneously propelling social liberals toward the Democrats.

Finally, the 1992 presidential campaign itself may have also contributed to the sudden emergence of mass party differences on cultural matters. Social issues became a more central subject of campaign rhetoric than they had been in preceding elections, due in large part to the decision of incumbent Republican president George H. W. Bush to adopt "family values" as a major theme of his reelection effort. In part, this strategy reflected political vulnerability: a serious national recession had deprived Bush of the ability to run on a record of economic prosperity, and his oft-repeated 1988 campaign pledge "Read my lips: no new taxes!" had been neutralized by a 1990 budget compromise with congressional Democrats that included tax increases. But Bush advisors also viewed moral issues as potentially favorable political terrain for their candidate due to Democratic opponent Bill Clinton's popular reputation as a womanizer with dubious personal integrity, and hoped that an emphasis on social issues would stimulate high levels of turnout by conservative voters who might otherwise lack strong enthusiasm for a second Bush term.[36] In contrast to other policy domains such as taxes and welfare, the Clinton campaign also did not attempt to challenge liberal Democratic orthodoxy on abortion or gay rights in 1992, further encouraging Bush's efforts to draw contrasts on cultural matters. Clinton called for an end to the U.S. military's ban on gay servicemembers and conspicuously declined to invite Pennsylvania governor Robert Casey Sr., a prominent pro-life Democrat, to address the party's national convention – a snub that received considerable media attention.

The Bush campaign's strategic approach had become apparent by the spring of 1992, when Vice President Dan Quayle delivered an attention-getting speech criticizing "our cultural leaders in Hollywood" who "routinely jeer at" traditional moral values; Quayle even singled out the television comedy *Murphy Brown* for "mocking the importance

---

[36] Andrew Rosenthal, "Bush Tries to Recoup from Harsh Tone on 'Values,'" *New York Times*, September 21, 1992, p. A1.

of fathers" by introducing a plotline in which the unmarried title character became pregnant and bore a child.[37] The Republican National
Convention, held in August in Bush's hometown of Houston, prominently
echoed this family values message, devoting an entire day of speeches to
the theme. With the Republican ticket trailing in the national opinion
polls, an atmosphere of urgency prevailed, and few convention speakers
aimed for rhetorical subtlety. Pat Robertson of the Christian Coalition
warned the audience that Clinton "wants to give your 13-year-old daugh-
ter the choice without your consent to destroy the life of her unborn
baby ... wants to repeal the ban on homosexuals in the military and
appoint homosexuals to his administration ... [and has] a radical plan to
destroy the traditional family and transfer many of its functions to the
federal government."[38] Vice President Quayle's wife Marilyn, like Clinton
a member of the Baby Boom generation that came of age in the 1960s,
indirectly referred to the Democratic nominee by noting pointedly that
"not everyone joined the counterculture. Not everyone demonstrated,
dropped out, took drugs, joined in the sexual revolution or dodged the
draft ... Most of us went to school, to church, and to work. We married and started families."[39] Perhaps the most memorable speech of the
convention was delivered by conservative columnist and former White
House aide Pat Buchanan, who had mounted a protest campaign against
Bush in the Republican presidential primaries earlier in the year. In the
most frequently quoted passage of his address, Buchanan claimed that
"there is a religious war going on in this country. It is a cultural war ...
for the soul of America. And in that struggle for the soul of America,
Clinton and Clinton are on the other side, and George Bush is on our
side."[40]

Buchanan's reference to "Clinton and Clinton" was no slip of the
tongue. Unusually for a candidate's spouse, Bill Clinton's wife Hillary
had become a prominent and polarizing figure in 1992. In contrast to
first lady Barbara Bush, who cultivated an apolitical, grandmotherly persona, Hillary Clinton gained a reputation as not only holding a great

---

[37] Dan Quayle, address to the Commonwealth Club of California, May 19, 1992, www
.vicepresidentdanquayle.com/speeches_standingfirm_ccc_1.html.
[38] Pat Robertson, "1992 Republican Convention," speech transcript at www.patrobertson
.com/Speeches/1992GOPConvention.asp.
[39] Quoted in Kathleen E. Kendall, ed., *Presidential Campaign Discourse: Strategic
Communication Problems* (Albany: State University of New York Press, 1995), p. 208.
[40] Patrick J. Buchanan, Address to the 1992 Republican National Convention, www
.americanrhetoric.com/speeches/patrickbuchanan1992rnc.htm.

deal of influence over the Clinton campaign – and, potentially, over a Clinton presidency – but also as more liberal and less conciliatory than her husband. Bush allies not infrequently launched rhetorical volleys in her direction, and her status as an ambitious professional woman and self-identified feminist effectively dovetailed with the emerging partisan divide over cultural traditionalism.

Many journalists have since viewed Buchanan's "culture war" speech (as it soon became known) as representing a turning point in American politics, marking the onset of a new, more heated style of partisan conflict over values and lifestyles that ultimately produced Clinton's 1998 impeachment over the Monica Lewinsky affair, the highly polarized reactions among political elites and voters alike to the socially conservative presidency of George W. Bush and the socially liberal administration of his successor Barack Obama, and a series of fierce battles over a set of issues – abortion, same-sex marriage, deference to religious faith in the public sphere – that seemed particularly unsuited to substantive compromise or temperate rhetoric. On the twentieth anniversary of the speech in 2012, Adam Nagourney of the *New York Times* noted in retrospect "the extent to which a Republican establishment that was once relatively moderate on social issues has been pushed rightward by grass-roots conservatives."[41] In the wake of the 1992 election, recalled Liz Marlantes of the *Christian Science Monitor*, "the culture gap exploded ... fostering a partisan divide that increasingly seems to be about identity. Voters are aligning with the party they feel best projects the values they want to pass on to their children."[42] Liberal journalist Thomas Frank wrote in a 2006 *New York Times* column that "the culture war has turned the politics of this country upside down."[43] By the 2010s, concluded the *Economist*, American politics had become "all culture war, all the time."[44]

The emergence of the contemporary regional divide in national elections after 2000 further convinced a number of political pundits that cultural differences now represented the primary fault line of partisan

[41] Adam Nagourney, "'Cultural War' of 1992 Moves in from the Fringe," *New York Times*, August 30, 2012, p. A15.

[42] Liz Marlantes, "Inside Red-and-Blue America," *Christian Science Monitor*, July 14, 2004, www.csmonitor.com/2004/0714/p01s03-usgn.html.

[43] Thomas Frank, "The Culture Crusade of Kansas," *New York Times*, August 8, 2006, p. A17.

[44] "We Are All Culture Warriors Now," *The Economist*, Democracy in America blog, February 29, 2012, www.economist.com/blogs/democracyinamerica/2012/02/republican-race-1.

conflict in the United States, not only separating Democratic leaders from their Republican counterparts but dividing the morally traditionalist inhabitants of the South and rural West from the cosmopolitan, progressive denizens of the coasts. According to this view, a political climate that was indeed "all culture war, all the time" left little room for the more venerable conflict over economic issues that had defined the party system since the New Deal era. Many analyses tacitly assumed, and a few explicitly asserted, that the new divide over social issues had largely eclipsed the old partisan battles over class interests and government activism.

Thomas Frank argued in the best-selling 2004 book *What's the Matter with Kansas?* that the results of the 2000 presidential election reflected the emergence of a new partisan divide along the fault line of socioeconomic status – not the New Deal–vintage party system defined by the conflicting material interests of affluent Republicans and blue-collar Democrats, but instead what he called a "remarkable inversion" of this traditional cleavage.[45] He described an intensifying cultural battle in which voters of modest means in the nation's interior – typified by the residents of Kansas, his own home state – had come to support the Republican Party in order to express sharp resentment of a bicoastal "liberal elite" whom they viewed as constituting "an overeducated ruling class that is contemptuous of the beliefs and practices of the masses of ordinary people" typified by "self-righteous young students," "the hippie set," "Ivy Leaguers," and "the haughty hedonists of Hollywood."[46] Frank credited right-wing political leaders with adeptly stoking a populist backlash against a Democratic Party that paradoxically best represented the economic concerns of many of its fiercest opponents, concluding that they had largely succeeded in convincing these voters "to renounce forever [their] middle-American prosperity in pursuit of a crimson fantasy of middle-American righteousness."[47]

Much of the scholarly response to the "red-versus-blue" genre of media commentary challenged this claim by demonstrating that economic views continue to exert a powerful influence over the partisan and electoral preferences of American citizens. Larry M. Bartels found in 2006 that social issues such as abortion and gay rights remained of secondary importance in accounting for the partisan preferences of

---

[45] Thomas Frank, *What's the Matter with Kansas? How Conservatives Won the Heart of America* (New York: Henry Holt, 2004), p. 15.

[46] Frank, *What's the Matter with Kansas?* pp. 115, 116, 117, 119.

[47] Frank, *What's the Matter with Kansas?* pp. 251.

voters compared to the more long-standing divide over economic ideology, including among members of the white working class whom many media analysts had portrayed as increasingly attracted to the Republican Party on the basis of shared social conservatism.[48] Stephen Ansolabehere, Jonathan Rodden, and James M. Snyder Jr. similarly confirmed that "economic issues have much more weight in voters' minds than moral issues," concluding that "the survey data roundly reject the basic claims of the culture war thesis."[49] Andrew Gelman showed that the propensity of the nation's poorest states to collectively favor Republican candidates, while the richest states correspondingly leaned Democratic, was not caused by a parallel increase in the Republican loyalties of poor voters (or a new-found Democratic preference among the prosperous).[50]

Most notably, the title of Morris P. Fiorina's study *Culture War? The Myth of a Polarized America* explicitly referred to Buchanan's 1992 convention speech and its frequent subsequent citations by journalists, for whom, in Fiorina's view, "division, polarization, battles, and war make better copy than agreement, consensus, moderation, cooperation, and peace."[51] Fiorina argued that many Americans hold centrist or internally conflicting views on cultural matters such as abortion, contradicting the assumption that such issues reliably divide the electorate into two corresponding camps of liberal and conservative absolutists. While Democratic and Republican politicians regularly engage in fierce rhetorical and legislative battles over these issues (egged on by highly attentive and mobilized interest groups on both sides), most citizens in Fiorina's account remain on the political sidelines, frustrated with this relentless ideological warfare.

Importantly, however, none of these accounts disputed the claim that social issues had become increasingly salient to voters as well as party elites after the 1980s – as seemingly confirmed by the growing partisan divide over abortion, political mobilization of the Christian right, and appearance of the "God gap." Perhaps the most elegant theoretical framework for understanding the changing relationship between

[48] Bartels, "What's the Matter with *What's the Matter with Kansas?*" *Quarterly Journal of Political Science* 1 (2006), pp. 201–226.

[49] Stephen Ansolabehere, Jonathan Rodden, and James M. Snyder Jr., "Purple America," *Journal of Economic Perspectives* 20 (Spring 1996), pp. 97–118, quotes on p. 99.

[50] Andrew Gelman, *Red States, Blue State, Rich State, Poor State: Why Americans Vote the Way They Do* (Princeton, NJ: Princeton University Press, 2008).

[51] Morris P. Fiorina with Samuel J. Abrams and Jeremy C. Pope, *Culture War? The Myth of a Polarized America*, 3rd edition (New York: Longman, 2011), p. 3.

partisanship and issue positions was proposed in 2002 by Geoffrey C. Layman and Thomas M. Carsey.[52] While they acknowledged the growing importance of cultural attitudes in motivating the partisan identification and vote choice of American citizens after 1988, Layman and Carsey noted that the emergence of a political divide in the mass public over social issues had not replaced the existing gap separating partisan identifiers on economic concerns. Instead, they argued, the electorate had undergone a "conflict extension" in which a second dimension of cultural differences simply augmented the enduring divide over economic policy. Democrats and Republicans still disagreed about the proper scope of government, generosity of public services, and optimal level of taxation just as much after 1992 as they had before (perhaps even more so, in fact), but now they also took increasingly divergent stances on the legality of abortion, the preferred societal role of religion, and other matters that had previously cut across party lines or remained of limited salience to voters. Partisans in the electorate, concluded Layman and Carsey, had found new things to fight about without resolving any of their old arguments.

For some scholars, the consistent finding across a number of empirical studies that cultural issues remained comparatively less important than economic issues in shaping the political orientation of most American voters, even after the post-1988 occurrence of the conflict extension described by Layman and Carsey, served as an effective refutation of the culture war hypothesis and, by extension, the tenor of much contemporary political punditry. Perhaps, as skeptics suggested, the extent of the divide between red states and blue states – often attributed to cultural polarization – had similarly been exaggerated by an overzealous news media that ignored the considerable degree of overlap in the political views of citizens residing in different regions of the nation. Yet the presence of winner-take-all elections has allowed even relatively modest variation in political preferences across geographic boundaries to produce vast partisan differences in electoral outcomes from place to place, and the sudden emergence of a notable, though secondary, division in the voting public over social issues and religiosity in the early 1990s indeed coincided with the appearance and subsequent persistence of the contemporary regional divide in presidential and congressional elections. One need not agree that American citizens are engaged in an all-out political "war" over culture (or anything else) in order to conclude that the

---

[52] Layman and Carsey, "Party Polarization and 'Conflict Extension' in the Mass Electorate."

rising salience of social issues after 1988 has largely fueled the widening partisan gap in electoral outcomes between Red and Blue America.

THE REGIONAL DISTINCTIVENESS
OF CULTURAL POLITICS

Scholarly critiques of the culture-war thesis express considerable frustration with journalistic accounts that appear to overestimate the depth of political divisions among the American public. During the Republican presidency of George W. Bush (2001–2009), these press reports often took the form of warnings (or reassurances, depending upon the perspective of the author) that the socially liberal coastal enclaves where most national media figures resided bore little resemblance to the ascendant "real America" of the nation's heartland. While the popular perception of a cultural divide remained intact after the national Democratic victories led by Barack Obama in 2008 and 2012, the tone shifted dramatically in response to the partisan change represented by Obama's electoral success. Now it was the Republican Party that had supposedly become trapped in a culturally obsolete regional bubble limited to the South and rural interior, leaving itself dangerously out of touch with the proudly progressive "new America" of the metropolitan North and coastal West. Once Donald Trump was elected to succeed Obama in 2016, however, this genre of media analysis mostly reverted to its Bush-era form, portraying Trump's rise to the presidency as representing a populist rebellion by middle America against an aloof class of cultural elites personified by Trump's Democratic opponent Hillary Clinton.

In concert with a larger Internet-age cultural zeitgeist in which consumer preferences play an increasingly central role as signifiers of personal identity, the red-versus-blue divide is now often viewed as extending to regionally divergent tastes in entertainment, recreation, and even cuisine. The posited association between these personal inclinations and more explicitly political characteristics such as party identification and choice of candidate often defies empirical verification – as Larry M. Bartels dryly noted, political surveys usually do not include "questions about windsurfing or latte-drinking" – and strikes some readers, not all of them academics, as more than a bit overstated.[53] Underneath these usually anecdotal (and thus easily discounted) accounts of geographic differences in popular consumption, however, lays a more serious set of claims: that

[53] Bartels, "What's the Matter ..." p. 217.

the American public exhibits regional variation in its collective religiosity and cultural character, that this variation becomes manifest on political issues that involve attitudes toward the sexual revolution in particular and adherence to moral traditionalism in general, and that the integration of this dimension of political conflict into the existing party system accounts, at least in significant part, for the emerging differences in partisan alignments between Red and Blue America in presidential and congressional elections. It is not necessary to believe that two halves of the American populace are waging an outright "war," or that social issues have superseded economic issues as the predominant policy dimension of partisan conflict, in order to conclude that underlying collective differences in citizen attitudes on cultural matters can account for much of the growing partisan gap between the electoral outcomes in Democratic-leaning states such as California and New York on one side and increasingly Republican states such as Alabama and Idaho on the other.

The impact of any particular causal factor on aggregate electoral outcomes is a function not only of its role in shaping the behavior of individuals, but also of the extent to which voters sharing similar characteristics are clustered within the same electoral constituencies. (For example, while gender is a demonstrably powerful variable in accounting for the political orientation of citizens, with women significantly more likely to identify as – and vote for – Democrats than men, it cannot explain significant geographic differences in election results due to the relatively even spatial distribution of men and women.) If cultural attitudes are dispersed less evenly than economic attitudes across geographic boundaries such as states and regions, the somewhat weaker influence of social issues on the partisan loyalties of individual citizens (as compared to economic views) can still exert a comparatively greater effect on the results of partisan elections.

Previous research has suggested that both the Republican realignment of the South over the past three decades and the simultaneous pro-Democratic shift in the Northeast were fueled in large part by the rising salience of cultural issues. Jonathan Knuckey's study of the changing partisanship of white southerners during the 1990s found that the prevailing social conservatism of these voters played a significant role in explaining their increasing Republican identity. "The effects of culture are evident," he concluded, "with both moral traditionalism and abortion attitudes becoming significant predictors of party identification."[54]

---

[54] Jonathan Knuckey, "Explaining Recent Changes in the Partisan Identifications of Southern Whites," *Political Research Quarterly* 59 (March 2006), pp. 57–70, quote on p. 64.

Likewise, Howard L. Reiter and Jeffrey M. Stonecash determined that party polarization on social issues has accounted for much of the increasing recent Democratic electoral dominance of the Northeast, noting that evaluations of the Republican Party among pro-choice northeasterners turned abruptly negative from the 1992 election onward.[55]

Figure 4.5 compares the aggregate economic and cultural attitudes of major-party voters residing in Red and Blue America. The figure displays the mean values of two indices constructed from items that have been consistently included on the survey instrument of the American National Election Studies since 1988.[56] The economic issues index is assembled from four measures of respondents' economic views: (1) relative preferences for a high-service, high-spending government as opposed to a lower-service, smaller government; (2) degree of agreement with the belief that the government should guarantee Americans a job and a sufficient standard of living;[57] (3) response to the claim that the government should play an active role in providing health care to all Americans; and (4) relative favorability ratings of big business and labor unions. The cultural issues index is an average of five components: (1) attitudes toward legalized abortion; (2) attitudes toward laws that shield gay people from job discrimination; (3) average response to a battery of four items measuring moral traditionalism; (4) respondents' relative favorability ratings of homosexuals and Christian fundamentalists; and (5) the self-reported importance of religion in the respondent's personal life.[58] Positive scores

---

[55] Howard L. Reiter and Jeffrey M. Stonecash, *Counter Realignment: Political Change in the Northeastern United States* (New York: Cambridge University Press, 2011), pp. 126–139.

[56] Data from the 2016 American National Election Studies (ANES) were not yet available at press time.

[57] The wording of this item admittedly seems somewhat antiquated from the perspective of contemporary politics. Yet it continues to capture an important component of respondents' economic views. Larry M. Bartels found in 2006 that the item has remained "powerfully relevant to ... electoral choices"; see Bartels, "What's the Matter ...," pp. 213–214, 216 (quote on p. 216).

[58] These indices are adapted from Laura Stoker and M. Kent Jennings, "Of Time and the Development of Partisan Polarization," *American Journal of Political Science* 52 (2008), pp. 619–635. The four items measuring moral traditionalism ask respondents to agree or disagree with the following statements: (1) "The newer lifestyles are contributing to the breakdown of our society"; (2) "The world is always changing and we should adjust our view of moral behavior to those changes"; (3) "This country would have many fewer problems if there were more emphasis on traditional family ties"; and (4) "We should be more tolerant of people who choose to live according to their own moral standards, even if they are very different from our own." The indices and their component variables are standardized to hold a mean of 0 and a standard deviation of 1; however, standardization does not significantly affect the results.

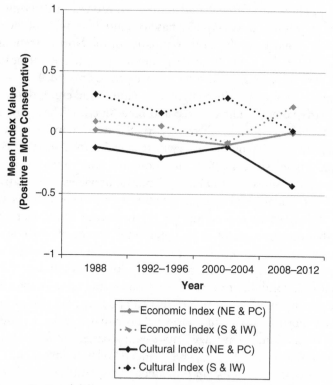

FIGURE 4.5. Regional differences in economic and cultural attitudes, 1988–2012.
Note: Major-party presidential voters only.
Source: Data from the American National Election Studies.

represent relative conservatism, and negative scores represent liberalism. Results are reported for major-party presidential voters only, and consecutive elections have been combined after 1988 in order to increase the number of observations.[59]

Figure 4.5 suggests that the collective attitudes of red-region and blue-region voters have indeed consistently differed more in the cultural than the economic domain since 1988. The cultural gap between Red and Blue America has remained relatively stable over time (roughly equaling one-half of a standard deviation on the standardized cultural issues index), with a parallel leftward shift after 2004 across regional boundaries that

[59] For certain elections, differences in the survey mode employed by the ANES prevented the collection of comparable measures on a large share of respondents; in particular, the significant proportion of the 2000 ANES that was conducted over the telephone could not be included in this analysis.

reflects an increasing nationwide tolerance of homosexuality. While voters in Red America have also tended to be somewhat more conservative than their Blue America counterparts on economic issues, the difference has been comparatively modest – although it notably widened in the Obama elections of 2008–2012, the gap in economic issue positions between red-region and blue-region residents remained smaller than the differences on the cultural index. It is possible that the solidifying Republican loyalties of the socially conservative residents of the South and interior West have also made them increasingly receptive to the party's economic message.

To be sure, the cultural divide separating the Northeast and Pacific Coast from the South and interior West falls well short of that portrayed by the most simplistic popular accounts. Not all of Blue America shares the zealous social liberalism of Berkeley, California; not all of Red America resembles the morally ultraconservative environment of Provo, Utah. In addition, Figure 4.5 provides no evidence to validate the assumption that the disagreement between residents of red and blue regions over cultural matters has deepened over time; a modest divergence between the two voting populations has only occurred on economic issues since 2004. However, the consistent cultural gap between Red and Blue America since 1988 could still account for the growing partisan differences in the electoral alignments of the two sets of regions if citizens are increasingly drawing upon their existing social-issue positions in order to determine their candidate preferences. The red-versus-blue divide over abortion, gay rights, and religiosity appears to have existed prior to the growth of regional differences in national election outcomes that began in the 1990s, but has perhaps become more electorally consequential as the salience of these issues has increased in the minds of voters, nudging the socially liberal inhabitants of Blue America toward Democratic candidates while the culturally conservative denizens of Red America take increasingly favorable views of the Republican Party.

In order to investigate this hypothesis, it is necessary to move to individual-level analysis of national survey data. Table 4.1 contains the results of a series of logit regression analyses based on responses to the American National Election Studies between 1988 and 2012. As in Figure 4.5, the elections of 1992 and 1996, 2000 and 2004, and 2008 and 2012 are paired in order to increase the number of respondents at each point in the timespan. The dependent variable in each regression is the two-party presidential vote (third-party voters and nonvoters are excluded).

TABLE 4.1. *How cultural views explain the regional gap in presidential elections, 1988–2012*

Independent variable	Model 1	Model 2	Model 3	Model 4
1988				
Regional category	−.135	−.267	−.321**	−.455**
	(.137)	(.192)	(.146)	(.202)
Economic index		1.578***		1.577***
		(.146)		(.149)
Cultural index			.406***	.418***
			(.077)	(.099)
Constant	.172	.226	.260	.301
N	866	623	836	605
1992–1996				
Regional category	.244*	.218	.027	−.032
	(.102)	(.137)	(.118)	(.158)
Economic index		1.705***		1.648***
		(.111)		(.118)
Cultural index			.817***	.780***
			(.063)	(.083)
Constant	−.545	−.611	−.503	−.517
N	1784	1377	1623	1258
2000–2004				
Regional category	.361**	.467**	.087	.210
	(.118)	(.192)	(.130)	(.203)
Economic index		1.869***		1.799***
		(.147)		(.155)
Cultural index			.716***	.620***
			(.067)	(.101)
Constant	−.220	−.003	−.103	.109
N	1418	835	1359	806
2008–2012				
Regional category	.472***	.380**	.134	.025
	(.081)	(.136)	(.128)	(.188)
Economic index		2.279***		2.162***
		(.107)		(.148)
Cultural index			.940***	.842***
			(.065)	(.089)
Constant	−.406	−.478	−.030	.022
N	4621	3292	2258	1864

†$p \le .10$ *$p \le .05$ **$p \le .01$ ***$p \le .001$

Note: Figures are estimated coefficients from logit regressions; standard errors are in parentheses. The dependent variable is the two-party presidential vote. The economic and cultural indices are standardized to hold a mean of 0 and standard deviation of 1.

Source: Data from American National Election Studies.

For each election or pair of elections, the first regression (Model 1) contains a single independent dummy variable corresponding to the respondent's residence in either a red (South or interior West) or blue (Northeast or Pacific Coast) state. (Midwestern voters are excluded from the analysis.) The estimated coefficient thus represents the lone "effect" of regional location on the likelihood of voting Democratic or Republican. Unsurprisingly, this variable produces insignificant results in the 1988 election, which occurred prior to the geographic polarization of presidential election outcomes, but is modestly associated with partisan vote choice in subsequent years. (Because many Democrats continue to live in majority-Republican regions and vice versa, knowing a respondent's state of residence alone can provide us with only a limited ability to predict his or her favored candidate in a presidential election.)

In Model 2, an additional independent variable is introduced: the economic issues index from Figure 4.5. Respondents' economic views perennially exhibit strong substantive and statistical significance with respect to the dependent variable of presidential vote choice over the entire timespan covered by the analysis. The evidence appears to refute claims that voters no longer view the parties as holding distinct positions on economic matters or choose candidates on the basis of economic policy. In fact, the estimated coefficients associated with the economic index increased in magnitude over the course of the 1988–2012 period, suggesting that – if anything – economic differences between the parties became more salient in the minds of voters after the 1980s. Yet the presence of the economic index in Model 2 exerts at best a modest influence on the estimated effect of the regional variable. In the 1992–1996 elections, the regional variable barely slips below the standard threshold of statistical significance, although the estimated coefficient hardly changes from its value in Model 1 upon the introduction of the economic index; in subsequent elections, the regional variable retains significance in the presence of the economic index. This pattern indicates that while economic views consistently maintain a powerful influence on individual voters' choice of presidential candidates, they cannot alone account for the aggregate partisan differences in electoral outcomes across regional borders that emerged in the 1990s.

Model 3 substitutes the cultural index for the economic index as a second independent variable alongside the regional dummy. Throughout the timespan covered by the analysis, voters' views on cultural matters also affect their presidential candidate preferences; consistent with the previous scholarship described earlier, the salience of cultural ideology appears to have increased between 1988 and 1992–1996. Although the estimated coefficients associated with the cultural index are consistently lower than those associated with the economic index in Model 2 for each election or pair of elections (suggesting that cultural concerns remain less powerful than economic views in shaping the partisan preferences of individual voters), the presence of the cultural index exerts a more notable influence on the estimated independent effect of region compared to the baseline value estimated in Model 1. In other words, the post-1992 regional gap in voting alignments between Red and Blue America appears to be primarily caused by geographic differences in cultural attitudes, even though economic views remain more salient in determining the partisan loyalties of individual citizens. Model 4 contains both the economic and cultural indices in a single regression analysis, confirming that the economic index continues to produce larger estimated coefficients than the cultural index when both are present.

Table 4.2 repeats the analysis reported in Table 4.1 on respondents' votes for the House of Representatives over the 1988–2012 period. On the whole, the results are quite similar, although the residual strength of Democratic congressional support in the South as late as the mid-1990s delays the appearance of strong regional differences in House voting until the 2000–2004 period. As with the presidential vote, economic concerns remain most important in explaining the choices of individual voters to support Democratic or Republican congressional candidates, while cultural matters hold disproportionate influence over the collective partisan gap between Red and Blue America.[60]

Table 4.3 presents yet another set of logit analyses using data from the General Social Survey (GSS), which confirms the centrality of cultural differences in accounting for the red–blue divide. The survey items included on the GSS differ somewhat from those of the ANES, most notably including measures of respondents' attitudes toward gun control and drug legalization that allow for the inclusion of these additional cultural issues in the analysis. The economic index included in Table 4.3 is based on five GSS items measuring respondents' attitudes toward the following: (1) whether the government should do more to solve our country's problems or should leave more autonomy to individuals and businesses; (2) whether the government should do more to improve citizens' standard of living; (3) whether the government should spend more on welfare

---

[60] Introducing the component variables as separate independent variables rather than as part of an economic or cultural index produces similar results.

TABLE 4.2. *How cultural views explain the regional gap in congressional elections, 1988–2012*

Independent variable	Model 1	Model 2	Model 3	Model 4
1988				
Regional category	−.283†	−.208	−.476**	−.388†
	(.151)	(.193)	(.162)	(.206)
Economic index		.952***		.932***
		(.124)		(.125)
Cultural index			.413***	.364***
			(.082)	(.102)
Constant	−.220	−.297	−.174	−.259
N	729	528	707	515
1992–1996				
Regional category	.139	.056	.007	−.042
	(.109)	(.139)	(.120)	(.149)
Economic index		1.240***		1.087***
		(.097)		(.100)
Cultural index			.495***	.406***
			(.059)	(.075)
Constant	−.272	−.189	−.202	−.107
N	1495	1158	1387	1076
2000–2004				
Regional category	.358***	.414**	.082	.201
	(.131)	(.194)	(.145)	(.206)
Economic index		1.478***		1.318***
		(.132)		(.135)
Cultural index			.774***	.633***
			(.073)	(.105)
Constant	−.282	−.269	−.167	−.198
N	1126	708	1076	683
2008–2012				
Regional category	.520***	.511***	.159	.154
	(.088)	(.135)	(.138)	(.181)
Economic index		1.878***		1.794***
		(.092)		(.125)
Cultural index			.760***	.604***
			(.071)	(.091)
Constant	−.283	−.397	.027	−.088
N	3784	2775	1856	1571

† p ≤ .10 *p ≤ .05 **p ≤ .01 ***p ≤ .001

Note: Figures are estimated coefficients from logit regressions; standard errors are in parentheses. The dependent variable is the two-party House vote. The economic and cultural indices are standardized to hold a mean of 0 and standard deviation of 1.

Source: Data from American National Election Studies.

TABLE 4.3. *Cultural views explain the regional divide,*
1984–2012 (General Social Survey data)

Independent variable	Model 1	Model 2	Model 3	Model 4
1984–1988				
Regional category	.017	−.180	−.109	−.207
	(.088)	(.199)	(.182)	(.379)
Economic index		.959***		1.201***
		(.119)		(.252)
Cultural index			.271**	−.232
			(.094)	(.204)
Constant	.436	.490	.213	.474
N	2172	498	561	152
1992–1996				
Regional category	.342***	.298†	−.083	.402
	(.075)	(.159)	(.170)	(.278)
Economic index		1.180***		1.099***
		(.095)		(.168)
Cultural index			.708***	.643***
			(.089)	(.148)
Constant	−.554	−.844	−.224	−.771
N	3015	869	662	305
2000–2004				
Regional category	.458***	.565**	.007	−.035
	(.070)	(.185)	(.204)	(.332)
Economic index		1.128***		1.153***
		(.111)		(.194)
Cultural index			.536***	.297*
			(.095)	(.153)
Constant	−.221	−.277	.300	.600
N	3404	629	473	225
2008–2012				
Regional category	.592***	.647**	.134	.229
	(.093)	(.211)	(.234)	(.443)
Economic index		1.517***		1.771***
		(.119)		(.277)
Cultural index			.808***	1.031***
			(.105)	(.224)
Constant	−.848	−1.328	−.137	−.729
N	2154	664	429	205

† $p \le .10$ *$p \le .05$ **$p \le .01$ ***$p \le .001$
Note: Figures are estimated coefficients from logit regressions; standard errors are in parentheses. The dependent variable is the two-party presidential vote. The economic and cultural indices are standardized to hold a mean of 0 and standard deviation of 1.
Source: Data from the General Social Survey.

programs; (4) whether the government should spend more on the nation's health; and (5) whether the government should spend more on the environment. The cultural index is based on the following: (1) an abortion index built from seven items measuring the specific legal restrictions that the respondent supports; (2) tolerance toward homosexuality; (3) support for gun control; (4) support for the legalization of marijuana; and (5) self-reported frequency of attendance of religious services (as a proxy for religiosity). The dependent variable is the two-party presidential vote; the GSS does not measure congressional voting.

Once again, the results reflect the modest regional differences in presidential vote preference that existed prior to the 1990s. The partisan divergence between the red and blue regions of America that first emerged in the 1992 election can be accounted for by the combined effect of the cultural measures included in the analysis, even though (as in the previous tables based on the ANES) economic views are more influential in guiding the vote choice of individual citizens.

These results are consistent with the findings of Benjamin Highton, who measured the relationship between public opinion and electoral preferences at the level of individual states after the 2012 presidential election. "Differences across the American states with regard to preferences on cultural policy were more strongly related to presidential outcomes in 2012 (and 2008) than differences in preferences on economic policy ... [reflecting] an ongoing transformation in the nature of party locations and cleavages in the US," concluded Highton. "Increasingly, states are sorted into 'Red' and 'Blue' based on cultural policy preferences."[61]

If the changing salience of social issues was indeed mostly responsible for producing greater state-level differences in electoral outcomes from 1992 to the present, steadily separating culturally conservative Red America from culturally liberal Blue America, we would expect the direction and magnitude of a state's aggregate partisan shift over the past several decades to reflect the prevailing cultural ideology and religious devotion of its inhabitants. Figure 4.6 summarizes the relationship between the aggregate level of religiosity in a state population (as indicated by two Gallup survey items measuring the frequency of respondents' attendance at religious services and the extent to which they consider religion central to their personal lives) and the partisan swing in

[61] Benjamin Highton, "Sorting the American States into Red and Blue: Culture, Economics, and the 2012 US Presidential Election in Historical Context," *The Forum* 10 (December 2012), pp. 11–19, at 17.

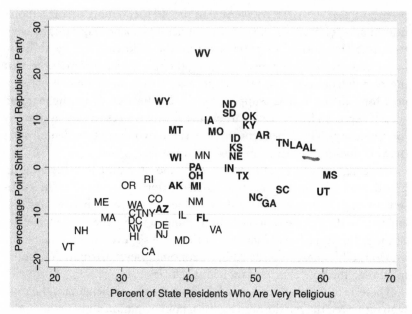

FIGURE 4.6. Relationship between state religiosity and party shift in presidential elections, 1988–2016.

Note: The *x* axis represents the percentage of state residents defined by Gallup in 2013 as "very religious"; these respondents reported that (1) religion is very important in their daily lives and (2) they attended religious services "almost every week" or more often. The *y* axis represents the difference in the share of the two-party statewide presidential vote won by the Republican candidate in 1988 and 2016 (positive values represent a pro-Republican shift over time). States in bold type were carried by Donald Trump in the 2016 presidential election.

Source: Religiosity data from Frank Newport, "Mississippi Most Religious State, Vermont Least Religious," Gallup Organization, February 3, 2014, www.gallup .com/poll/167267/mississippi-religious-vermont-least-religious-state.aspx.

the state's two-party presidential vote between the 1988 and 2016 elections. As expected, states with the lowest aggregate levels of religiosity – located mainly in the Northeast and along the Pacific Coast – moved sharply toward the Democratic Party over this period, while the relatively devout populations of most southern and many interior western states voted even more decisively for Donald Trump over Hillary Clinton in 2016 than they had for George H. W. Bush over Michael Dukakis in 1988. The Pearson correlation coefficient representing the association between state religiosity and aggregate partisan shift is .48.

As Gary Miller and Norman Schofield pointed out in 2003, the state-level coalitions of the two parties almost completely reversed over the course of the twentieth century. "If one were to predict that a Republican state in 1896 would be Democratic in 2000," they observed, "one would get all but five states correct."[62] Miller and Schofield argued that the parties engaged in a series of mutual strategic flanking maneuvers around a two-dimensional issue space that collectively produced this remarkably near-perfect exchange of geographic constituencies over one hundred years of presidential elections. By the 1990s, they wrote, many culturally liberal voters who were "historically loyal to the Republican Party" had become disillusioned with a new generation of Republican leaders who "aggressively pushed traditional social values."[63] At the same time, "the Democratic Party had irrevocably lost a vital component of the successful New Deal coalitions: the South. As a result, [Bill] Clinton had only one choice: he could keep the Democratic Party as a minority party ... or he could reach out to ... cosmopolitans" by dissociating himself from liberal economic policies while embracing cultural progressivism.[64] This analysis may understate the continuing relevance of economic views to the partisan preferences of individual voters, and it does not acknowledge that Clinton himself attempted to return the South to the Democratic coalition in 1992, albeit with limited ultimate success. But it recognizes that the modern Democratic Party is now strongly rooted in the most secular and socially liberal precincts of the nation, while the Republican Party draws its most loyal aggregate support in both presidential and congressional elections from the heaviest geographic concentrations of religious devotion in the American population. Even if cultural ideology is not the primary factor motivating individual citizens to choose Democratic or Republican candidates, it does an excellent job – as Figure 4.6 demonstrates – of explaining why American states and regions now vote the way they do.

THE CULTURE SKIRMISH

While many news media commentators have concluded that contemporary regional partisan coalitions primarily reflect a growing conflict over social issues, two other explanations for the rise of the red–blue divide have also received considerable popular attention in recent years. The first

[62] Gary Miller and Norman Schofield, "Activists and Partisan Realignment in the United States," *American Political Science Review* 97 (May 2003), pp. 245–260, at 246.
[63] Miller and Schofield, "Activists and Partisan Realignment," p. 257.
[64] Miller and Schofield, "Activists and Partisan Realignment," p. 258.

alternative account emphasizes the role of residential clustering in producing the increasingly stark geographic divisions now visible in American election returns. Former *Austin American-Statesman* reporter Bill Bishop argued in his 2008 book *The Big Sort* that Americans were increasingly choosing to settle among politically like-minded neighbors, thus producing a rise in aggregate electoral polarization at the regional, state, and county level. While Bishop acknowledged that a relatively small proportion of Americans consciously placed the partisan composition of their prospective neighborhood ahead of other considerations when selecting a place to live, he nonetheless contended that the factors weighed by migrants increasingly contained inherent political associations:

Between 4 and 5 percent of the population moves each year from one county to the other ... to take jobs, to be close to family, or to follow the sun. When they look for a place to live, they run through a checklist of amenities: Is there the right kind of church nearby? The right kind of coffee shop? How close is the neighborhood to the center of the city? What are the rents? Is the place safe? When people move, they also make choices about who their neighbors will be and who will share their new lives. Those are now political decisions, and they are having a profound effect on the nation's public life.[65]

The phenomenon described by Bishop no doubt plays a role in producing a degree of partisan variation across neighborhood, municipal, and metropolitan boundaries, and surely rings true as a matter of personal experience for many Americans. Yet it is difficult to credit residential sorting with the rise of the larger regional divide. Rather than arising gradually over the course of several decades, most of the geographic divergence in electoral outcomes occurred over a relatively short period in the 1990s and early 2000s, strongly suggesting a change in the prevailing partisan alignments of existing populations of voters rather than the large-scale reshuffling of loyal Democratic and Republican supporters around the nation. In addition, some of the greatest partisan shifts during this time occurred in states with comparatively low levels of residential in-migration, such as Louisiana and West Virginia. Finally, the ANES data summarized in Figure 4.5 indicate that the inhabitants of Red and Blue America are not actually becoming more divergent over time in their collective cultural ideology; instead, electoral polarization has progressed as existing attitudes on social issues have become increasingly powerful in shaping partisan voting preferences.

[65] Bill Bishop with Robert G. Cushing, *The Big Sort: Why the Clustering of Like-Minded America Is Tearing Us Apart* (Boston: Houghton Mifflin, 2008), p. 5.

The second alternative explanation for the growing regional divide concerns race and ethnicity. The growing racial diversity of the American public since the 1980s has intensified the salience of immigration, affirmative action, bilingual education, and other relevant political issues while simultaneously altering the demographic complexion of the national electorate, particularly within the Democratic Party. Demonstrating the increasing electoral power of racial minorities, Barack Obama won reelection in 2012 despite losing the white vote to Mitt Romney by a margin of 20 percentage points (59 percent to 39 percent), according to the national media exit poll. Obama attracted support from 80 percent of the nation's nonwhite voters, who represented 44 percent of his total electoral base.[66]

Some commentators have explained the rise of a reliable Democratic geographic base after the 1980s by citing the growing electoral clout – and increasing Democratic loyalties – of minority groups concentrated in urban areas along the nation's East and West coasts. For example, many political observers agree that the transformation of California from a competitive or even Republican-leaning state to a solid Democratic bastion in the 1990s was significantly advanced by Republican endorsements of restrictive immigration laws – especially Proposition 187, championed by then-governor Pete Wilson and approved by California voters in 1994 – which stoked a massive partisan backlash among Latinos. The *Orange County Register* reflected this conventional wisdom in a retrospective on the twentieth anniversary of Proposition 187's passage by crediting a "wave of Latino activism and changing demographics" with making California "a solid blue state in presidential elections."[67] "How did California go from a Republican stronghold to a Democratic lock?" asked political analysts David Damore and Adrian Pantoja. "The answer is clear – anti-immigrant policy and a frustrated and mobilized Latino vote."[68]

Though the highly visible and often bitter partisan conflict over the immigration issue may well have produced a rise in the political participation and Democratic identification of Latinos in California and

---

[66] Pew Research Center, "Changing Face of America Helps Assure Obama Victory," November 7, 2012, www.people-press.org/2012/11/07/changing-face-of-america-helps-assure-obama-victory/; *Washington Post*, "Exit Polls 2012: How the Vote Has Shifted," www.washingtonpost.com/wp-srv/special/politics/2012-exit-polls/table.html.

[67] Roxana Kopetman, "20 Years After Prop. 187, O.C. Group That Created It Is Pushing for Same Goals," *Orange County Register*, October 31, 2014, www.ocregister.com/articles/immigration-640538-california-group.html.

[68] David Damore and Adrian Pantoja, "Anti-Immigrant Politics and Lessons for the GOP from California," Latino Decisions, 2013, www.latinodecisions.com/blog/wp-content/uploads/2013/10/Prop187Effect.pdf.

elsewhere, it cannot alone account for the state's firmly blue electoral status in contemporary national elections. California first shifted into the Democratic column in the 1992 election – two years before Proposition 187 appeared on the ballot – when it gave Bill Clinton an 18-point margin in the two-party popular vote and elected two new Democratic senators. According to exit polls, Clinton carried the white vote in California by 7 points in 1992.[69] While the growing share of racial minorities in the state's electorate has contributed significantly to its now-formidable Democratic advantage, the changing partisan preferences of socially liberal white voters after the 1988 election appears to represent the initial catalyst for the political transformation of California and other states that habitually voted Republican in the 1970s and 1980s but turned reliably blue thereafter.

To be sure, the rapidly changing demographic composition of the American electorate promises to exert a significant influence on future electoral outcomes; absent a major change in the social coalitions of the parties, the rising proportion of nonwhite voters can be expected to benefit Democratic candidates in racially diverse electoral constituencies such as Nevada, New Jersey, and Virginia. But the current regional pattern of red and blue territory does not principally reflect the geographic distribution of racial groups in the electorate. In fact, three of the four states with the nation's highest percentage of non-Hispanic whites – the adjacent states of Maine (94.4 percent white, as of the 2010 U.S. census), Vermont (94.3 percent), and New Hampshire (92.3 percent) – are all former Republican bastions that moved in a Democratic direction after the 1980s. As in the rest of the country, the contemporary partisan alignment of these three states arises less from their racial composition than from the cultural ideology of their residents – as Figure 4.6 illustrates, the collective religiosity of upper New Englanders ranks as the lowest in the entire nation.

Social issues have become incorporated into the national party system in recent decades, first separating Democratic from Republican officeholders and activists in the 1960s and 1970s and ultimately differentiating partisans in the mass electorate as well, especially after 1992. This process has occurred via the "conflict extension" model described by Layman and Carsey: the new cultural divide has augmented rather than replaced the existing partisan divergence over economic policy, opening up a new dimension of issue-related conflict without extinguishing or even reducing

[69] CNN, "1992 California Exit Polls Results," www.cnn.com/ELECTION/1998/states/CA/polls/CA92PH.html.

the importance of the previous one. While political disputes over abortion, gay rights, religious liberty, and similar matters still constitute a secondary axis of political competition, maintaining less influence over the partisan choices of individual American voters than the economic issues and interests that have distinguished Democrats from Republicans since the New Deal era, existing regional variations in the distribution of cultural views and rates of religious observance are sufficiently strong under winner-take-all electoral rules to shift the socially liberal states of the Northeast and Pacific Coast in a collectively Democratic direction in both presidential and congressional elections while solidifying the ascendancy of the Republican Party in the culturally conservative South and interior West.

To some scholars, claims of a polarized public cleft in two by a "culture war" is a thoroughly unfounded myth; to others, the polarization of political elites has simply reflected the corresponding polarization of the masses. Yet neither account fully captures the complexity of the association between the increasing partisan salience of cultural differences in the electorate and the changes that occurred in the regional alignments of the parties after the 1980s. A complete appraisal of this relationship requires an acknowledgment of the central role played by the American electoral system in translating individual votes into aggregate outcomes.

American politics is by no means "all culture war, all the time." Social issues do not divide the public more than economic issues do, nor are they more powerful in convincing citizens to join a specific party or support a particular candidate. Views on abortion – usually portrayed as a "hot button" issue that produces fervently held and morally absolutist opinions – are frequently nuanced or ambivalent; most Americans believe that abortion should be legal in certain circumstances but not in others.[70] Public opinion on cultural issues among red- and blue-state inhabitants similarly exhibits substantial overlap in its distribution, with a significant population of cultural liberals residing in Red America and cultural conservatives remaining in Blue America. Even within the ranks of party identifiers, ideological sorting on social issues is far from complete; a Pew Research Center survey conducted in September 2015 found that 27 percent of Democrats favored prohibiting abortion in all or most cases, while 28 percent of Republicans supported continued legalization.[71]

---

[70] Fiorina, *Culture War?* pp. 79–108.
[71] Pew Research Center, "Majority Says Any Budget Deal Must Include Planned Parenthood Funding," September 28, 2015, www.people-press.org/2015/09/28/majority-says-any-budget-deal-must-include-planned-parenthood-funding/.

Yet culture war skeptics risk understating the political divisions that do exist over social issues among American voters, as well as the substantial electoral consequences of conflict extension in the contemporary party system. Differences in public opinion across regional lines may be regularly exaggerated by an excitable news media, but they can still be responsible for very different partisan outcomes from one constituency to the next. Social issues have exerted a disproportionate impact on the collective alignment of states and regions, due to their significant spatial variation across geographic borders. Popular assumptions that the growing politicization of cultural and religious differences since the 1980s has made red states redder and blue states bluer – with attendant implications for the national balance, electoral strategy, and ideological polarization of the national parties – are, in fact, fundamentally sound, despite the tendency of scholars who question the existence of mass polarization to minimize the presence of political divisions in the mass public.

At the same time, it is difficult to identify a straightforward causal relationship between mass and elite polarization on cultural issues. While the residents of Red and Blue America have become increasingly distinct in their respective partisan preferences over time, the evidence presented here suggests that the relative cultural attitudes of red-state and blue-state residents exhibit stability, not divergence. For example, while the voters of the South and interior West have become increasingly likely over the past 20 years to support socially conservative Republican candidates for federal office, this trend does not reflect a corresponding shift to the right in their own cultural views. The magnifying effect of winner-take-all elections likewise produces a much larger regional gap in partisan outcomes than would be warranted based on the much more modest cross-regional differences in public opinion visible in Figure 4.5.

Should we then hold the parties responsible for systematically distorting the true preferences of the citizenry by deferring more frequently to the extreme views of activists and financial donors than the moderate and open-minded ordinary American? This is a popular view in an age of widespread dissatisfaction with the persistence of elite-level polarization. But the system of democratic representation in the United States is highly complex, and a mismatch between the distribution of opinion in the mass public and the aggregation of policy positions in elective institutions does not necessarily reflect the destructive influence of rank partisanship, requiring the imposition of institutional reforms to beat back its malign effects.

Under the American form of government, elected officials represent specific geographic constituencies: congressional districts, states, and (for presidents) groups of states. More precisely, they represent a majority, or even plurality, of participating voters within those electoral units. Views that are held by even a slim preponderance of participating citizens across a large proportion of constituencies will likely achieve ample representation, while the nature of the electoral rules now in place is systematically insensitive to the preferences of electoral minorities – even those of substantial size. Whether the margin of victory is one vote or a million, the winner takes all and the loser gets nothing.

The degree of conflict extension in the electorate since the 1980s has proven sufficiently sizable to transform most culturally liberal constituencies into secure territory for Democratic candidates while rendering most culturally conservative areas safely Republican. As a result, while the national population indeed still contains a substantial share of socially liberal Republicans and socially conservative Democrats, both groups rarely constitute a majority in a particular state or district – thus ensuring their perennial underrepresentation in political office. Because nearly all elected Democrats now represent constituencies in which cultural liberalism commands majority support – while Republican officeholders overwhelmingly represent constituencies in which cultural conservatism likewise prevails – there is little incentive for leaders of either party to moderate their positions or encourage the emergence of a dissenting faction within party ranks. With no realistic chance of competing across much of the South and interior West in the immediate future, national Democratic candidates are free to take sharply liberal positions on cultural matters, while Republicans, openly conceding the Northeast and Pacific Coast, can likewise represent the regional majorities that elected them by remaining strongly conservative.

Such a process of representation is far from simple, but it is representation all the same. Contemporary elites are notably more polarized on political issues, including cultural issues, than the mass public as a whole, yet a visible connection still exists between the preferences of individual constituencies and the positions taken by their favored candidates. The extension of partisan conflict into the cultural domain since the 1980s has had the effect of increasing the proportion of the nation that is safely red or blue in both presidential and congressional voting, resulting in a series of nationally competitive elections between increasingly polarized parties. While the conflict in the mass public over social issues resembles a mere skirmish more than a true culture war, its effects are all the more consequential because the participants largely line up on opposite sides of the nation's regional boundaries.

5

Regional Polarization and Partisan Change in the U.S. Congress

THE CASE OF THE VANISHING MODERATES

To some critics of elite polarization, the disappearance from Congress of members with moderate policy positions and bipartisan styles of governing amounts to a serious failure of representational legitimacy. In their view, today's parties are led by two warring sets of politicians who have become more sensitive to the demands of a relatively small population of zealous issue activists, interest groups, and primary electorates on the ideological left or right than to the concerns of a larger, more open-minded American public. "A ... problem with cohesive parties that offer voters a clear choice is that voters may not like clear choices," argues Morris P. Fiorina. "Voters may not want a clear choice between a constitutional prohibition of abortion and abortion on demand, between privatizing Social Security and ignoring unsustainable fiscal imbalances, between launching wars of choice and ignoring developing threats. Given that the issue positions of the electorate as a whole are not polarized, it is likely that many voters today would prefer a fuzzier choice than typically provided by the candidates on their ballots."[1]

Yet according to Alan I. Abramowitz and like-minded analysts who dispute this view, "there is no disconnect between political elites and the public," especially among the "politically engaged [citizens] whose opinions are of greatest concern to candidates and elected officials."[2]

---

[1] Morris P. Fiorina with Samuel J. Abrams, *Disconnect: The Breakdown of Representation in American Politics* (Norman: University of Oklahoma Press, 2009), p. 155.
[2] Alan I. Abramowitz, *The Disappearing Center: Engaged Citizens, Polarization, and American Democracy* (New Haven, CT: Yale University Press, 2010), pp. 5, 37.

Abramowitz draws a direct connection between the ideological divergence of partisan officeholders and the changing policy preferences of their constituents, concluding that "members of Congress generally reflect the views of their parties' electoral bases: Republicans reflect the views of their party's conservative electoral base, and Democrats reflect the views of their party's liberal electoral base. Polarization in Congress reflects polarization in the American electorate."[3]

This chapter examines how the rise of well-defined and temporally stable partisan geographic coalitions has influenced the operation of Congress. It focuses in particular on two major trends that have transformed the legislative branch over the past three decades: the steady polarization of the congressional parties and the increased success of Republican candidates in both House and Senate elections. The consolidation of Democratic electoral support in the blue regions of the Northeast and Pacific Coast, along with even more substantial gains achieved by Republicans in the red South and interior West since the early 1990s, has contributed to elite polarization by significantly reducing the proportion of moderate officeholders. Congressional Republicans, in particular, have almost completely shed their centrist wing in both chambers, as the party has become dominated by an increasingly numerous bloc of very conservative members elected from southern and interior western constituencies.

The growing popularity of the congressional Republican Party among the inhabitants of Red America in the years after 1992 has allowed it to compete consistently, and usually with success, for control of both legislative chambers for the first sustained period since the 1920s. In fact, Republicans now benefit from a systematically favorable geographic distribution of support in the electorate that gives their party an easier path than the Democratic opposition to assembling a national majority in both houses of Congress. For Democrats, the steady departure of moderate southern and interior western incumbents from elective office has become a particularly formidable obstacle to winning and holding control of the legislative branch; the party had traditionally demonstrated the ability to win elections in otherwise Republican-leaning constituencies by nominating centrist candidates who could once attract substantial popular support from Republican presidential voters.

These developments illustrate the complexity of the contemporary relationship between elite polarization and the preferences of the

---

[3] Abramowitz, *Disappearing Center*, p. 157.

mass public. Analysts who wish to hold the American citizenry fully exempt from responsibility for an increasingly polarized Congress risk minimizing the influence of electoral trends in reducing the proportion of ideological centrists in office. When offered the choice between a moderate incumbent of one party and a more extreme challenger from the other, voters have increasingly opted for the latter, replacing many moderate Democrats with conservative Republicans in the red states and a smaller number of moderate Republicans with liberal Democrats in the blue states. Claims that the American electorate has been denied the opportunity to express its collectively centrist, pragmatic preferences by a party system that only provides it with an excessively "clear choice" between unattractively polarized options fail to acknowledge the contribution that changes in the behavior of regional electorates have made to the ideological divergence of the parties in government. In fact, the leadership of the congressional Republican Party pursued a strategy of intentionally drawing sharper contrasts with their Democratic opponents beginning in the 1980s as an ultimately successful means of mobilizing greater electoral support for the party in conservative-leaning constituencies, challenging the commonly held assumption that legislative parties necessarily risk losing popularity among a collectively moderate American public by visibly shifting away from the ideological center.

At the same time, these trends do not demonstrate that a newly polarized electorate now prefers ideological extremity to moderation when party affiliation is held constant, as might be implied by analyses that describe the ideological divergence of partisan officeholders as a simple democratic response to polarization among citizens. There is little evidence that ideologically doctrinaire candidates perform better in general elections than more centrist candidates of the same party, for example, or that the emergence of strong regional alignments in congressional elections is primarily a consequence of popular demands for a more polarized politics. Democrats and Republicans have increasingly voted differently on the floor of Congress in part because the geographic constituencies that once elected maverick partisans to office in significant numbers have become more secure in their preferences for candidates of the opposite party regardless of their policy positions. The declining proportion of congressional moderates does not necessarily indicate that voters no longer hold moderate views themselves or have come to eschew conciliatory approaches to policymaking; rather, the state and district electorates that select members of Congress are now collectively more likely to prioritize a candidate's party affiliation over his or her ideological profile, rarely departing from their normal partisan alignments in order to support even a moderate candidate nominated by the opposition.

A set of complex constitutional and electoral rules governs the process by which the votes of individual citizens are translated into the composition of Congress. As a result, political analysts should be especially reluctant to assume a simple connection between the opinions of the electorate and the behavior of officeholders – or, alternatively, to view the lack of such a correspondence as necessarily representing a serious deficiency of the political parties. The extent to which the partisan, ideological, and policy-related preferences of the public receive proportionate representation in elective institutions also depends crucially upon the interaction between the spatial distribution of votes and the effects of electoral procedures, constitutional provisions, and other factors. The emergence of regional patterns of party support in congressional voting since the early 1990s has rapidly produced massive differences across geographic borders in the collective voting records of senators and House members – differences that cannot be explained as simply reflecting a parallel divergence in the political views of regional electorates. As the previous chapter demonstrated, differences in issue positions between the inhabitants of Red and Blue America have not become dramatically polarized over the past three decades – yet the congressional representatives of these two sets of regions have rapidly shifted in opposite ideological directions during the same period.

Even the partisan allegiances of the American public, as measured simply by the total number of votes received by each congressional party, do not correspond precisely to the relative share of seats awarded to Democratic and Republican senators and representatives. In the current era, for example, Republicans hold a structural advantage that has allowed them on several occasions to gain majority control of one or both chambers of Congress without winning a plurality of the national vote. The representation of citizens is thus fundamentally shaped by the geographically based electoral institutions that determine the composition of the House and the Senate. As Americans have become more consistent and more regionally distinct in their partisan voting habits, they have encouraged – whether intentionally or not – the emergence of a more polarized, and more Republican, legislative branch.

IDEOLOGY AND SHIFTING PARTISANSHIP IN TWO
CONGRESSIONAL CONSTITUENCIES

South of metropolitan Atlanta, suburban sprawl gradually gives way to the more rural environs of central Georgia, where the hilly terrain of the Piedmont plateau meets the flatter landscape of the Atlantic coastal plain. While there are a few medium-sized cities in the area, including Macon and Warner Robins, much of the region still consists of small towns and countryside, with peanut and soybean farms dotting what once was the heart of the Cotton Belt. Central Georgia also features rich deposits of kaolin, a white clay commonly used as a component of porcelain and for various industrial processes, which is mined across the region and exported both domestically and abroad.[4]

Union General William Tecumseh Sherman marched through the area on his devastating Savannah Campaign in November 1864, hastening the end of the Civil War and cementing Georgia's antipathy to the North (and to the Republican Party that presided over the war and Reconstruction) for generations. Democratic candidates routinely received 80 to 95 percent of the popular vote in most central Georgia counties as late as the mid-twentieth century – even in the 1952 and 1956 elections, when the Republican presidential nominee was Dwight D. Eisenhower, a national military hero. As in most of the Deep South, this long era of single-party politics ended in central Georgia with the advent of the civil rights movement. In rural Pulaski County, for example, the Democratic share of the two-party presidential vote dropped from 89 percent in 1956 to just 35 percent in 1964. But the partisan change that immediately occurred in presidential elections after the passage of the Civil Rights Act did not extend to voting for Congress and other down-ballot offices for decades thereafter. Much of central Georgia lies within the 8th Congressional District, which voted overwhelmingly for Republican presidential nominee Barry Goldwater in 1964 even as its incumbent Democratic congressman, James Russell Tuten, ran unopposed for reelection. Tuten was one of a long succession of moderate-to-conservative Democrats who represented the region; the neighboring 6th District was the home of Carl Vinson, the hawkish long-standing chair of the House Armed Services Committee who, at the time of his retirement in 1965, had represented Georgia in the

---

[4] Ronald Smothers, "White Georgia Clay Turns into Cash," *New York Times*, December 12, 1987, sec. I, p. 12.

House for more than 50 years – a tenure of service that was unequaled at the time in American history.

Another full generation elapsed before competitive congressional elections finally arrived in central Georgia, even as the region routinely supported Republican presidential candidates from Goldwater forward (except in 1968, when the third-party candidacy of racial segregationist George Wallace attracted a substantial proportion of the Georgia vote, and in 1976 and 1980, when favorite son Jimmy Carter topped the Democratic ticket). The Democratic share of the House vote in the 8th District dropped below 69 percent only once before the 1990s; as late as 1988, Republicans didn't even bother to field a candidate for the seat. But five-term incumbent Democrat J. Roy Rowland was held to 56 percent of the vote in 1992, foreshadowing the partisan change to come. Rowland retired from Congress two years later, just ahead of a 52-seat national Republican gain that ended four decades of Democratic control of the House and produced a Republican majority in the South for the first time since Reconstruction. The 8th District mirrored this national trend, electing Republican Saxby Chambliss to succeed Rowland by a 26-point margin and finally breaking the Democrats' century-long hold on congressional politics in central Georgia.

While Republicans became favored in southern congressional elections after 1994, two-party competition did not immediately vanish from conservative-leaning constituencies in the region. When Chambliss vacated the seat in 2002 in order to mount a campaign for the U.S. Senate, he was succeeded in the House by a Democrat named Jim Marshall, who was a decorated ex-Army Ranger and former mayor of Macon.[5] In an otherwise unfavorable year for Democratic congressional candidates due to the popularity of President George W. Bush, Marshall narrowly regained the seat for his party.

Like his Democratic predecessors from central Georgia, Marshall compiled a centrist voting record in the House, regularly breaking ranks with his party's left wing on particularly prominent or controversial issues. Among other departures from the Democratic party line, Marshall opposed the expansion of federally funded stem cell research; voted against 2007 legislation proposed by the Democratic House leadership to require the withdrawal of American troops from Iraq; and opposed the Affordable Care Act, Barack Obama's 2010 health care reform initiative.

---

[5] The 8th District in Georgia was temporarily renumbered as the 3rd District between 2002 and 2006.

These demonstrations of partisan independence represented smart political maneuvering for a southern congressman with right-of-center constituents who were increasingly suspicious of the Democratic label – and who may have felt even more distant from the national party after Nancy Pelosi of California became speaker of the House in 2007. A television advertisement produced by Marshall's 2010 reelection campaign featured a folksy-sounding narrator drawling that "Georgia is a long way from San Francisco, and Jim Marshall is a long way from Nancy Pelosi," as a series of visual images contrasted a trio of bandana-clad hippies with a shot of Marshall chatting amiably with an elderly war veteran. The ad proceeded to tout Marshall's vote against the Affordable Care Act and his endorsement by the National Rifle Association, National Right to Life Committee, and U.S. Chamber of Commerce, bragging that these traditionally conservative interest groups "wouldn't have anything to do with a Nancy Pelosi supporter."[6]

For a time, Marshall's moderate ideological profile allowed him to remain in Congress by attracting sufficient support from constituents who voted Republican at the top of the ticket; he outran Democratic presidential candidates John Kerry and Barack Obama in his district by 19 and 14 percentage points, respectively, in the 2004 and 2008 elections. Despite his voting record, however, Marshall never enjoyed the easy reelection victories that his 8th District predecessors achieved in the 1970s and 1980s – in five total elections, he received at least 60 percent of the vote only once – reflecting the increased Republican electoral strength in nonpresidential contests that emerged across the South in the early 1990s and intensified thereafter. He was finally swept from office by the Republican landslide in the 2010 midterm election, which netted the party 63 House seats nationwide. Despite a more favorable national climate in 2012, Democrats failed to recruit even a token challenger to Marshall's Republican successor, Austin Scott, indicating that the 8th District had finally become as securely Republican in congressional elections in the 2010s as it had been in presidential contests since the 1980s. Scott ran unopposed for reelection again in 2014 and easily defeated a nominal challenger in 2016.

In another corner of America located a thousand miles to the north, the course of congressional politics has run in the opposite partisan direction. Fairfield County occupies the southwestern corner of Connecticut,

---

[6] "Long Way," Jim Marshall for Congress 2010 advertisement, www.youtube.com/watch?v=dngrecgvv4k.

bordered on the west by the New York state line, on the northeast by the Housatonic River, and on the southeast by 30 miles of coastline facing Long Island Sound. A string of towns along the shore constitutes Connecticut's "Gold Coast," one of the most affluent areas in the United States. While Fairfield County has long been home to the families of well-to-do business executives and professionals who commute daily to Manhattan – *The Stepford Wives*, a 1975 cinematic satire of upper-class suburban life, was set in a fictionalized Gold Coast community and filmed in the town of Fairfield – a number of corporate headquarters and financial services companies are now based in the area as well.

Reflecting the dominant socioeconomic status of its electorate, Fairfield County consistently leaned decidedly Republican for most of the twentieth century in both presidential and congressional elections. Fairfield voters made a rare exception in 1964, joining the rest of the Northeast in strongly preferring Lyndon B. Johnson to Barry Goldwater. But Richard Nixon won Fairfield County easily in both 1968 and 1972, Gerald Ford defeated Jimmy Carter there by 17 percentage points in 1976, Ronald Reagan won the county twice by 20-point margins in 1980 and 1984, and George H. W. Bush carried it in both his 1988 national victory and his 1992 defeat. Republicans maintained a corresponding dominance in elections for the House of Representatives over the same period, holding Connecticut's Fairfield-based 4th Congressional District for 40 consecutive years after the 1968 election.

The Republicans who represented the 4th District reliably belonged to the moderate wing of the party popularly identified in the 1960s with New York governor Nelson Rockefeller. Lowell Weicker (served 1969–1971) earned a reputation as a party maverick via numerous well-publicized legislative battles with fellow Republicans; his support of school busing programs to promote racial desegregation and federally funded abortions for poor women, among other causes, placed him to the ideological left even of many congressional Democrats of his era, especially on cultural issues. Weicker became a U.S. senator after a single term in the House; his successor in the 4th District seat, Stewart B. McKinney (served 1971–1987), was a socially liberal former business executive and self-styled "urbanist" who used his position as ranking minority member of the House Committee on the District of Columbia to advocate for D.C. home rule.[7] (After McKinney's death in office, Congress named the first major federal assistance bill for the homeless in his honor.) The

---

[7] Alan Ehrenhalt, ed., *Politics in America, 1982* (Washington, DC: CQ Press, 1981), p. 210.

next representative of the 4th District, Chris Shays (served 1987–2009), was another moderate who frequently differed with his party on social issues such as abortion, gun control, and federally funded stem cell research. While in office, Shays was perhaps best known for cosponsoring the Bipartisan Campaign Reform Act of 2002 (popularly known as the "McCain–Feingold" legislation after its fellow sponsors in the Senate) – a cause that also placed him at odds with most of his Republican congressional colleagues.

Like many other suburban areas in the metropolitan North, Fairfield County began to shift in the Democratic direction in the 1990s, as the national Republican Party continued its rightward turn on social issues. Bill Clinton, who narrowly lost the county in 1992, carried it in 1996, as did the subsequent Democratic presidential nominees Al Gore in 2000, John Kerry in 2004, Barack Obama in 2008 and 2012, and Hillary Clinton in 2016. Even Donald Trump's biography as a New York–based business leader failed to win him substantial support among the prosperous residents of southwestern Connecticut. Trump attracted only 38 percent of the Fairfield vote in 2016 – the lowest share received by a Republican presidential nominee in the county since the three-way election of 1912.

Just as the moderate Democrats in the Georgia House delegation did not become electorally endangered for decades after their constituents began to vote Republican for president, Chris Shays was initially insulated from his district's general pro-Democratic trend, receiving an average of 67 percent of the vote over the six elections between 1992 and 2002. In 2004, however, Shays faced a serious challenge from a Democratic opponent for the first time in his congressional career. Shays narrowly survived that year and again in 2006, when he won a tenth full term with 52 percent of the vote, but he was finally defeated in 2008 by Democratic challenger Jim Himes of Greenwich, a former vice president at the Goldman Sachs investment banking firm. Himes has held the seat ever since, winning a fifth term in 2016 by a 20-point margin over his Republican challenger.

Though they belonged to different parties, took opposite positions on social issues, and represented very dissimilar constituencies, Jim Marshall and Chris Shays also shared a common challenge. Both officeholders belonged to regional factions within their respective parties that had long maintained public distance from national party leaders – a strategy that became more critical over time in maintaining their political standing among the voters whose support was required to remain in office.

For Marshall and Shays, as well as many other red-state Democrats and blue-state Republicans, assiduously tended records of conspicuous independence came to serve as bulwarks against the prevailing partisan tides within their home districts. These fortifications remained intact for a time, but a combination of increasing party loyalty among American voters and particularly adverse short-term national electoral forces ultimately swept both incumbents, and many of their fellow moderates, out of Congress in favor of politically orthodox members of the opposite party, in what has proven to be a durable change in the partisan alignment of their former constituencies.

The increasing regional polarization of partisan outcomes in federal elections has thus contributed to the ideological polarization of the congressional parties. While the widening policy gap between Democratic and Republican officeholders over the past several decades is too complex and multifaceted to arise from a single cause, the declining share of political centrists in both parties has been visibly accelerated by the growing partisan divergence between Red and Blue America. Historically, the majority of moderate-to-conservative congressional Democrats represented southern or interior western constituencies that have become more reliably Republican over the past several decades, while most moderate-to-liberal Republicans were elected from the now solidly Democratic Northeast and coastal West. For much of the twentieth century, these dissident partisans constituted a significant share of the membership of both houses of Congress, especially on the Democratic side; today, each faction resembles a critically endangered species of wildlife that only survives in a few isolated sanctuaries within its formerly extensive geographic range.

In presidential elections, the resurgence of regional divisions after the 1980s worked to the net advantage of the Democratic Party by creating a safe electoral base for its candidates in the socially liberal environs of the metropolitan North and coastal West, contributing to four Democratic victories (and six first-place finishes in the national popular vote) in the seven elections after 1992. However, the growth of geographic polarization has had the opposite effect on the national balance of party strength in Congress. The widening of the regional gap in House and Senate elections has been primarily driven by the growing Republican loyalties of culturally conservative voters, especially in the South. Congressional Republicans have therefore captured many more additional seats in Red America over the past two decades, such as those once held by Jim Marshall and other Democratic moderates, than Democrats have gained in Blue America at the expense of centrist Republicans such as Chris

Shays – a development that has allowed Republicans to compete for, and often attain, a national majority in both houses of Congress after more than 60 years of Democratic dominance. While conventional wisdom often urges parties to respond to electoral defeat by adopting a more moderate set of policy positions, the congressional GOP managed to achieve this popular resurgence while shifting even further in a rightward direction, due to increasing success after 1994 in conservative-leaning electoral constituencies that have become particularly sympathetic to the appeals of Republican candidates.

CONGRESSIONAL REPUBLICANS SINCE THE 1980S: FEWER MODERATES, MORE SEATS

The series of decisive losses suffered by Democratic presidential candidates between 1968 and 1988 convinced many party leaders and voters alike that ideological moderation was necessary to achieve electoral victory – a view that was seemingly vindicated by the triumph of Bill Clinton in 1992 and 1996 in the wake of unsuccessful candidacies by more liberal nominees Walter Mondale and Michael Dukakis. While congressional Republicans endured an even more severe record of futility after losing control of both chambers during the Eisenhower administration – with the exception of a temporary period of Senate control between 1980 and 1986 – Republican leaders ultimately reached a very different conclusion about the strategic direction that would improve their electoral fortunes. The party reforms enacted by ruling Democrats in the House during the 1970s centralized institutional power within the party leadership and caucus (and thus discouraged committee chairs from developing legislation via bipartisan collaboration), ultimately leading many congressional Republicans to agree that the only remaining path to achieving substantive influence lay in capturing a majority themselves.[8] Instead of moving closer to the ideological center in order to broaden the party's appeal in a mirror image of the approach recommended to the opposition Democrats by the Democratic Leadership Council, Republicans adopted a strategy of intensifying substantive and procedural confrontation with the opposition in order to discredit Democratic rule and energize conservative support in the electorate on behalf of a prospective Republican Congress.

---

[8] Nelson W. Polsby, *How Congress Evolves: Social Bases of Institutional Change* (New York: Oxford University Press, 2004).

The primary force behind this approach within the House Republican conference was the Conservative Opportunity Society (COS), founded after the disappointing election of 1982 (in which House Republicans fell to a 269–166 minority after suffering a net loss of 26 seats). The COS was the brainchild of Georgia congressman Newt Gingrich, originally elected in 1978 from a suburban Atlanta district that had previously been represented by 12-term conservative Democrat Jack Flynt; when he first took office, Gingrich was the only Republican in the Georgia congressional delegation. Gingrich soon became the chief proponent within the House Republican Party of adopting a more aggressive stance toward the Democratic opposition, though his ambition of achieving a Republican majority was initially dismissed as unrealistic by many of his fellow partisans. Fellow COS member Vin Weber of Minnesota later recalled that "the most important thing that I remember from my early conversations with Newt is that he believed that we could be in the majority. He also understood that the major impediment to becoming a majority was our own mind set, the minority party mind set, as we put it. It was the sense that we couldn't become a majority and since probably a majority of the members in the Republican Party believed that, even if they didn't articulate it, it drove them to behave in ways that hurt the Republicans. So it became a self-fulfilling prophecy."[9]

The COS may have faced considerable skepticism at first within Republican ranks, but Gingrich's institutional activism began to win over colleagues who had become frustrated with life in the minority under an increasingly unaccommodating House Democratic Party. He filed ethics charges against Democratic Speaker Jim Wright, a strongly partisan leader who was a particular nemesis of House Republicans, over Wright's personal finances; the controversy ultimately led to the speaker's resignation from the House in June 1989. In the midst of the Wright investigation, Gingrich ran for the minority whip position left vacant when Dick Cheney of Wyoming resigned from the House to become U.S. Secretary of Defense, prevailing over Edward Madigan of Illinois, an ally of Minority Leader Bob Michel, by a margin of 87 to 85. The following year, Gingrich broke with Republican president George H. W. Bush over his tax-raising budget agreement with congressional Democrats, leading 126 of 173 House Republicans to oppose the legislation. By 1993, Gingrich was beginning to signal that he would mount a direct challenge to Michel, prompting the minority leader to announce his retirement rather than risk a publicly embarrassing ouster.[10] The path was now clear for Gingrich to assume the leadership of the party as it closed in on four consecutive decades of minority status in the House of Representatives.

The central assumption underlying Gingrich's strategic approach – that House Republicans would benefit from taking more conservative issue positions and from adopting a more confrontational attitude toward the Democratic opposition – directly contradicted the conventional wisdom of politics (formalized by Anthony Downs in *An Economic Theory of Democracy*) that parties in a two-party system achieve increasing electoral success as they move closer to the ideological center.[11] Perhaps House Republicans had become increasingly skeptical of the validity of this model of party competition during their long years in the minority, in which a go-along, get-along approach toward the Democrats had sometimes resulted in achieving policy influence yet had seldom paid electoral dividends. But Gingrich's argument was also bolstered by considerations of political geography, which seemed to suggest that the prospect of gaining seats by moving ideologically rightward was not as counterintuitive as it might first appear.

To congressional Republicans of the 1980s and early 1990s, the most promising electoral targets among the ranks of Democratic-held districts were those with conservative-leaning inhabitants who already voted for Republican presidential nominees in large numbers; many of these districts were located in the South. Republican candidates for the House had so far been unable to match the landslide victories of Nixon, Reagan, and George H. W. Bush within most of these constituencies, which were frequently represented by moderate Democratic incumbents who had cultivated personal popularity that allowed them to regularly outrun their own party's presidential nominees by double-digit popular margins. In addition, the South's traditional partisan legacy had left state and local offices overwhelmingly under Democratic control, depriving the Republican Party of a valuable source of future congressional candidates.

---

[10] Jackie Calmes, "As Michel Leaves Top House GOP Post, Young Generation Flexes for Fights," *Wall Street Journal*, October 5, 1993, p. A18.

[11] Anthony Downs, *An Economic Theory of Democracy* (New York: Harper, 1957). For a broader argument that contemporary Republican leaders largely reject Downsian logic, see Justin Buchler, "Asymmetric Polarization and Asymmetric Models: Democratic and Republican Interpretations of Electoral Dynamics," paper presented at the Annual Meeting of the Midwest Political Science Association, Chicago, IL, April 16–19, 2015.

Gingrich and his allies believed that an organized effort to intensify the ideological contrast between the congressional parties would allow the Republicans to make electoral inroads in the South. They worked energetically to tie individual Democratic incumbents to the party's more liberal national leadership while simultaneously raising highly charged cultural issues in Congress, such as proposed constitutional amendments to allow prayer in public schools and to ban the burning of the American flag, on which conservative positions were widely popular – especially among southern voters.[12] Gingrich also initiated an ambitious effort to recruit and fund strong Republican candidates in a number of Democratic-held districts in the South; true to their region, these southern Republicans nearly always represented the staunchly conservative wing of the party.

The 1994 midterm election resulted in a national landslide, producing new Republican majorities in both chambers while installing Gingrich as speaker of the House. The party achieved significant electoral inroads in the South and rural West, benefiting from a conservative backlash to the first two years of Bill Clinton's presidential administration. Republicans portrayed Clinton as an economic and cultural liberal who had engineered the "biggest tax increase in history," who had attempted to permit openly gay people to serve in the military, and who had signed a crime bill that contained unacceptably restrictive gun control measures. Even moderate Democrats who had opposed some or all of these policies found themselves relentlessly tied to Clinton; a then-innovative visual effect allowed Republican television ads to "morph" the face of Democratic congressional candidates into the visage of the unpopular president.[13] Five incumbent House Democrats and two Democratic senators, all from southern or interior western states, switched their affiliation to the ruling Republican Party after the election, further cementing the GOP's newly won regional advantage.

The Republican Revolution of 1994 suggested to many journalists and commentators that a party realignment was under way, soon establishing the Republicans as the new national majority. In the months after the election, Washington-based media coverage portrayed Bill Clinton as merely a placeholder figure who was marking time until his likely

---

[12] James Salzer, "Gingrich's Language Set New Course," *Atlanta Journal-Constitution*, January 29, 2012, http://www.ajc.com/news/local-govt--politics/gingrich-language-set-new-course/O5bgK6lY2wQ3KwEZsYTBlO/

[13] Robin Toner, "In a Cynical Election Season, the Ads Tell an Angry Tale," *New York Times*, October 24, 1994, p. A1.

defeat two years later. One reporter at an April 1995 presidential press conference noted that "Republicans have dominated political debate in this country since they took over Congress" before asking Clinton, "Do you worry about making sure that your voice is heard in the coming months?" "The President is relevant here," insisted Clinton in response, in what was widely interpreted as an expression of political desperation.[14]

The results of 1994 were also considered a personal triumph for Newt Gingrich, whose personally blunt and outspokenly conservative brand of politics had been vindicated by the shocking electoral outcome. "There is no close historical comparison to Newt Gingrich's role in leading the House Republicans to their majority," concluded Ronald M. Peters Jr. after the election. "He was actively involved in recruiting candidates for office, he provided training for them through ... workshops, he articulated their campaign themes on audiotapes that most of them drew upon, he planned campaign strategy for the party, he raised vast sums of money for candidates, he organized the incumbent GOP members to contribute to the campaigns of nonincumbent GOP candidates, he planned the 1994 'Contract with America' strategy [of nationalizing the election by pledging Republican support for a series of popular reforms and legislative measures] – in short there was no aspect of the Republican effort to elect a House majority that he was not responsible for initiating and leading."[15] More than any speaker before or since, Gingrich had become both the strategic architect and public face of his party.

But it did not take long before Gingrich himself became the center of controversy. The new speaker's enthusiasm for courting media attention (during the first several months of his speakership, Gingrich held a daily televised news conference) mixed badly with his penchant for making impolitic off-the-cuff remarks, and the sharply conservative policy direction pursued by the Republican-led Congress attracted declining mass support outside the reddening constituencies of the South and rural West. By the time that Gingrich emerged from a damaging fight with the White House over cuts to federal entitlement programs – a standoff that led to a series of government shutdowns in late 1995 and early 1996 – public opinion surveys revealed that he had become the most disliked politician

---

[14] Transcript of Clinton's April 18, 1995 press conference, available at www.presidency.ucsb.edu/ws/?pid=51237.

[15] Ronald M. Peters Jr., "Institutional Context and Leadership Style: The Case of Newt Gingrich," in Nicol C. Rae and Colton C. Campbell, eds., *New Majority or Old Minority? The Impact of Republicans on Congress* (Lanham, MD: Rowman & Littlefield, 1999), pp. 43–68, at 50.

in America. He thus represented an increasingly useful political foil for Clinton, who, facing Senate Majority Leader Bob Dole in the 1996 presidential election, adopted a strategy of explicitly running against the "Dole–Gingrich Congress."

Gingrich's sinking public reputation (a March 1996 CNN poll found that 58 percent of respondents held an unfavorable view of the speaker, as compared to just 25 percent who viewed him favorably) soon became a political liability for other Republicans as well.[16] Democratic-sponsored advertising campaigns attempted to associate rank-and-file Republican House members with their increasingly prominent leader, especially in blue states where Gingrich's public persona – and fiery, southern-style conservatism in general – proved particularly unpopular. Moderate Republican Peter Blute, who represented a district in central Massachusetts, was unlucky enough to have a name that rhymed with the divisive speaker's own distinctive moniker; "if you wouldn't vote for Newt," asked a television ad produced on behalf of Democratic challenger Jim McGovern, "why would you vote for Blute?"[17] Other Republican incumbents in politically marginal districts hurriedly took measures to distance themselves publicly from their leader. By the summer of 1996, Republican freshman Jim Longley of Maine had even established a habit of regularly voting against the routine approval of the previous day's journal on the floor of the House, prompting speculation that he was merely attempting to reduce the proportion of recorded floor votes in which he supported Gingrich's position in order to defuse Democratic attacks that he was a right-wing loyalist.[18] Both Blute and Longley ultimately lost their bids for reelection in 1996.

The new Republican congressional leadership displayed little interest in protecting the political interests of moderate members of the party, even though most of them represented Democratic-leaning districts and were therefore potentially vulnerable in general elections. Instead, moderates were treated like vestigial relics of a bygone era whose continued presence in office only served to frustrate the GOP's single-minded pursuit of a conservative legislative agenda. Rather than work to fortify the political strength of blue-state incumbents, Republican leaders preferred

---

[16] Survey results from Alec Tyson and Carroll Doherty, "Lessons from the Last Government Shutdown," Pew Research Center, September 27, 2013, www.pewresearch.org/fact-tank/2013/09/27/lessons-from-the-last-government-shutdown/.

[17] I thank Darshan J. Goux, who coined the quote, for supplying this example.

[18] Guy Gugliotta, "GOP Freshmen with No Time for the Minutes," *Washington Post*, July 6, 1996, p. A12.

to further build the party's standing in the South, where newly elected Republicans would almost certainly hold loyally conservative positions on both economic and social issues. While campaigning for southern Republican challengers in the fall of 1996, House Majority Leader Dick Armey of Texas argued publicly that additional victories in the region would particularly benefit the party precisely because they would deprive moderate Republicans of a pivotal position in floor votes. "One of the things we've learned is that we've got to be strong enough to outvote our own moderates," remarked Armey. "We tossed them a bone and they bit us in the leg."[19]

Ill feeling between House Republican moderates and the party leadership occasionally erupted openly in subsequent years. In the spring of 2000, a group of moderate incumbents threatened to withhold their dues to the National Republican Congressional Committee to protest what they believed was tacit support by Armey and Majority Whip Tom DeLay of Texas for conservative primary challengers to several of their members, especially Marge Roukema of New Jersey. Roukema narrowly prevailed in the 2000 Republican primary over a state assemblyman named Scott Garrett, who enjoyed support from the Club for Growth, a conservative political action committee whose claimed mission was "to rankle and ruffle the feathers of the [Republican] moderates," according to cofounder Stephen Moore, who added, "We feel like they've been the enemy of progress."[20] Though Roukema won reelection, she lost the competition for the chair of the House Banking Committee the following year to a more conservative colleague, despite being next in line under the seniority system, and retired from the House in 2002 – to be succeeded by Garrett.

Moderate Republicans also repeatedly complained about perceived snubs by the party leadership in the selection of committee chairs and slots on desirable committees. After the 2002 election, Speaker Dennis Hastert and his political ally Tom DeLay, who had become majority leader upon the retirement of Dick Armey, announced that Appropriations Subcommittee chairs, popularly known as the "cardinals," would be selected by the leadership-controlled Republican Steering Committee. Hastert and DeLay were seen as responding to complaints by

[19] Dan Balz, "GOP Moderates Seeking 'Meaningful Role' in Party," *Washington Post*, November 24, 1996, p. A10.
[20] John Bresnahan and Susan Crabtree, "Moderates Fume at GOP Leaders," *Roll Call*, March 16, 2000.

conservatives that the Appropriations Committee was too moderate and free-spending. They also punished dissident Republicans by excluding them from top assignments on other committees.[21] Chris Shays, the senior Republican on the Government Reform Committee, was denied the chair in large part for his role in enacting the Bipartisan Campaign Reform Act over the objections of conservatives.[22] Moderate Wayne Gilchrest of Maryland, among those passed over for the chair of the House Resources Committee, expressed his unhappiness: "If you bypass the seniority system for political purposes, you've disrupted the orderly operations of the House."[23] Mike Castle of Delaware, a key moderate leader, told *Roll Call*, "I have a continuing and abiding concern that moderates are uncomfortable in the Conference and that becoming chairs of committees has come down to a litmus test on voting. I don't think that's conducive to the Conference as a whole."[24] The revelation that a political action committee (PAC) controlled by Majority Leader DeLay had donated $50,000 to the Club for Growth during the 2002 campaign contributed further to the moderates' sense of being unwelcome in their own party.

Moderate Republicans in a House ruled by vocal conservatives attempted to navigate between the demands of their party leadership on one side and their often blue-tinged constituencies on the other. Robin Kolodny argues that moderate Republicans exercised substantial influence over their party in private, becoming "most effective at limiting objectionable items" on the party agenda while seeking "to protect their party from being embroiled in controversial issues that would obscure the core set of issues that united them all ... This is consistent with their general belief that they must be supportive of the party leadership as much as possible to preserve their majority position. The Tuesday Group [an alliance of moderate House Republicans] would prefer to have family feuds be private rather than public matters."[25]

But conservatives in the party did not always oblige this goal, requiring moderates to choose between going along with their party and openly

---

[21] Alexander Bolton, "House Leaders Tighten Grip, Anger Centrists," *The Hill*, January 13, 2003, p. 1.

[22] Jim VandeiHei and Juliet Eilperin, "GOP Leaders Tighten Hold on House," *Washington Post*, January 13, 2003, p. A01.

[23] "Rep. Pombo Wins Resources Chair," *Sacramento Bee*, January 9, 2003, p. A6.

[24] Susan Crabtree, "DeLay, Moderates Mend Fences," *Roll Call*, January 29, 2003.

[25] Robin Kolodny, "Moderate Success: Majority Status and the Changing Nature of Factionalism in the House Republican Party," in Rae and Campbell, eds., *New Majority or Old Minority?* pp. 153–172, at 158.

allying with Democrats against the position of the leadership. Moderates were reluctant to defect on floor votes if doing so would deprive the Republican agenda of a voting majority, even as they repeatedly expressed misgivings with the party's ideological direction to reporters and constituents. This approach was exemplified by the response of moderate Republicans to the DeLay-led impeachment of Bill Clinton in 1998–1999. Under heavy pressure from Republican leaders and activists to support the unpopular impeachment effort, most moderate Republicans voted in favor of at least two of the four proposed articles. But four prominent moderates then immediately sent a letter to Senate Majority Leader Trent Lott that was also released publicly, stating that "we are not convinced, and do not want our votes interpreted to mean, that we view removal from office as the only reasonable conclusion of this case," an act that struck some critics as trying to have the issue both ways.[26]

As American voters become less likely to split their partisan tickets, the electoral standing of moderate Republicans became increasingly vulnerable, especially in years when the political climate had become unfavorable for their party. The presidential administration of George W. Bush suffered declining public approval rates over the course of his second term in office, due to growing popular dissatisfaction with the Iraq War and the onset of a serious economic recession in December 2007 that sparked a crisis in the American financial industry. As a result, Democrats gained 30 seats in the 2006 midterm election, reversing partisan control of the House, and netted a further 21 seats along with Barack Obama's election as president in 2008. Because opposition to Bush was most strongly concentrated in Blue America, Republican moderates absorbed much of this electoral damage, notwithstanding their attempts at personal ideological differentiation. "There was just the antipathy to the president, to some of the things the right wing of my party has espoused, to Iraq," lamented Nancy Johnson of Connecticut, a leading House Republican moderate who lost her bid for a thirteenth term in the Democratic wave of 2006. "And it added up, for the first time in my 30 years in political life, to actually the individual member and their record not mattering."[27]

Republican moderates had long argued that the party's ability to maintain control of Congress depended upon their own continued electoral

---

[26] David W. Chen, "His Public Faults Lawmaker Who Voted to Impeach, Then Leaned to Censure," *New York Times*, December 23, 1998, p. A24.

[27] Kwame Holman, "Midterm Elections Oust Several Moderate Republicans," *PBS Newshour*, November 24, 2006, transcript at www.pbs.org/newshour/bb/politics-july-dec06-gop_11-24/.

success; as Shays told the *New York Times* in 2002, "Any leadership that does not value its moderates will soon be in the minority."[28] Yet House Republicans did not respond to the losses of 2006 and 2008 by adopting a more centrist or conciliatory posture in an attempt to bolster the party's standing in blue states. Instead, Republican leaders expressed strong and vehement opposition to the legislative agenda of the Obama administration – an approach further encouraged by the rise of the Tea Party movement in 2009 and 2010, which regularly accused Republican office-holders of demonstrating insufficient loyalty to conservative principles and of failing to block Obama's liberal policy initiatives. This strategy was seemingly vindicated by the results of the 2010 midterm election, in which a 63-seat national Republican gain returned the GOP to power in the House of Representatives. Rather than reinstalling blue-state moderates in office, the results of 2010 (and the similarly favorable 2014 midterm elections) further bolstered the ranks of strongly conservative Republicans elected from friendly partisan constituencies elsewhere in the nation.

By the mid-2010s, it had become clear that the Republican Party did not require a sizable bloc of moderate members in order to achieve substantial electoral success. House Republicans gained 247 seats in the 2014 elections – the party's highest share since 1928 – yet only a few scattered members mostly representing districts in the Northeast, such as Chris Smith of New Jersey and Charlie Dent of Pennsylvania, could be properly classified as ideological moderates. Though congressional Republicans suffered from substantial internal disunity during the Obama presidency, divisions within Republican ranks instead separated "establishment" conservatives allied with John Boehner of Ohio (who served as speaker between 2011 and 2015) from insurgent or Tea Party conservatives, who claimed to embody superior ideological purity.

House Republicans have repeatedly demonstrated the ability to capture a solid national majority without the need to appeal to left-leaning voters in pro-Democratic blue-state constituencies. Of the 247 House Republicans who served in the 2015–2016 Congress, 222 represented districts carried by Mitt Romney in the 2012 presidential election, while 218 of the 241 Republicans in the 2017–2018 House represented districts carried by Donald Trump in 2016 – even though neither Romney

[28] Steven R. Weisman, "An Incumbent on Top of the Republicans' List of Endangered Species," *New York Times*, September 29, 2002, www.nytimes.com/2002/09/29/opinion/an-incumbent-on-top-of-the-republicans-list-of-endangered-species.html.

nor Trump won the national popular vote. Republicans have benefited from increasing electoral dominance within their own geographic base, holding 74 percent of the congressional districts in the South and 71 percent of those in the interior West after the 2016 election. Without the need to compete in Democratic-leaning seats in order to maintain national control of Congress, there is little strategic incentive for party leaders to tack in a moderate direction; the trajectory of the past thirty years, during which the party has simultaneously grown in numbers and moved substantially to the ideological right, represents an apparent practical disproof of Downsian predictions.

Senate Republicans followed a similar path over the past three decades. While the weaker party leadership, stronger norms of individualism, and greater respect for the seniority system in the upper chamber have largely spared Republican moderates in the Senate from the degree of internal marginalization suffered by their counterparts in the House, moderate senators from socially liberal regions have still found themselves trapped between pro-Democratic general electorates and increasingly conservative primary voters. Moderate senator Arlen Specter of Pennsylvania was nearly defeated for renomination in 2004 by Representative Pat Toomey, a more conservative rival; when Toomey (who in the interim had led the antimoderate Club for Growth) signaled in 2009 that he would seek a rematch the following year, Specter switched to the Democratic Party rather than risk a loss in the Republican primary. A similar conservative challenge nearly denied renomination to fellow moderate Lincoln Chafee of Rhode Island in 2006. In 2010, Senator Lisa Murkowski of Alaska lost the Republican primary to a right-wing opponent, forcing her to (successfully) seek reelection by means of a write-in campaign; the same year, former governor and nine-term congressman Mike Castle of Delaware lost the Republican nomination for the Senate to conservative neophyte Christine O'Donnell. In 2012, six-term senator Richard Lugar of Indiana, whose record in office was substantially less moderate than those of Chafee, Specter, Murkowski, or Castle, was nonetheless defeated in the Republican primary by a more conservative challenger, Indiana state treasurer Richard Mourdock.

These acts of ideological purification, which become more frequent after the Tea Party movement gained influence in primary elections, undoubtedly cost the Republican Party several seats in the Senate; Castle and Lugar, for example, were both strong favorites to prevail in the general election, while their primary opponents ultimately lost to Democratic nominees. As in the House, however, the rightward collective turn of the Senate Republican Party has not prevented it from gaining a national majority, as it did following the 2014 and 2016 elections. Instead of competing in Democratic-leaning constituencies, Senate Republicans have simply consolidated their advantage in Red America, capturing the vast majority of seats from the South (86 percent in the 2017–2018 Congress) and interior West (77 percent) while almost entirely conceding the Northeast and Pacific Coast – once fertile ground for the election of moderate Republican senators – to the Democratic opposition. As of 2017, only two Republican senators – Toomey of Pennsylvania and Susan Collins of Maine – represented any of the 15 states located in these two regions of the nation.

CONGRESSIONAL DEMOCRATS SINCE THE 1980s: THE DECLINE OF BLUE DOGS IN RED STATES

The remarkable Democratic dominance of Congress over a 62-year period between 1932 and 1994 often came at the price of internal factionalism along ideological and regional lines. Even after the effects of the Voting Rights Act (1965) and the rise of the southern Republican Party had succeeded in removing many of the most conservative Dixiecrats from party ranks, Democratic congressional leaders still faced challenges in keeping their party unified on contentious issues. Scores of moderate southern Democrats, known at the time as "Boll Weevils," crossed party lines to support elements of Ronald Reagan's agenda in the 1980s, while Bill Clinton's 1993 budget deficit reduction legislation passed both houses of a Democratic-controlled Congress by a single vote in each chamber due to significant defection from members of his own party. Other Clinton proposals, most notably his universal health care plan and effort to repeal the ban on gay members of the military, ultimately foundered in Congress due to the opposition of moderate Democrats.

After the Democratic losses in the 1994 midterm election, which were disproportionately suffered by party centrists, a group of 21 remaining moderates founded the Blue Dog Coalition, an organization intended to provide both a means of acquiring a stronger voice in party affairs and a public brand name for members seeking to cement their reputation as a "different kind of Democrat." (The name of the group was supposedly intended to denote "yellow-dog [i.e., loyal] Democrats choked blue by the party leadership.")[29] While the nominal policy agenda of the Blue Dog

---

[29] Gabriel Kahn, "In Major Break with Own Leadership, Conservative Democrats Launch Group," *Roll Call*, February 13, 1995.

Coalition emphasized fiscal responsibility, members staked out distinct positions from the liberal wing of the party on a variety of issues, and the term "Blue Dog" soon won widespread use as a synonym for "southern moderate Democrat." Many Blue Dogs represented red-state constituencies that were particularly out-of-step with national Democrats on social and cultural issues such as abortion and gay rights, and voted accordingly when such matters arose on the floor of the House. Liberal Democrats often complained about the defection of moderate party members on controversial issues, but most grudgingly recognized that their colleagues were "voting the district" in order to protect their personal electoral standing. Efforts to impose greater party discipline on the Blue Dogs might further endanger their chances of reelection at a time when the party did not have seats to spare, tempt them to retire and leave an open seat vulnerable to Republican capture, or even provoke them to switch parties (as several southern Democrats did anyway in the mid-1990s).

While a few normally Democratic-leaning seats in Blue America flipped to the Republicans in the national wave of 1994, most soon returned to their natural party affiliation within a few elections (with help from a popular backlash in Democratic regions of the nation against the Gingrich speakership and the impeachment of Bill Clinton). But House Democrats narrowly remained in the minority for another decade. Party leaders seeking additional gains lacked the obvious targets of opportunity on the electoral map that their Republican counterparts enjoyed in the South and rural West. Returning the party to majority status therefore virtually necessitated winning seats that fundamentally leaned Republican in presidential elections.

Rahm Emanuel, a former Clinton White House aide who chaired the Democratic Congressional Campaign Committee for the 2006 election (and who later served as Barack Obama's first presidential chief of staff before becoming mayor of Chicago in 2011), recognized that the Democratic Party needed to expand its appeal into red state constituencies in order to put enough seats in play to win back control of the House. His aggressive candidate recruitment efforts in these districts especially prized politicians with decidedly moderate ideological profiles. Emanuel was known to brag to journalists that the Democratic candidate in a southern or rural district opposed abortion, supported gun rights, or took other positions at odds with the national party, viewing such departures from orthodoxy as indicators of electoral strength. One of Emanuel's prized recruits was Heath Shuler, a native of Bryson City, North Carolina (population 1,411), who had led his rural high school to three state football championships as a quarterback before winning the Heisman Trophy at the University of Tennessee and playing briefly in the National Football League. Shuler built his successful 2006 congressional campaign around the theme of "mountain values," emphasizing his evangelical Christian faith (one television ad featured him standing in front of his boyhood church, while another depicted his young son kneeling in prayer as Shuler and his wife watched with smiles) and socially conservative views.[30]

Taking advantage of George W. Bush's sliding popularity, House Democrats indeed achieved substantial gains in normally Republican-leaning territory in the 2006 and 2008 elections, which resulted in a new congressional majority made possible by the election of a sizable bloc of moderate Democratic candidates from districts that had supported Bush in 2000 and 2004. By 2009, the Blue Dog Coalition had grown to 52 members, or 20 percent of the House Democratic caucus. Recognizing that Blue Dogs were "majority makers," in Speaker Nancy Pelosi's oft-repeated term, few faced the threats to their institutional power that Republican moderates had suffered during their own time in the majority. House Democrats nearly always respected seniority in the assignment of committee chairs, allowing moderates Collin Peterson (Agriculture), Ike Skelton (Armed Services), Bart Gordon (Science), and John Spratt (Budget) to hold gavels in the Pelosi-led Congress. "When we agree with her, we help her," said Blue Dog member Allen Boyd of Florida in reference to Pelosi. "When we disagree with her, she knows that we will stand up to her and disagree with her."[31]

Such disagreements became far more consequential after the election of Barack Obama as president in November 2008. Obama took office in the midst of a deep national recession and two wars in the Middle East, but was also intent on pursuing an ambitious domestic policy agenda that included a large economic stimulus package, more aggressive regulation of the financial services industry, mandated carbon emission reductions to combat climate change, repeal of the U.S. military's prohibition on openly gay servicemembers, and – most notably – a federal program to provide Americans with universal health insurance. Near-unanimous Republican opposition to most of these initiatives increased the political

---

[30] Naftali Bendavid, *The Thumpin': How Rahm Emanuel and the Democrats Learned to Be Ruthless and Ended the Republican Revolution* (New York: Doubleday, 2007), pp. 104–106.

[31] Sarah Lueck, "In Congress, a Pack of 'Blue Dogs' Gains Ground," *Wall Street Journal*, June 2, 2008, p. A3.

pressure on moderate Democrats, who found themselves casting a series of potentially pivotal votes that forced them to choose between satisfying a president and congressional leadership of their own party and mollifying constituents who were increasingly dissatisfied with Obama's policies, especially in Red America.

Democratic leaders were forced to repeatedly revise legislative proposals in order to meet moderate demands; even so, passage was not always assured. The Affordable Care Act (ACA), the centerpiece of Obama's first-term agenda, ultimately won approval from a closely divided House in March 2010, with 34 Democratic defectors (23 of whom represented southern or interior western constituencies and 26 of whom represented districts carried by John McCain in 2008); it was not clear that the bill would pass until the afternoon before the vote. For many Blue Dogs, however, their efforts at maintaining visible distance from Obama and Pelosi ultimately failed to protect them from a strong popular backlash in the 2010 midterm elections, which decisively returned Republicans to power in the House. The results of 2010 especially decimated the ranks of moderate Democratic officeholders, reducing the size of the Blue Dog Coalition by more than half in a single blow. After another series of Republican victories in 2014, the Blue Dog Coalition declined to just 15 members; only three of the 34 Democratic opponents of the ACA in 2010 still remained in office five years later. With the defeat of five-term representative John Barrow of Georgia in the 2014 election, no Democrat in either chamber of Congress represented a majority-white Deep South constituency for the first time since the party's founding in the nineteenth century.

In the Senate, the convergence of party voting in the South and interior West beginning in 1994 increased the size of the Republican conference while pushing it farther to the ideological right. For a time, a cluster of popular Democratic incumbents (including Mary Landrieu of Louisiana, Ernest "Fritz" Hollings of South Carolina, Tim Johnson of South Dakota, Max Baucus of Montana, Ben Nelson of Nebraska, Kent Conrad and Byron Dorgan of North Dakota, and Robert Byrd and Jay Rockefeller of West Virginia) managed to fend off Republican challengers, even as their states became safely Republican in presidential elections. With the Northeast and Pacific Coast swinging more reliably toward Senate Democrats, the party managed to achieve a national tie in the 2000 election and an outright majority from 2006 to 2014 that briefly reached 60 seats between the middle of 2009, when Senator Al Franken of Minnesota was seated following a lengthy ballot recount, and January 2010, when Republican Scott Brown won an upset victory in a special election in Massachusetts. Beginning in the 2010 midterm election, however, moderate Democrats found it increasingly difficult to run far enough ahead of their party's presidential nominees to prevail in Republican-leaning states. Eight moderate Democratic senators retired or were defeated between 2012 and 2014; all but two were succeeded by conservative Republicans.[32] By 2017, the South and interior West were collectively represented by 44 Republicans and just 10 Democrats. Most of these remaining Democrats, including Joe Manchin of West Virginia, Jon Tester of Montana, and Heidi Heitkamp of North Dakota, were red-state moderates who faced the prospect of serious challenge in the 2018 election or thereafter.

In 2006 and 2008, the congressional Democratic Party benefited from both a relatively aggressive recruitment of moderate candidates and a notably tolerant treatment of Blue Dogs (and their ideological counter-parts in the Senate) once in office, building majorities in both houses of Congress by achieving numerous electoral victories in constituencies that voted Republican in presidential elections. The Democratic attitude toward party mavericks contrasted with that of Republican leaders, who often marginalized centrist members within their ranks and demonstrated little interest in strengthening their party in Blue America by encourag-ing moderate candidates to run for Congress. Unlike Republicans, most Democratic officials continued to perceive the existence of a trade-off between doctrinal purity and electoral success. But the Democratic con-gressional leadership's relatively accommodationist approach to the moderate bloc within party ranks ultimately failed to protect those mem-bers from the electoral threat posed by regional polarization. The Blue Dogs' regular strategic demonstrations of political independence proved to be an insufficient defense against the trend of increasing party-line voting for Congress as well as the presidency, especially in combination with intense popular dissatisfaction in the conservative regions of the nation with the policies of national Democratic leaders from 2010 for-ward. Voters may often claim to support "the person, not the party," but the stances and records of individual candidates now appear to weigh much less than their partisan label in determining electoral outcomes – a

---

[32] Joe Lieberman of Connecticut, Ben Nelson of Nebraska, and Jim Webb of Virginia retired in 2012; Max Baucus of Montana retired in 2014; and Mark Begich of Alaska, Mark Pryor of Arkansas, Mary Landrieu of Louisiana, and Kay Hagan of North Carolina were all defeated in the 2014 general election. Only Lieberman and Webb were succeeded by fellow Democrats.

development that has hastened the decline of the moderate wing within both parties, but has been particularly costly and frustrating to congressional Democrats.

HOW THE REGIONAL POLARIZATION OF ELECTIONS ENCOURAGES PARTISAN POLARIZATION IN CONGRESS

Anecdotal evidence that moderate members of Congress have been steadily replaced with more extreme successors in both chambers over the past three decades can be confirmed by more systematic analyses of incumbents' roll-call voting.[33] Figure 5.1 demonstrates that moderates have become an ever-smaller share of both party caucuses in the House of Representatives over the past four decades, as measured by DW-NOMINATE common-space scores developed by Keith T. Poole and Howard Rosenthal. This decline accelerated after 1992 – a pattern consistent with the regional shifts that replaced moderate Democrats with conservative Republicans in Red America and moderate Republicans with liberal Democrats in Blue America. The total proportion of moderates in the House declined from 32 percent after the 1990 election to just 7 percent after the 2014 election, with a temporary reversal due to the short-term success of a number of Rahm Emanuel's moderate recruits in the pro-Democratic elections of 2006 and 2008.

Figure 5.2 reveals that the share of moderate senators also declined over the same period, although centrists have continued to represent a significant share of the Democratic Party in the Senate. This remaining moderate bloc is mostly comprised of incumbents from Republican-leaning states in the South, Midwest, and rural West whose electoral success is necessary to the party's ability to fight for a national majority but who are increasingly vulnerable to Republican challenge. Moderates have almost entirely disappeared from the ranks of the Senate Republican Party even as the GOP has held majority control of the Senate for more than 14 of the 24 years between 1994 and 2018, demonstrating that the party does not need to maintain a large centrist bloc in order to compete effectively for control of the chamber.

---

[33] Keith T. Poole and Howard Rosenthal, *Ideology and Congress* (New Brunswick, NJ: Transaction, 2007); Richard Fleisher and John R. Bond, "The Shrinking Middle in the US Congress," *British Journal of Political Science* 34 (2004), pp. 429–451.

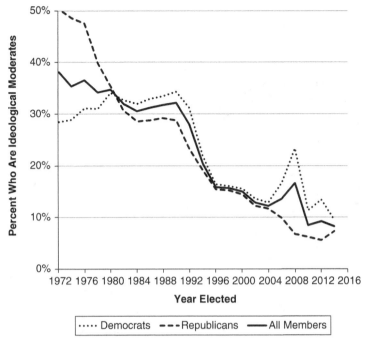

FIGURE 5.1. The decline of ideological moderates in the U.S. House of Representatives, 1972–2016.
Source: Calculated by author from DW-NOMINATE common-space scores developed by Keith Poole and Howard Rosenthal, www.voteview.com. Moderates are classified as incumbent members of Congress whose DW-NOMINATE common-space score fell within ±0.25 points of the mean score (−0.002) for the entire period under study.

Figures 5.3 and 5.4 reveal the extent to which the disappearance of moderate members of Congress is a product of regional polarization. In Figure 5.3, the congressional seats in Red America (the South and interior West) are classified into four categories on the basis of the party and ideology of their inhabitants elected between 1972 and 2014, while Figure 5.4 displays the identical findings for Blue America (the Northeast and Pacific Coast). House and Senate results are averaged together for ease of presentation.

As Figure 5.3 demonstrates, the congressional seats in Red America have come to be dominated by conservative Republicans, who made particularly successful inroads in these constituencies between 1992 and 1996 but have increased their advantage further in more recent elections. While liberal Democrats have become more scarce in red states

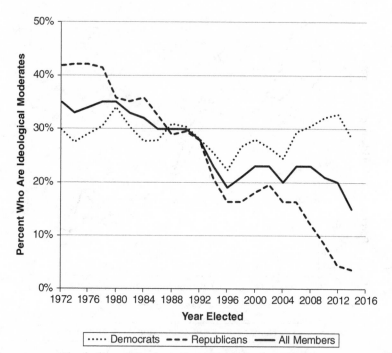

FIGURE 5.2. The decline of ideological moderates in the U.S. Senate, 1972–2016. *Source*: See Figure 5.1.

since the 1970s, most of the Republican gains over the past four decades have occurred at the expense of moderate Democrats. Moderate Republicans were never numerous in what are now known as the red states, though they too have declined in number over time. Prior to the 1990s, the majority of red-state Democrats were ideological moderates; even in recent years, nearly half have been members of the party's centrist bloc.

Figure 5.4 finds an almost perfect mirror image of this trend in Blue America, where liberal Democrats have become more numerous as moderate Republicans have nearly disappeared. Conservative Republicans, in contrast, have remained at a relatively steady share of seats (about 20 percent) since the early 1980s. Until 1994, most blue-state Republicans were moderates rather than conservatives, although the moderate bloc has declined substantially over the last two decades even in its traditional regional bases of the Northeast and coastal West. Blue-region Democrats have consistently been dominated by the party's liberal wing.

As Figure 5.5 confirms, the compilation of a moderate voting record can represent an electoral survival strategy for incumbents representing

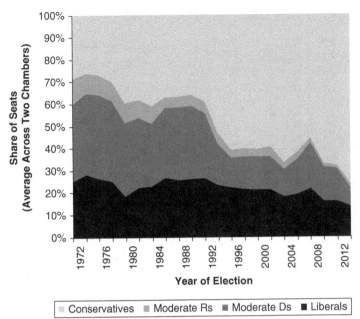

FIGURE 5.3. Party and ideology among House and Senate members in Red America, 1972–2016.
Source: See Figure 5.1.

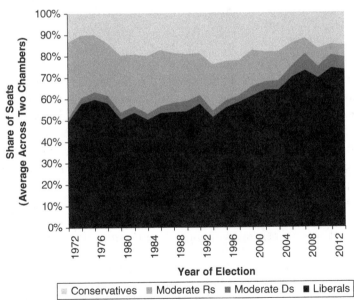

FIGURE 5.4. Party and ideology among House and Senate members in Blue America, 1972–2016.
Source: See Figure 5.1.

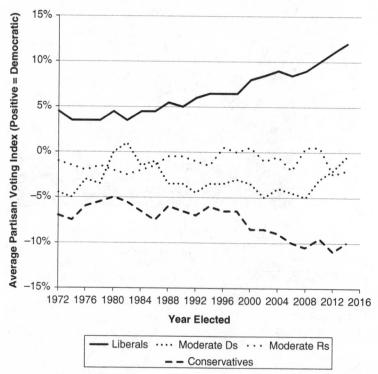

FIGURE 5.5. Constituency partisanship and member ideology, 1972–2016 (average across House and Senate).
Source: See Figure 5.1.

marginal, or even relatively hostile, partisan constituencies.[34] The figure employs the Partisan Voting Index (PVI), a commonly used measure of partisanship calculated by averaging together a state or district's relative partisan lean compared to the nation as a whole in the previous two presidential elections. As more congressional constituencies have become strongly Democratic or Republican in their partisan character, the mean PVI scores of the states and districts represented by liberal Democrats and conservative Republicans have diverged significantly over time. By 2010, the average liberal Democrat in Congress represented a constituency that was 10 percentage points more Democratic than the national

---

[34] Other studies confirm that candidates benefit electorally from adopting moderate positions. See Barry C. Burden, "Candidate Positioning in U.S. Congressional Elections," *British Journal of Political Science* 34 (2004), pp. 211–227; Brandice Canes-Wrone, David W. Brady, and John F. Cogan, "Out of Step, Out of Office: Electoral Accountability and House Members' Voting," *American Political Science Review* 96 (2002), pp. 127–140.

average, while the typical conservative Republican incumbent similarly represented a state or district that was 10 points more Republican than the nation as a whole.

Until the 2014 election, the average moderate Democrat in the House or Senate usually represented a constituency that was more fundamentally Republican than Democratic, as denoted by Figure 5.5. In fact, moderate Democrats collectively represented more Republican-leaning constituencies than did moderate Republicans between 1986 and 2012. This somewhat curious pattern reflected the fact that congressional Democrats historically found much more success in appealing to Republican presidential voters than Republican members found in attracting votes from Democratic identifiers in the electorate. The underlying partisan alignment of the constituencies of moderates in both parties (as measured by the PVI) has changed little since the 1980s.

While the tendency for incumbents from unfavorable partisan constituencies to adopt relatively moderate issue positions has remained consistent over time, the electoral benefit to doing so has seemingly decreased in recent years, as voters have increasingly deposed incumbents such as Jim Marshall and Chris Shays in favor of politically orthodox challengers from the opposite party. Figure 5.6 demonstrates that the reelection rate of moderate House incumbents, which was virtually identical in the 1970s to that of liberal or conservative members, has dropped significantly in recent years. Moderates are now substantially more vulnerable to defeat in general elections than they were in the past, and much more so than their more party-loyal peers.

This pattern holds in the Senate as well, as depicted by Figure 5.7. In fact, moderate Senate incumbents were slightly more likely to win reelection than nonmoderates in the 1970s. While liberals and conservatives have become more electorally secure over time, moderates became increasingly endangered after the 1990s.

In principle, these unsuccessful incumbents could have been defeated by fellow moderates from the opposite party, which would not reduce the total proportion of moderates in office. The trends depicted in Figures 5.3 and 5.4 appear to suggest that this possibility is unlikely in practice, as the ranks of moderate Republicans from red states and moderate Democrats from blue states have not grown in proportion to the decline of their counterparts on the other side of the aisle. Moreover, a focus on reelection rates may even systematically underestimate the electoral vulnerability of moderate members of Congress, as it does not reflect the tendency for electorally vulnerable incumbents facing an unfavorable

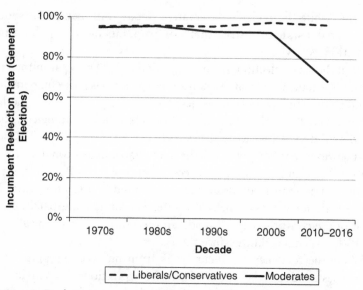

FIGURE 5.6. Reelection rate in the U.S. House of Representatives by incumbent ideology, 1972–2016.
Source: See Figure 5.1.

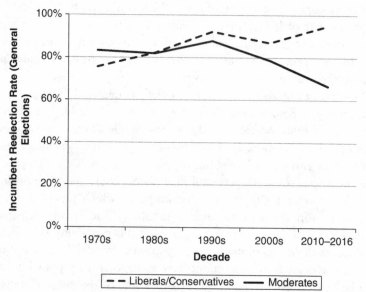

FIGURE 5.7. Reelection rate in the U.S. Senate by incumbent ideology, 1972–2016.
Source: See Figure 5.1.

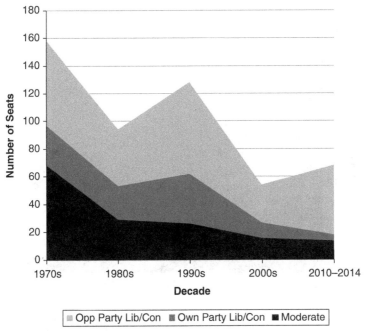

FIGURE 5.8. Most House moderates are replaced by nonmoderates from the opposite party.
Source: See Figure 5.1.

political climate to strategically retire or seek another office rather than risk an embarrassing defeat at the polls.

Figure 5.8 takes both of these additional considerations into account by compiling the partisanship and ideology of House members who succeeded a defeated or retiring moderate incumbent. Over time, departing moderates have become less likely to be replaced by a fellow moderate (of either party). Instead, most are now succeeded in their seats by ideologically orthodox members of the opposite party. Moderate incumbents often hold politically marginal districts until they either suffer defeat by a more extreme challenger or choose to retire and leave the seat open to capture by the partisan opposition. Even if the nominee of the retiring member's party attempts to replicate his or her electoral success by adopting similarly moderate issue positions, the results displayed in Figure 5.8 suggest that this strategy does not commonly lead to victory for the incumbent's would-be successor.

Figure 5.9 repeats this analysis for departing moderates in the Senate. Once again, moderate incumbents have become very likely to cede their

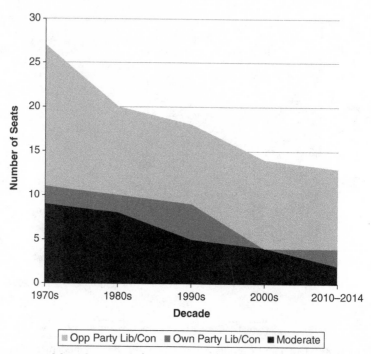

FIGURE 5.9. Most Senate moderates are replaced by nonmoderates from the opposite party.
Source: See Figure 5.1.

seats to liberals or conservatives of the opposite party. By the 2010s, 74 percent of moderate House members and 69 percent of moderate senators were succeeded by nonmoderates from the other side of the partisan aisle. The seats that were held by party moderates in the 1970s and 1980s are now likely to be inhabited by more doctrinaire members of the opposition; just as liberal Democrats Chuck Schumer of New York and Jeff Merkley of Oregon now hold the seats that were long occupied by moderate Republicans Jacob Javits and Mark Hatfield, respectively, the contemporary successors to moderate Democrats Lloyd Bentsen of Texas and Dennis DeConcini of Arizona are conservative Republicans Ted Cruz and Jeff Flake.

Frances E. Lee has argued that measures such as NOMINATE scores that are derived from the roll-call votes of congressional incumbents should not be interpreted as strictly reflecting members' ideological positions.[35]

---

[35] Frances E. Lee, *Beyond Ideology: Politics, Principles, and Partisanship in the U.S. Senate* (Chicago: University of Chicago Press, 2009).

She demonstrates that the congressional parties have also diverged over time on legislation addressing topics that are not fundamentally ideological in nature – such as measures increasing government efficiency or making technical revisions to the formulas governing the distribution of existing funds within federal programs – and have increasingly acted strategically to support the initiatives proposed by presidents of their own party while obstructing those proposed by presidents of the opposite party. Rather than view Democratic and Republican members of Congress as merely adopting increasingly dissimilar political philosophies, she argues, we should acknowledge the extent to which the two sides have also become more cohesive partisan teams that increasingly battle over power and procedure. However, Lee's interpretation of changes in congressional roll-call voting as reflecting the growing strength of partisanship as well as ideological orthodoxy does not challenge the findings presented in the preceding figures. Whether the rise of polarization in the House and Senate is best viewed as representing the growth of ideological extremity in office at the expense of centrism or instead as the growth of party loyalty at the expense of bipartisanship, this trend has been demonstrably furthered by the advent of the regional partisan divide.

Observers who are troubled by the emergence of polarization in Congress often blame the creation of safe partisan districts via gerrymandering or the nomination of extreme candidates by equally extreme primary voters, implying that the general electorate has played little part in furthering the policy divergence of the congressional parties.[36] Yet if even incumbents – who nearly always hold substantial advantages in name recognition and fundraising prowess, who have demonstrated an ability to run skilled campaigns and appeal to the voters of their home state or district, and who can exploit the institution of Congress to communicate their moderate positions to the public via roll-call voting and bill sponsorship – are increasingly vulnerable to defeat in general elections by liberal or conservative challengers of the opposite party, it is difficult to conclude that the American electorate is entirely devoid of responsibility for a progressively polarizing legislative branch. The findings presented here reveal a set of fundamental changes in the relationship between elected representatives and their constituents over the past 40 years. While it was once possible for many members of Congress to attract a "personal

---

[36] For a reply to these arguments, see Nolan M. McCarty, "The Limits of Electoral and Legislative Reform in Addressing Polarization," *California Law Review* 99 (April 2011), pp. 359–371.

vote" via strategic position taking on issues of interest to their states and districts, the cultivation of an attractive presentation of self, a reputation for effective constituent casework, and other activities,[37] the American electorate now seems to weigh party affiliation far more than these other considerations when choosing among congressional candidates. Many citizens may express frustration with the bitter partisan warfare that has become the norm in Congress, but they seldom act to discourage it by supporting centrist or maverick aspirants for office if it requires departing from their usual party preferences to do so.

Of course, the declining electoral fortunes of red-state Democrats and blue-state Republicans are not the only reason why the parties are becoming more polarized. For example, the growing influence of ideologically motivated party actors, especially on the Republican side, has clearly played an important role in causing incumbents who hold safe party seats to take increasingly extreme policy positions over time.[38] But the notable and enduring partisan change within the electoral constituencies that once supplied the House and Senate with the bulk of their moderate members has had visible effects on the collective composition of both chambers. The policy preferences of Red and Blue America do not appear to have been fundamentally transformed since the 1980s; instead, voters in the two sets of regions have become more loyal supporters of the party that best represents these preferences, especially on cultural matters. Voters may not have sought to elect a more polarized legislative branch, but they have helped to do so all the same – demonstrating the capacity of even minor changes at the mass level to produce large, and perhaps unintended, aggregate consequences for the direction of government under the American political system.

GEOGRAPHIC POLARIZATION AND THE REPUBLICAN ADVANTAGE IN CONGRESSIONAL ELECTIONS

The increasing regional divide in congressional elections since the early 1990s has worked to the net benefit of House and Senate Republicans

---

[37] David R. Mayhew, *Congress: The Electoral Connection* (New Haven, CT: Yale University Press, 1974); Richard F. Fenno Jr., *Home Style: House Members in Their Districts* (Boston: Little, Brown, 1978); Bruce Cain, John Ferejohn, and Morris Fiorina, *The Personal Vote: Constituency Service and Electoral Independence* (Cambridge, MA: Harvard University Press, 1987).

[38] Jacob S. Hacker and Paul Pierson, *Off Center: The Republican Revolution and the Erosion of American Democracy* (New Haven, CT: Yale University Press, 2005); Matt

by allowing the GOP to capture more seats in red states once held by Democrats than it has cost the party in blue states. But Republicans maintain an even more fundamental advantage due to the nature of congressional apportionment. The number of Republican-leaning states and congressional districts significantly exceeds the number of pro-Democratic constituencies in both chambers, giving Republicans a sizable head start in the race to assemble national House and Senate majorities. Congressional Democrats can win control of either chamber by performing much better in normally red seats than Republicans do in traditionally blue seats, but the Democratic Party's ability to contest fundamentally Republican-leaning seats by nominating moderate candidates has become increasingly threatened by the decline of ticket-splitting and the rise of party-line voting in the American electorate.

Figure 5.10 summarizes the underlying partisan orientation of House districts in place for the 114th Congress (2015–2016), using the Partisan Voting Index as a measure of constituency partisanship. PVI scores represent a district's relative distance from the national two-party popular vote in the previous two presidential elections (in this case, 2008 and 2012) in either partisan direction. In a district with a PVI of Democratic +5, for example, the share of the popular vote received by Barack Obama in 2008 and 2012 was, on average, 5 percentage points higher than in the nation as a whole.

As Figure 5.10 indicates, fundamentally Republican-leaning districts outnumbered Democratic-leaning districts after 2012 by a margin of 247 to 188. In addition, there are more overwhelmingly Democratic districts than equally lopsided Republican districts; 17 of the 20 most strongly partisan districts are pro-Democratic. This imbalance reflects the over-concentration of Democratic voters in highly noncompetitive seats, where their votes are effectively wasted. For example, Obama received 97 percent of the two-party vote in 2012 within the nation's most Democratic House seat, the South Bronx–based 15th District of New York, represented since 1990 by Representative José Serrano. Serrano enjoys as much job security as any incumbent could possibly hold in a general election, but many of his constituents cast effectively meaningless votes; they would be much more strategically valuable to their party if they could be redistributed to a politically competitive district elsewhere in the nation.

In part, this underlying Republican advantage represents a consequence of the Voting Rights Act, which mandates the creation of districts

Grossmann and David A. Hopkins, *Asymmetric Politics: Ideological Republicans and Group Interest Democrats* (New York: Oxford University Press, 2016).

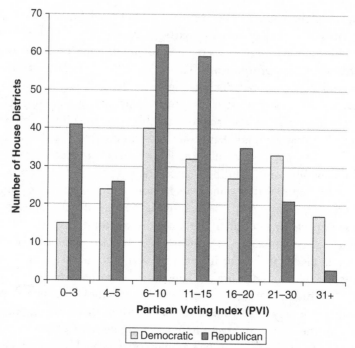

FIGURE 5.10. The fundamental Republican advantage in House elections.

dominated by racial minorities who usually vote heavily Democratic. "Packing" these voters into seats in which they constitute electorally potent supermajorities often works to the net advantage of Republican candidates in adjacent districts who are deprived of constituents unlikely to support them, thus boosting the descriptive representation of minority groups at the expense of their substantive representation.[39] Even without the effects of intentional gerrymandering, however, Democratic voters tend to be heavily clustered in large urban areas, making this partisan asymmetry somewhat inevitable in a single-member-district electoral system in which district contiguity and respect for existing political boundaries are often considerations during the redistricting process.[40] It is difficult to imagine how mapmakers could draw a politically competitive House district in Democratic strongholds like the Bronx, the cities

---

[39] David Lublin, *The Paradox of Representation: Racial Gerrymandering and Minority Interests in Congress* (Princeton, NJ: Princeton University Press, 1997).

[40] Jowei Chen and Jonathan Rodden, "Unintentional Gerrymandering: Political Geography and Electoral Bias in Legislatures," *Quarterly Journal of Political Science* 8 (2013), pp. 239–269.

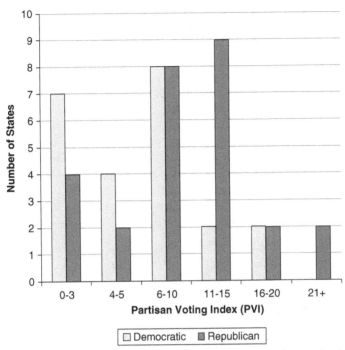

FIGURE 5.11. The fundamental Republican advantage in Senate elections.

of Chicago and Los Angeles, or the San Francisco Bay Area even if they endeavored to do so.

In the Senate, Republicans maintain a similar fundamental advantage due to the constitutionally prescribed equal representation of states regardless of population. Figure 5.11 displays the distribution of PVI scores across states after the 2012 election. Today, 27 states are more Republican-leaning than the national average while just 23 states are more Democratic. Most of the states that closely follow the national outcome lean very slightly in the Democratic direction; if the states with a PVI of 3 points or less in either direction are classified as swing states rather than essentially red or blue, the Republican advantage in states grows to 23–16, which corresponds to a 46–32 margin in Senate seats. In presidential elections, this partisan imbalance is at least partially counteracted by the large number of electoral votes cast by safely Democratic states such as California and New York, but the GOP's small-state advantage is more consequential in the battle for a Senate majority. In the recent past, a number of states with pro-Republican PVI scores of 10 or more regularly elected moderate Democratic senators (including Arkansas,

TABLE 5.1. *The regional distribution of congressional seats, 2012–2020*

	Pct House seats	Pct Senate seats
Blue regions		
Northeast	20%	22%
Pacific Coast	16	8
Total	36	30
Red regions		
South	35	28
Interior West	9	26
Total	44	54
Midwest	20	16

Louisiana, Nebraska, and both Dakotas), thus allowing Senate Democrats to assemble a national majority by extending their electoral reach into Red America, but the declining inclination of red-state voters to split their tickets in congressional elections threatens the future viability of this strategy.

The overrepresentation of the thinly populated interior West is a particular impediment to the ambitions of Senate Democrats. Table 5.1 summarizes the regional distribution of seats across the five regions in both houses of Congress after the post-2010 census apportionment. While the South and Midwest are somewhat underrepresented in the Senate (compared to the House, which closely reflects the populations of the component states within each region) and the Northeast is slightly overrepresented, the largest representational discrepancies occur in the two western regions. The 14 states of the interior West are collectively apportioned only 56 percent as many House seats as the four Pacific Coast states, yet elect 3.25 times as many senators. A Senate Republican Party that can achieve electoral dominance in the two reddest regions of the nation can therefore capture an overall majority without the need to compete effectively in the other three regions. The numerical advantage that the interior West region provides to Senate Republicans is not purely accidental; the admission of new states to the Union was intentionally manipulated by Republican leaders in the late nineteenth century to provide just such a structural benefit (for example, by splitting the former Dakota Territory into two separate states).[41]

---

[41] See Charles Stewart III and Barry R. Weingast, "Stacking the Senate, Changing the Nation: Republican Rotten Boroughs, Statehood Politics, and American Political Development," *Studies in American Political Development* 6 (Fall 1992), pp. 223–271.

The underlying Republican advantage in congressional elections also allows the party to capture a majority of seats in both chambers without winning a plurality of votes nationwide. Table 5.2 summarizes the partisan distribution of the two-party popular vote and the share of seats in the House and Senate since 1972. For the Senate, the figures represent an average of the previous three elections in order to compensate for the body's staggered six-year terms. The party winning the most popular votes has failed to achieve a majority of seats twice in the House and seven times in the Senate over the past 35 years.[42] In every one of these nine cases, it was the Democratic Party that was denied institutional control despite attracting more total votes than the Republican opposition.

Previous studies have established that the polarization of the congressional parties is primarily due to the rightward drift of the congressional Republican Party over the past four decades – a development that in part reflects the rising influence of conservative activists, including cultural traditionalists, within the party itself.[43] Some veteran scholars of Congress have lamented the changes that polarization – and, in particular, the increasingly aggressive governing style of Republican leaders – has introduced to the institution.[44] A conservative party that was required to seriously compete among left-leaning electoral constituencies in order to achieve a national majority might be forced to temper its ideological purity or risk its hold on power. However, House and Senate Republicans face relatively little electoral incentive to collectively shift further toward the political center, even if the considerable contemporary pressure from party activists and primary voters to reject moderate positions and bipartisan dealmaking were to abate in the future.

---

[42] David R. Mayhew notes that the 1996 House election contains several idiosyncratic attributes that complicate attempts to determine which party received more total votes that year; see Mayhew, "Earning More Seats with Fewer Votes," The Monkey Cage blog, December 6, 2012, themonkeycage.org/2012/12/earning-more-seats-with-fewer-votes-why-the-1996-house-election-results-are-not-necessarily-a-good-analogy-for-2012/.

[43] Poole and Rosenthal, *Ideology and Congress*; Hacker and Pierson, *Off Center*.

[44] Thomas E. Mann and Norman J. Ornstein, *The Broken Branch: How Congress Is Failing America and How to Get It Back on Track* (New York: Oxford University Press, 2006); Mann and Ornstein, *It's Even Worse Than It Looks: How The American Constitutional System Collided with the New Politics of Extremism* (New York: Basic Books, 2012).

TABLE 5.2. *Partisan popular vote and congressional seat shares, 1972–2016*

Year	House pct popular vote	House pct seats	Sen pct popular vote	Sen pct seats
1972	52.9	55.9	51.3	57.0
1974	58.6	66.9	53.7	62.0
1976	57.2	67.1	53.6	62.0
1978	54.3	63.7	55.3	59.0
1980	51.2	55.9	53.6*	47.0*
1982	56.1	61.8	53.2*	46.0*
1984	52.6	58.2	52.5*	47.0*
1986	55.0	59.3	51.8	55.0
1988	53.9	59.8	51.0	55.0
1990	54.1	61.6	52.0	56.0
1992	52.8	59.5	52.6	57.0
1994	46.6	47.1	50.6*	48.0*
1996	50.0*	47.8*	49.6	45.0
1998	49.5	48.7	49.1	45.0
2000	49.8	49.0	50.1*	50.0*
2002	47.6	47.4	49.7	49.0
2004	48.7	46.7	50.1*	45.0*
2006	54.1	53.6	52.1	51.0
2008	55.5	59.1	54.1	59.0
2010	46.5	44.4	52.3	53.0
2012	50.5*	46.2*	52.4	55.0
2014	47.3	43.2	49.9	46.0
2016	49.3	44.6	52.2*	48.0*

Note: Figures denote the Democratic share of the two-party vote (or seats in chamber). In races with more than one candidate from a single party (as can occur in the "top-two" runoff system used in California, Louisiana, and Washington), votes are counted only for the highest vote-getter from each party. Victorious independent candidates are treated as members of the party with which they caucus in Congress. The Senate figures represent a rolling average of the national two-party Democratic vote share from the previous three Senate elections (in order to compensate for turnout differences between presidential-year and midterm elections). Asterisks and bold type indicate years in which a partisan discrepancy exists between the party winning a popular plurality and the party holding majority control in the chamber after the election.

CONCLUSION: A CONGRESS POLARIZED
BY REGION

The twenty-first-century Congress is sharply polarized not only by party and by ideology but also by geography. As Figures 5.12 and 5.13 reveal, the ideological gap between the elected representatives of the red and blue regions widened dramatically after 1992 in both the House and the Senate. Even the 1940s and 1950s, when political conflict frequently took the form of battles between northern and southern members of Congress, did not result in large aggregate ideological differences between the regions; southern Democrats were collectively more conservative than northern (and far western) Democrats, but northern voters were also more likely during that era to elect Republican senators and representatives who also held right-of-center issue positions. Today, in contrast, regional delegations differ markedly in their roll-call voting habits in both houses of Congress. Attentive viewers of the deliberations of the legislative branch (as broadcast live on the C-SPAN cable television network) can predict with increasing confidence that a member who rises to speak with a southern drawl will be more likely to respond to the policy proposal of a New York–accented colleague by voicing strong opposition than by expressing enthusiastic support.

As the figures show, the growing regional separation of congressional voting patterns is principally driven on the House side by the strong rightward shift of the delegations from the South and interior West, while representatives from the Northeast and Pacific Coast have remained more stable in their average ideological positioning. In the Senate, by contrast, senators from red and blue regions alike have collectively moved apart in a more symmetric pattern. This notable difference between the chambers demonstrates the potentially significant consequences of vote aggregation at different geographic levels. The Northeast and Pacific Coast both contain pockets of Republican electoral strength large enough to elect a minority of House members. These enclaves are mostly concentrated in the Northeast in the rural areas of upstate New York and central Pennsylvania or the exurbs of New Jersey, and are centered in the Pacific Coast states along a band extending south from inland eastern Washington to the Inland Empire and suburban San Diego in California. Nearly all of the House Republicans representing these constituencies are strong conservatives, especially in the Pacific Coast states; the California delegation alone has supplied some of the congressional Republican Party's most prominent conservative members, from Robert

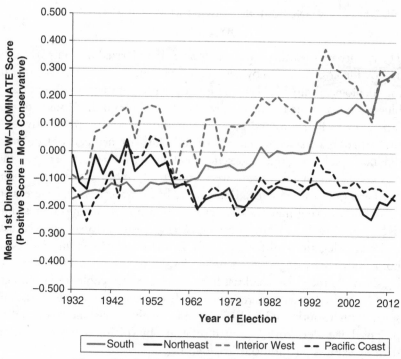

FIGURE 5.12. The regional polarization of the U.S. House of Representatives, 1932–2016.
Source: See Figure 5.1.

Dornan and Chris Cox in the 1990s to Tom McClintock, Darrell Issa, and Kevin McCarthy today. Their continued presence and further right-ward shift over time – the Republican California delegation held a mean DW-NOMINATE score of 0.476 in the 1991–1992 Congress and 0.728 in the Congress of 2011–2012 – has largely counteracted the region's increasing population of Democratic representatives in terms of the mean ideology of Blue America representatives.

In the Senate, however, Republicans – especially conservative Republicans – constitute a small and declining proportion of northeastern and coastal western delegations; after the 2008 defeat of two-term incumbent Gordon Smith of Oregon, no Senate Republican remains in office from any of the four Pacific Coast states. The Republican vote in these states is large and geographically concentrated enough to elect multiple House members, but is consistently outnumbered at the state level by Democratic support-ers. The Senate contingent from Blue America has therefore collectively

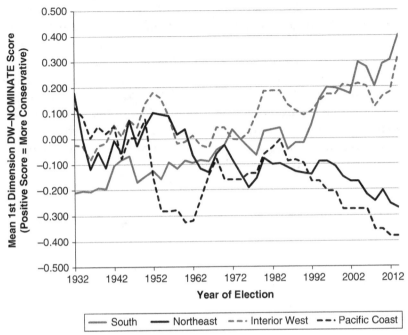

FIGURE 5.13. The regional polarization of the U.S. Senate, 1932–2016.
Source: See Figure 5.1.

shifted in a liberal direction over time without being significantly affected by a countervailing trend of increasing conservatism among congressional Republicans.

The polarization of the congressional parties over the past forty years is a complex, multifaceted process that encompasses institutional reform, the strategies of presidents and other party leaders both within and outside the legislative branch, changes in party coalitions, the rise of new issues, and the impact of numerous salient political events (Watergate, the Reagan Revolution, the Iraq War, and so forth). As such, it is neither a simple reflection of changes in the preferences of the mass public nor wholly insulated from them. But the influence of American citizens over the identity and behavior of their elected officials must be viewed in the context of the complicated means by which democratic representation is realized in the United States. The geographic polarization of winner-take-all electoral outcomes in races for House and Senate seats, when combined with the emergence of a fundamental Republican advantage in elections for both chambers, has contributed significantly to the transformation of Congress from a relatively moderate, regularly bipartisan, and Democratic-dominated branch of government to a highly polarized, overwhelmingly partisan, and mostly Republican-ruled institution over the course of the last several decades. Millions of Democratic supporters continue to reside in the South or interior West, just as the population of the Northeast and coastal West is still far from devoid of Republican-leaning citizens, but both of these voting blocs have suffered a significant erosion (and, in the Senate, a near-extinction) of their representation in the legislative branch of government at the hands of increasingly entrenched regional majorities.

6

Rural Red, Big-City Blue, and the Pivotal
Purple Midwest

THE NEW DIVIDE BETWEEN CITY AND COUNTRY

The partisan divergence between red and blue geographic territory does not merely separate New York from North Dakota and Oklahoma from Oregon. Geographic polarization has progressed below the level of states and regions as well, widening the electoral rift between the residents of populous metropolitan areas and their cousins in small-town and rural America. Just as a number of states that once remained open to persuasion by both Democrats and Republicans have evolved over the past three decades to become reliable bastions of a single party, many localities within individual states deliver increasingly lopsided majorities to either one side or the other in national elections.

The political geography inside most states has thus similarly settled into a stable pattern of partisan alignments. The deepest shades of blue on the electoral map are dependably located in the largest population centers of the North and coastal West. Most large cities outside the South have leaned Democratic since the 1930s, though this partisan advantage has become even more pronounced over time. Since 1992, Democratic presidential candidates have also drawn significant electoral support from suburbs surrounding these urban cores, allowing them to establish a solid regional base in the blue states even as suburban population growth has outpaced that of most northern cities over the past several decades.

The Republican Party has countered this trend by consolidating its advantage in the smaller cities, towns, and countryside of the South, Midwest, and interior West. Much of the small-town South retained a degree of residual loyalty to Democratic candidates into the 1990s, as did adjacent areas of the Midwest. The rural West also maintained a tradition of "prairie populism" that regularly resulted in the election of Democratic members of Congress from Montana, Nebraska, and the Dakotas into the early years of the twenty-first century. But these areas' subsequent marked shift in a Republican direction has solidified the party's majority status across what has become known as Red America.

It is hardly a coincidence that the rising salience of cultural issues after the 1980s that increasingly divided the Northeast and coastal West from the South and interior West also produced a substantial partisan gap between the socially progressive residents of large metropolitan areas and the more traditionalist inhabitants of less populous communities. As James G. Gimpel and Kimberly A. Karnes noted in 2006, "the 'red' vs. 'blue' Election Night maps really mask an urban-rural divide *within* states – a gap that has increased in recent years according to a range of definitions ... Nearly all contemporary surveys show that rural Americans are more religiously and morally conservative than those living elsewhere."[1]

The increasingly lopsided Democratic alignment of populous metropolitan areas have helped to push the states where they contain a majority of the electorate into the Democratic column in national elections, while the growing preference of the inhabitants of smaller communities for Republican candidates has likewise contributed to a countervailing shift elsewhere in the nation. In the Midwest, which contains several large metro areas but is also home to a significant small-town vote, these two trends have usually canceled each other out in the aggregate – leaving a closely divided overall partisan balance in most midwestern states that has masked significant geographic polarization at the local level. As the results of 2016 demonstrate, the Midwest remains the nation's most politically pivotal region, and even minor shifts in the voting preferences of midwestern residents can easily prove decisive to the national outcome in an era of routinely close-fought presidential and congressional elections.

THE NORTHEAST AND PACIFIC COAST: REALM OF THE METROPOLITAN DEMOCRATS

The Democrats have been the party of the big city for generations, but only since the 1990s have they established themselves as the party of the big metropolis. This distinction is important: the explosive population

[1] James G. Gimpel and Kimberly A. Karnes, "The Rural Side of the Urban-Rural Gap," *PS: Political Science and Politics* 40 (July 2006), pp. 467–472, at 467, 471.

growth of American suburbs from the mid-twentieth century to the present has reduced the relative voting power of central cities, requiring Democratic candidates to expand their appeal to suburban dwellers in order to remain electorally competitive. Today, Democrats can usually expect to receive 70 percent or more of the vote in nearly every large city outside the South, but the narrower margins that the party attracts in populous surrounding suburbs are often crucial to supplying the raw number of ballots needed to prevail statewide.

Figure 6.1 illustrates the sizable pro-Democratic shift that has occurred in the large metropolitan areas of Blue America. Of the 20 largest metropolitan areas in the nation (as measured by 2010 census figures), collectively representing 45 percent of the American voting population as of 2016, nine are wholly or partially located in the Northeast or Pacific Coast, including six of the top seven (New York, Los Angeles, Washington–Baltimore, San Jose–San Francisco, Boston–Providence, and Philadelphia). Ronald Reagan received 55 percent of the total two-party vote within these nine metro areas in both 1980 and 1984, while George H. W. Bush and his Democratic opponent Michael Dukakis each received 50 percent in 1988. Ever since, however, the Democratic presidential candidate has won at least 60 percent of the collective vote in large blue-state metro areas. Barack Obama carried them by a nearly two-to-one ratio in both 2008 and 2012, and Hillary Clinton prevailed over Donald Trump by an even wider margin, 66 percent to 34 percent, in 2016.

As a result, northeastern and coastal western states in which a large proportion of the population resides within large metropolitan areas became some of the most safely Democratic states in the nation after 1992. For example, the Los Angeles, San Jose–San Francisco, and San Diego metro areas together constituted 77 percent of the California electorate in 2012; Obama's electoral success in these vote-rich areas allowed him to defeat Mitt Romney by a statewide margin of 62 percent to 38 percent in the two-party vote. (Obama still would have carried California if every one of his supporters in the rest of the state had voted for Romney instead.) Washington and Oregon are similarly reliable blue states in federal elections due to the Democratic Party's formidable electoral advantage in metropolitan Seattle and Portland. In 2016, Hillary Clinton won 67 percent of the two-party vote in greater Seattle and 61 percent in greater Portland, allowing her to carry Washington and Oregon by double-digit statewide margins even though the remainder of the electorate in both states preferred Donald Trump by a margin of 55 percent to 45 percent.

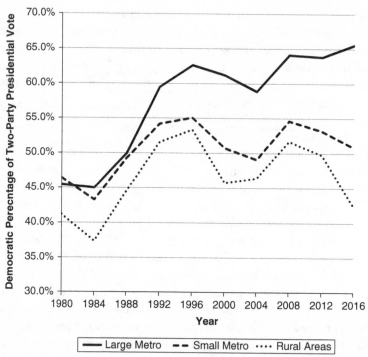

FIGURE 6.1. The geographic polarization of the Northeast and Pacific Coast, 1980–2016.
Note: "Large Metro" includes the counties classified by the federal Office of Management and Budget as part of the 20 most populous Metropolitan Statistical Areas (MSAs) or Combined Metropolitan Statistical Areas (CMSAs) as of 2015: (1) New York, (2) Los Angeles, (3) Chicago, (4) Washington–Baltimore, (5) San Jose–San Francisco, (6) Boston–Providence, (7) Philadelphia, (8) Dallas, (9) Miami, (10) Houston, (11) Atlanta, (12) Detroit, (13) Phoenix, (14) Seattle, (15) Minneapolis, (16) Cleveland, (17) San Diego, (18) Denver, (19) Portland, and (20) Orlando. Counties within all other MSAs or CMSAs are classified as "Small Metro"; nonmetropolitan counties are classified as "Rural Areas."

A chain of four nearly contiguous large metro areas in the northeastern United States (greater Boston–Providence, New York, Philadelphia, and Washington–Baltimore) stretches from southern New Hampshire to northern Virginia, containing all or part of ten states (plus the District of Columbia) worth a combined 118 electoral votes. Since 1992, this "megalopolis" has provided Democratic candidates with a massive popular advantage across most of the Northeast, shifting the former swing states of Connecticut, New Jersey, Maryland, and Delaware into safely blue status while helping to transform historically Republican-leaning

New Hampshire into a perennial electoral battleground. Even Virginia, a geographically southern state that was safely Republican in presidential elections as late as 2000, has since become politically competitive – led by the populous northern Virginia counties that lie within the greater Washington metropolitan area and are more northeastern than southern in their prevailing culture. In 2016, the Republican presidential candidate narrowly carried Pennsylvania for the first time since 1988, but this widely unexpected outcome reflected a pro-Republican shift in the central and western sections of the state rather than a decline of Democratic support in metro Philadelphia (where Hillary Clinton received 61 percent of the two-party vote, nearly matching Obama's 62 percent in 2012).

John B. Judis and Ruy Teixeira have noted that Democrats benefited from the rise of "postindustrial metropolitan area[s]" serving as "headquarters for the production of ideas." Many of the large population centers that now anchor the Democratic electoral advantage in the Northeast and coastal West are ethnically diverse and culturally cosmopolitan, populated by "new professionals who live according to ... socially liberal values."[2] After the parties polarized on cultural issues, these voters increasingly viewed the Democratic Party as their natural home in national elections, producing a sizable partisan advantage throughout the Northeast Corridor and along the Pacific Coast.

Figure 6.1 illustrates how the pro-Democratic shift across Blue America after 1988 was particularly concentrated within the largest metropolitan areas. Before 1992, large metro areas in the Northeast and Pacific Coast did not vote much differently from their small metro counterparts in the two regions. Beginning with the Bill Clinton elections of the 1990s, however, a gap suddenly emerged between large and small metro areas that grew to a magnitude of 15 percentage points by 2016. The smaller metro areas located in blue states are collectively representative of the national electorate as a whole, leaning slightly but not securely in the Democratic direction after 1992. Non-metro counties, even in the blue states, have consistently voted more Republican than the national average since the 1990s, with a particular marked pro-Republican shift occurring between 2012 and 2016; only in Hawaii and parts of New England does the small-town vote favor Democratic candidates.

Significant pockets of Republican voters still remain within some large coastal metropolitan areas, including on New York's Long Island,

---

[2] John B. Judis and Ruy Teixeira, *The Emerging Democratic Majority* (New York: Scribner, 2002), pp. 8, 9.

in exurban New Jersey, and in the prosperous suburbs surrounding Philadelphia, San Diego, and Seattle. But the trajectory of recent election results suggests that the party's electoral strength is likely to decline in the future even within these remaining islands of Republican red. A party that is increasingly associated with social conservatism and Donald Trump–style nationalism faces a steep barrier to competing effectively in the culturally progressive environs of the largest metropolitan areas of the North and Far West. In Pennsylvania, where less than 40 percent of the population resides within greater Philadelphia and where the remainder of the state contains a significant small-metro and small-town vote, statewide electoral trends are not unfavorable to Republican ambitions, and Trump's particularly strong appeal in rural areas also allowed him to carry Maine's northern congressional district in 2016.[3] But the rest of Blue America appears destined, absent a fundamental transformation in the social coalitions of the parties, to become even bluer in the future due to the growing Democratic character of its largest metropolitan areas.

THE SOUTH AND INTERIOR WEST: REPUBLICAN ASCENDANCE IN THE HEARTLAND

While the New Deal–era Democratic dominance of the South and (to a lesser degree) the interior West in presidential voting had begun to decay as early as the Eisenhower elections of the 1950s, the extension of partisan policy conflict in the mass electorate to the realm of social issues four decades later significantly accelerated the growing Republican cast of the two regions in congressional as well as presidential contests. Southern, prairie, and mountain states have historically been prone to bouts of economic populism that in certain past eras placed them to the ideological left of the more affluent cities of the Northeast, but the prevailing party politics of the 1990s and thereafter has established them as the regional anchors of the contemporary Republican geographic base.

In a number of southern states, party realignment proceeded first in urban areas before extending to rural communities; the cities of Alexandria, Virginia; St. Petersburg, Florida; Dallas, Texas; and Mobile, Alabama were among the first southern constituencies outside Appalachia to elect Republican members of Congress in the years after World War II. As Figure 6.2 reveals, the rural vote in the South and interior West was

---

[3] Brandon Finnegan, "Why Trump Can Win Pennsylvania," *National Review*, July 25, 2016, www.nationalreview.com/article/438269/donald-trump-pennsylvania-path-white-house.

slightly less Republican-leaning than the urban vote as late as 1980, and even the elections of 1992 and 1996 did not produce a dramatic difference in the partisan alignments of large metropolitan areas, small metro areas, and rural counties. But the urban and rural vote diverged markedly in the 2000 election and thereafter, producing a pattern of geographic polarization below the state level that mirrors the gap that had emerged in the blue states during the 1990s. As in the rest of the nation, large Red America metropolitan areas are now consistently the most Democratic-leaning localities within their region while rural areas are collectively the most pro-Republican; the numerical difference between them now represents more than 20 percentage points in the two-party vote.

But even the large metro areas of the South and interior West are not universally Democratic bastions, reflecting these regions' relative cultural traditionalism. Greater Miami and Denver stand out as liberal enclaves within their more conservative regional surroundings, both becoming sufficiently pro-Democratic since the 1990s to transform their home states of Florida and Colorado – both once safely Republican – into highly competitive electoral battlegrounds. Other major population centers in Red America, such as metropolitan Dallas, Houston, Atlanta, and Phoenix, are either closely divided between the parties or lean slightly Republican, especially within their populous suburban outskirts. As Figure 6.2 shows, the large metro vote in Red America is indeed becoming more Democratic over time – an especially large pro-Democratic shift occurred in 2016, reflecting Trump's unpopularity among urban and suburban college-educated whites – but is not yet sufficiently lopsided to counteract the more decisive Republican tilt of the small-metro and rural counties across the two regions. The dramatic population growth of many southern and southwestern metro areas over the past several decades has resulted in the reapportionment of congressional seats to red states such as Georgia, Texas, and Arizona at the expense of the bluer Northeast and Midwest – a trend that has worked to the advantage of the Republican Party in both the House of Representatives and the electoral college.

Not only do the largest metropolitan areas of the South and interior West fail to vote as decisively for Democratic candidates as their counterparts in the North and along the Pacific Coast, but they also represent a much smaller proportion of the regional electorate. In the 2016 election, large metro areas collectively contained 71 percent of the voters in Blue America but only 28 percent of the voters in the two Republican-leaning regions. As Figure 6.2 demonstrates, the rural vote

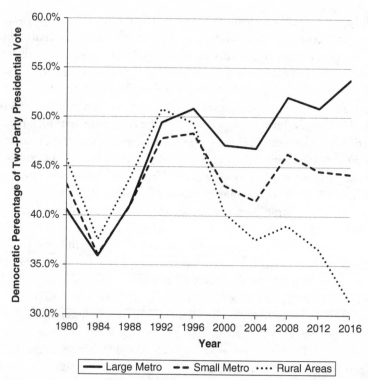

FIGURE 6.2. The geographic polarization of the South and interior West, 1980–2016.

Note: "Large Metro" includes the counties classified by the federal Office of Management and Budget as part of the 20 most populous Metropolitan Statistical Areas or Combined Metropolitan Statistical Areas as of 2015: (1) New York, (2) Los Angeles, (3) Chicago, (4) Washington–Baltimore, (5) San Jose–San Francisco, (6) Boston–Providence, (7) Philadelphia, (8) Dallas, (9) Miami, (10) Houston, (11) Atlanta, (12) Detroit, (13) Phoenix, (14) Seattle, (15) Minneapolis, (16) Cleveland, (17) San Diego, (18) Denver, (19) Portland, and (20) Orlando. Counties within all other MSAs or CMSAs are classified as "Small Metro"; nonmetropolitan counties are classified as "Rural Areas."

in the South and interior West remained evenly split between the parties in the 1990s but immediately shifted in a Republican direction thereafter. George W. Bush defeated Al Gore among these voters by a margin of 60 percent to 40 percent in the 2000 election, and subsequent elections produced even more decisive Republican advantages. Both Mitt Romney in 2012 and (especially) Donald Trump in 2016 won a greater share of the rural vote in the South and interior West than Ronald Reagan had received in his 49-state 1984 landslide; Trump outpolled

Hillary Clinton in the two regions' rural counties by a collective margin of 69 percent to 31 percent.

The collapse of the small-town Democratic vote in Red America has put states such as Arkansas, Kentucky, and Montana – all won at least once by Bill Clinton in the 1990s – out of reach for the party's candidates in presidential elections. If Gore had been able to carry his native Tennessee, where he had twice been elected statewide to the U.S. Senate, he would have won the presidency in 2000 regardless of the outcome in Florida. West Virginia, once so loyal to the Democratic Party that it was one of only six states to support Jimmy Carter over Ronald Reagan in 1980 and one of ten to prefer Michael Dukakis over George H. W. Bush in 1988, is now one of the most heavily Republican states in the nation, giving Romney a 27-point victory over Obama in 2012 and Trump a 42-point landslide over Hillary Clinton in 2016.

Republican success in consolidating popular support across much of the South and West has increasingly extended to congressional elections as well. The party now holds a reliable electoral dominance over both regions, constrained only by the federally required creation where feasible of majority-minority House districts (which tend to be safely Democratic) and by the presence of a few islands of liberal sentiment elsewhere, usually in communities populated by migrants from the Northeast and California such as Denver, Colorado; Raleigh, North Carolina; and Austin, Texas. A Democratic Party increasingly identified in the public mind with cultural liberalism is increasingly unable to compete effectively against the ascendant red-state Republicans, even when it nominates socially conservative candidates for office – leaving the majority of both regions to unchallenged Republican rule and giving the congressional GOP a formidable advantage in the battle for control of the House and Senate.

Of the 27 states located in the South and interior West, seven can be classified as more politically "purple" than safely red – an exception to the larger regional trend that is of limited benefit to the Democratic Party in Senate elections but more consequential in presidential contests (since several of these states have large caches of electoral votes). Florida, Virginia, North Carolina, New Mexico, Colorado, and Nevada all combine significant populations of racial minorities with sufficiently large concentrations of white cultural liberals to render their states politically competitive, especially in presidential elections when voter turnout reaches its peak. Obama carried all seven of these states in 2008 and six (all but North Carolina) in 2012, but the return of Florida to the

Republican column by a narrow margin provided Donald Trump with a key swing-state victory four years later. If current trends continue, the largest metropolitan areas of the Sun Belt may eventually become sufficiently Democratic to transform the currently Republican states of Georgia and Arizona into electoral battlegrounds and the current swing states of Virginia and Colorado into Democratic-leaning constituencies, but the substantial Republican vote still remaining in large-metro Red America, in combination with a Republican-leaning small metro population and an overwhelmingly pro-Republican rural vote, has so far preserved the GOP's dominance across both regions.

THE MIDWEST: AMERICA'S REMAINING PARTISAN BATTLEFIELD

Democratic presidential nominee Bill Clinton, his vice presidential running mate Al Gore, and their wives Hillary Clinton and Tipper Gore embarked together on a three-day bus caravan in the late summer of 1992 through a string of small cities and towns, stopping frequently along the way to hold public rallies and meet voters informally in town squares, diners, and community centers. This extended road trip represented a noteworthy departure from what had become the standard practice of presidential campaigning, in which each member of the national ticket jetted separately around the country from one large metropolis to another in order to appear before the maximum number of potential supporters. While the bus tour was received favorably by the national press due to its novelty and appealingly homespun flavor (the Clintons and Gores strove for picturesque portrayals of themselves as regular folks in touch with the American heartland by tossing footballs at rest stops, traipsing through barnyards, and even stopping to play a round of miniature golf), it was also intentionally designed to create attention and excitement for the Democratic Party in less populous communities that were not accustomed to hosting personal appearances from national candidates. "With the bus, the campaign is able to attract news reports in towns that are too small to have airports," observed the *New York Times*, and the resulting media coverage was generous to the Clinton–Gore ticket both in its overwhelmingly positive disposition and its sheer volume. One edition of a local newspaper contained "seven articles on the candidates' visit, plus a full page of photographs," while a television station preempted its usual morning schedule of game shows in order to devote extensive live coverage to the arrival of the prospective president and vice president – even rebroadcasting the footage that evening for the benefit of any viewers who wished to relive the experience.[4]

Impressed by the favorable attention that the Clinton–Gore tour received, candidates have often organized similar ground-level excursions in subsequent campaigns. Gore, seeking to succeed Clinton as president eight years later, and running mate Joe Lieberman traveled together by riverboat over four days in the summer of 2000. Incumbent president George W. Bush held his own bus tour in 2004, while his Democratic opponent John Kerry joined vice presidential nominee Senator John Edwards of North Carolina on a multistate railroad expedition. By 2012, bus tours had acquired slogans coined by political advisors to advertise the candidate's message of the hour; while sitting president Barack Obama embarked on the "Betting on America" tour, his challenger, Mitt Romney, countered with a motorcoach convoy of his own dubbed "Every Town Counts."

Now a familiar staple of quadrennial campaign pageantry, these extended forays by candidates into small-town America via back roads, train tracks, and waterways shared a common geographic setting: they all occurred largely or entirely within the Midwest. This single region exerts a predictable gravitational pull over the travel itineraries of contemporary presidential aspirants, who frequently find themselves returning again and again to the same cluster of eight states – or a subset thereof – over the course of a long campaign. With most of the nation now safely red or blue territory in presidential elections, the Midwest is the last remaining corner of America where a contiguous set of vote-rich "purple" states remains open to persuasion by either side, offering a strategic location conducive to the extended campaign road trip. Candidates reckon that a long weekend spent delivering speeches and shaking hands along the byways of central Ohio, eastern Iowa, or western Wisconsin could plausibly reap enough popular support to tip a closely divided state in their direction; if the election is very competitive nationally – as most recent contests have been – the outcome in that single state could potentially determine the identity of the next president.

The Midwest stands apart not because its residents are insulated from the large-scale political changes that have influenced the rest of the nation over the past several decades, but because these trends have caused the aggregate partisan balance within most midwestern states to remain

[4] Richard L. Berke, "Clinton Bus Tour Woos and Wows Local Press," *New York Times*, August 9, 1992, sec. 1, p. 30.

relatively even over time – thus preserving the competitiveness of state-wide elections in an era of strong party loyalty. Just as the near-equal strength of the two national parties conceals significant regional differences in electoral outcomes, the purple states of the Midwest contain internal geographic concentrations of loyal Democratic and Republican sentiment that happen to have nearly canceled each other out once aggregated at the state level. While references to the Midwest as the location of a uniquely authentic "true" America are too often expressed as tired clichés characteristic of unimaginative candidates or pundits, the region is indeed the most politically representative – and, thus, strategically critical – part of the nation within which it lies.

The electoral typicality of the Midwest is a long-standing attribute of American politics. The winning presidential candidate has also carried the Midwest in 27 of the 31 elections held since 1896; the four exceptions – the elections of 1916, 1960, 1976, and 2000 – were all unusually close national contests in which the winner narrowly failed to place first in the midwestern vote. National party leaders are well aware of the Midwest's role as an electoral bellwether. Of the 34 presidential elections between 1860 and 1992, in only three – the elections of 1928, 1932, and 1960 – was the Midwest unrepresented on the national ticket of either party; in fully half of these elections, both parties nominated a presidential or vice presidential candidate from one of the eight states of the region.[5]

As other regions have evolved into Democratic or Republican strongholds over time, the Midwest's persistent national representativeness has become more distinctive. Figure 6.3 displays the partisan deviation in the regional two-party popular vote for president from the national vote for the Midwest and the two sets of red and blue regions over the 1968–2016 period. The measure is scored such that a value of 5 percent indicates that the Democratic candidate performed 5 percentage points better in the denoted region or regions than in the total national vote; negative values indicate that the Republican candidate outran his national performance. While the rest of the nation diverged in one partisan direction or the other after the 1980s, the Midwest has remained collectively competitive, closely mirroring the national distribution of the presidential vote.

Figure 6.4 similarly presents the regional alignment of the vote for the House of Representatives between 1968 and 2016, once again comparing

---

[5] Senator Thomas Eagleton of Missouri, the original vice presidential nominee of the Democratic Party in 1972, resigned from the ticket during the campaign and was replaced by a nonmidwesterner, Sargent Shriver of Massachusetts.

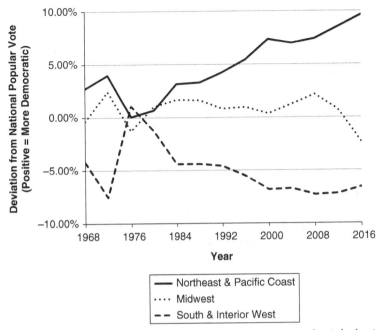

FIGURE 6.3. The representativeness of the Midwest in presidential elections, 1968–2016.

the popular vote results in Red America, Blue America, and the Midwest to the national partisan vote distribution during the same election. Prior to the 1990s, the Midwest was consistently more Republican-leaning in its congressional voting habits than the nation as a whole, due principally to the remaining Democratic support in the South (which rendered the Midwest more Republican in national comparison). After the regional divergence of the Northeast and Pacific Coast from the South and interior West began to occur during the 1990s, the Midwest assumed its familiar place in between the two sets of party-aligned regions, closely mirroring the national partisan trend from one election to the next.

As the nation's most politically representative – and competitive – region, the Midwest holds an unmatched pivotal position. It constitutes much of the active battleground during any particular national campaign; in a typical election, most of the midwestern states are subjected to frequent candidate visits, advertising blitzes, and get-out-the-vote initiatives on behalf of both parties. The prevalence of strong two-party competition in the Midwest is not only reflected in the degree of presidential campaign activity directed its way every four years, but also remains evident

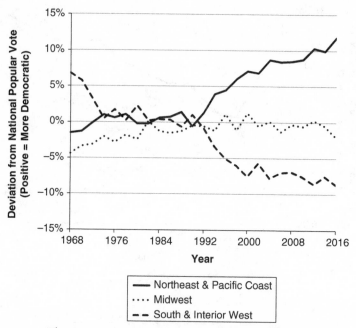

FIGURE 6.4. The representativeness of the Midwest in House elections, 1968–2016.

in the enduringly high frequency of split partisan Senate delegations among the eight states of the region. As Figure 6.5 demonstrates, the incidence of split delegations – which occur when a state's two Senate seats are divided between the parties – has declined over time in the rest of the nation, as the states of the Northeast and Pacific Coast have become more likely to elect two Democrats apiece to the upper chamber while states from the South and interior West have increasingly sent a pair of Republicans to Washington. However, many midwestern states have continued to elect one member of each party to the Senate; in the 2013–2014 session of Congress, six of the region's eight states were represented by one Democratic and one Republican senator.

Critics of partisan polarization in Congress might understandably look to the politically competitive "purple" states of the Midwest as a valuable source of ideologically moderate representatives. Indeed, several midwestern state parties have long-standing traditions of regularly electing relative moderates to statewide office: the Democratic Party in Indiana and Missouri and the Republican Party in Illinois and Minnesota. But the region's partisan marginality does not guarantee ideological

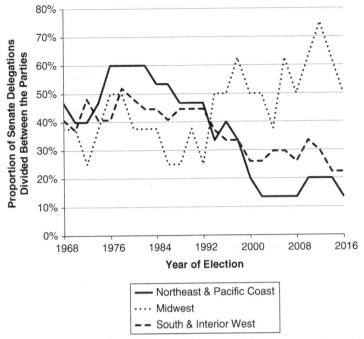

FIGURE 6.5. The persistence of split Senate delegations in the Midwest, 1968–2016.

centrism among its elected officials. In the Senate, many leading liberal Democrats of the past and present have represented midwestern states; recent examples include Paul Wellstone of Minnesota, Russ Feingold of Wisconsin, Carl Levin of Michigan, and Sherrod Brown of Ohio. Likewise, the Midwest has recently supplied the Senate with several conservative Republicans of note, including Ron Johnson of Wisconsin, Dan Coats of Indiana, and John Ashcroft and Roy Blunt of Missouri. For the 30 years between 1985 and 2015, Iowa was simultaneously represented by conservative Republican Chuck Grassley and liberal Democrat Tom Harkin – the second-longest tenure of a split state partisan delegation in the history of the Senate.[6] A significant fraction of Iowans thus did not hesitate to repeatedly elect a pair of senators who could be expected to cancel out each other's votes on most prominent issues that came before the chamber.

[6] The record is held by Republican Strom Thurmond and Democrat Ernest "Fritz" Hollings, who represented South Carolina between 1967 and 2003.

THE EFFECTS OF LOCAL GEOGRAPHIC
POLARIZATION IN THE MIDWEST

The trend of geographically polarized county-level election outcomes, in which large metropolitan areas have become increasingly Democratic-leaning over time while rural America has produced a growing electoral shift to the Republican Party, has occurred in the Midwest as well as the rest of the nation. As Figure 6.6 demonstrates, Democratic presidential candidates have established a persistent advantage in the four largest population centers of the region (greater Chicago, Detroit, Minneapolis, and Cleveland), but – as in the South and interior West – this trend has been balanced or even outweighed by the solidifying Republican loyalties of small-town and rural electorates. Some of the most dramatic electoral gains made by Republican presidential and congressional candidates alike over the past three decades have occurred in the sections of Ohio, Indiana, Illinois, and Missouri that lie adjacent to the southern states of West Virginia, Kentucky, and Arkansas. Sharing many cultural commonalities with the South proper, these areas once contained substantial Democratic electoral strength; as late as 1992, Bill Clinton carried every county along the southern borders of Illinois and Indiana while winning broadly across Appalachian Ohio and southeastern Missouri. In more recent elections, the downstate Midwest has become solidly Republican, in parallel with contiguous constituencies across state lines to the south. By 2012 and 2016, for example, the only county in southeastern Ohio that remained Democratic was Athens County, reflecting the unique liberal college-town vote surrounding the University of Ohio.

Democratic electoral strength in the Midwest, as in other regions, has thus become more heavily concentrated over time in large metropolitan areas. For example, Bill Clinton in 1992 and Barack Obama in 2012 both received an identical share of the two-party vote in Illinois (58.6 percent in each election), yet Clinton placed first in 73 of the state's 102 counties while Obama carried just 23. In Ohio, Obama performed slightly better than Clinton – winning 51.5 of the state two-party vote compared to 51.2 for his predecessor – yet carried just 17 of 88 counties (Clinton had carried 31). The two candidates likewise nearly matched their statewide performance in Michigan (Clinton won 54.6 percent of the two-party vote in 1992, while Obama won 54.8 percent in 2012) on the basis of very different county-level results (Clinton carried 50 of 83 counties, compared to 20 for Obama). This trend has furthered the underlying Republican advantage in the geographic distribution of electoral support

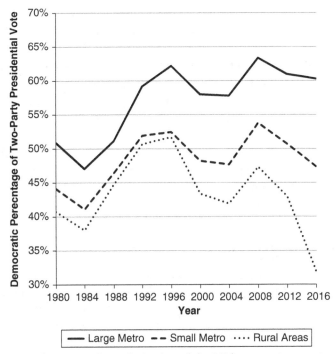

FIGURE 6.6. The geographic polarization of the Midwest, 1980–2016.
Note: "Large Metro" includes the counties classified by the federal Office of Management and Budget as part of the 20 most populous Metropolitan Statistical Areas or Combined Metropolitan Statistical Areas as of 2015, four of which are located in the Midwest (Chicago, Detroit, Minneapolis, and Cleveland). Counties within all other MSAs or CMSAs are classified as "Small Metro"; nonmetropolitan counties are classified as "Rural Areas."

within individual states. The southern border areas of Ohio, Indiana, Illinois, and Missouri that once regularly elected Democrats to the House of Representatives now strongly favor Republican candidates in congressional elections; while Democrats may effectively compensate in statewide races by increasing their popular margins in major urban centers, these votes are largely "wasted" within metropolitan House districts that already tend to be safe Democratic seats.

When combined with friendly district drawing by Republican-controlled state governments, the more efficient distribution of Republican votes across the Midwest can produce sizable partisan seat advantages. Under a district map approved by the Republican legislature in Ohio after the 2010 national census, Republican congressional candidates received

52 percent of the state two-party vote in 2012 and wound up holding 12 of the state's 16 seats in the House of Representatives. Winning 54 percent of the two-party vote in Indiana similarly delivered 7 of 9 seats to the GOP, while a cleverly designed set of congressional boundaries in Michigan resulted in a nine-to-five Republican edge in seats despite a Democratic victory in the combined popular vote of 53 percent to 47 percent. The battle for control of governorships and legislatures in state-level elections preceding the decennial redistricting process often determines the partisan composition of congressional delegations from closely divided midwestern states, where the strategic placement of district lines can represent the difference between a Democratic and a Republican majority.

THE PIVOTAL MIDWEST IN 2016 AND BEYOND

The Midwest's decisive role in national elections was demonstrated to dramatic effect in the 2016 presidential contest. Hillary Clinton entered Election Day as the heavy favorite in the eyes of political analysts, based on a combination of national polls that gave her a consistent lead and state-level surveys that indicated a solid Democratic advantage in the electoral college. Clinton indeed won the national popular vote as expected, but Republican nominee Donald Trump outperformed the polls in enough battleground states to unexpectedly capture an electoral majority. Crucially, Trump defeated Clinton in four midwestern states that had been carried by Barack Obama in both 2008 and 2012 – Iowa, Michigan, Ohio, and Wisconsin – and came within 45,000 votes of capturing a fifth (Minnesota). For the second time in just 16 years, stunned Democrats were forced to accept defeat in the electoral college despite attracting more popular support nationwide than their Republican opponents.

Prior to the election, some political commentators had identified much of the Midwest as part of a "blue wall" of states stretching west from the Northeast that had reliably provided Democratic candidates with electoral victory in previous presidential contests. Democratic presidential nominees had indeed won Illinois, Michigan, Minnesota, and Wisconsin in all six of the elections between 1992 and 2012, and had carried Iowa in five (all but 2004). The characterization of these states as solidly "blue," however, was fundamentally misleading. Democrats had often won midwestern states by narrow margins – for example, John Kerry defeated George W. Bush in Wisconsin by just 0.42 percentage points in 2004 – and the party was particularly dependent on the support of white voters without a college degree residing in small cities or towns to achieve electoral success in the region. Only Illinois, where approximately two-thirds of the state electorate is located within the large metropolis of greater Chicago, is reliably Democratic-leaning; elsewhere in the Midwest, Democratic candidates need to attract substantial support from the residents of smaller metro areas (such as Youngstown, Ohio; Duluth, Minnesota; or Saginaw, Michigan) and rural counties (as in much of Iowa and Wisconsin) in order to prevail statewide.

Whether due to Trump's unusual strengths, Clinton's personal flaws, or a combination of the two, the 2016 election produced what turned out to be an electorally decisive shift in the preferences of midwestern voters – especially in rural areas. As Figure 6.6 indicates, the partisan gap among rural midwesterners widened from a 14-point Republican advantage in the two-party vote (57 percent for Romney, 43 percent for Obama) in 2012 to a 36-point landslide (68 percent for Trump, 32 percent for Clinton) just four years later. This regional success for the GOP extended to congressional elections as well, contributing to Republican victories in key Senate races in Indiana, Missouri, Ohio, and Wisconsin that preserved a 52–48 national Republican majority in the upper chamber for the 2017–2018 session of Congress.

In the wake of the unexpected 2016 outcome, many observers – including a number of bitter Democrats – faulted Hillary Clinton's campaign for failing to recognize its electoral vulnerability in the Midwest early in the race and to devote sufficient energy to defending the region against Donald Trump's candidacy. It is possible that a more generously funded set of television advertisements and a more aggressive schedule of personal appearances could have produced greater electoral success for Clinton, at least in Michigan and Wisconsin (two states where she lost to Trump by narrow popular margins). However, both the simultaneous defeat of Democratic candidates for other offices across the Midwest in 2016 and the long-term trend toward geographic polarization (which has provided Republicans with a widening relative advantage among small-town and rural electorates for at least two full decades) suggest that the Democratic Party may face a growing challenge in the nation's most pivotal region that extends beyond the tactical errors of a single campaign or the unusual appeal of a single opponent.

Most studies of past elections have tended to conclude that the electoral college was not strongly or consistently biased in favor of either political party.[7] But this finding is not guaranteed to hold indefinitely. The use of winner-take-all elections held within 51 separate geographic constituencies is very sensitive to marginal variations or trends that push one party across the threshold of 50 percent of the two-party vote, and insensitive to differences or changes of equal or greater magnitude that fail to affect the candidates' order of finish. In the long term, Democratic presidential and congressional candidates' improving performance in large metropolitan areas, even in Red America, may give the party a valuable electoral edge in several populous southern or southwestern states that could ultimately compensate for, or even outweigh, any countervailing pro-Republican trend now under way in the small cities and towns of the Rust Belt. In 2016, however, the modest collective tilt of the Midwest toward the Republican Party proved sufficient to decide party control of both the executive and legislative branches, rendering the unlikely presidency of Donald Trump an indisputable symbol of the central importance of partisan geography to the course of political events in the United States – and, thus, the entire world.

[7] For example, John E. Berthoud, "The Electoral Lock Thesis: The Weighting Bias Component," *PS: Political Science and Politics* 30 (1997), pp. 189–193, I. M. Destler, "The Myth of the Electoral Lock," *PS: Political Science and Politics* 29 (1996), pp. 491–494; James C. Garand & T. Wayne Parent, "Representation, Swing, and Bias in U.S. Presidential Elections, 1872–1988," *American Journal of Political Science* 35 (1991), pp. 1011–1031, Bernard Grofman, Thomas L. Brunell, and Janet Campagna, "Distinguishing the Difference Between Swing Ratio and Bias," *Electoral Studies* 16, pp. 471–487 (1997).

7

A Locked-Up Nation

THE CONTEMPORARY PARTIES: NATIONAL
BALANCE AND REGIONAL DOMINANCE

Once the outcome of a presidential election becomes clear from the aggregated reports of the many thousands of voting precincts across the United States, a number of prominent journalists, pundits, and party leaders will predictably declare that the results signal the formation of an enduring, or even "permanent," national majority. This common interpretation is partially a legacy of traditional party realignment theory, which still shapes the understanding of many commentators and which predicts that a single party will predominate in any given electoral period. But it surely also reveals a temptation in the wake of a long campaign – especially one that produces an apparently decisive conclusion – to treat the outcome as holding much larger historical importance, marking the beginning, or at least the continuation, of an entire political epoch. As the winning party struts the stage while the losers retreat to lament their fate and assign blame for their predicament, it is only natural for observers to assume that these dramatic tableaux of victory and defeat reflect a partisan climate that is unlikely to change very easily or very soon. But another presidential contest is always four short years away – and the congressional midterms, capable of delivering an unfavorable popular referendum on the governing record of the president's party, await in only 24 months.

The tendency of even experienced and well-informed analysts to over-extrapolate from the politics of the moment, assuming that partisan trends in motion will necessarily remain in motion, has led to a series of electoral proclamations that events have subsequently overruled – sometimes with astonishing rapidity. Kevin Phillips's *The Emerging Republican Majority* (1969), though frequently cited for its perceptive identification of the ideological, social, and geographic bases of support that would elect a series of Republican presidents in the 1970s and 1980s, could not account for the continued Democratic dominance of congressional and state-level elections over the same period.[1] The Republican "electoral lock" hypothesis seemingly explained the party's 1980s-era success in presidential elections until a poorly timed national recession spoiled the reelection chances of George H. W. Bush in 1992, dooming such titles as *Getting the Donkey Out of the Ditch* and *Minority Party: Why the Democrats Face Defeat in 1992 and Beyond* to immediate obsolescence.[2] John B. Judis and Ruy Teixeira published *The Emerging Democratic Majority* after the Democratic Party had achieved its third consecutive popular-vote presidential plurality in 2000; the book accurately identified the importance of culturally liberal metropolitan areas as sources of Democratic electoral support in the twenty-first century but had the misfortune to appear in advance of the Republican victories of 2002 and 2004.[3] George W. Bush's reelection alongside a Republican-controlled Congress prompted his chief political advisor Karl Rove to claim credit for engineering a "rolling realignment" in which "incremental but … persistent change" would produce increasingly decisive Republican victories in future elections – a theory that was eagerly accepted by many conservative pundits before it was swiftly refuted by the Democratic victories of 2006 and 2008.[4]

---

[1] Kevin P. Phillips, *The Emerging Republican Majority* (New Rochelle, NY: Arlington House, 1969).

[2] Carolina Arden, *Getting the Donkey Out of the Ditch: The Democratic Party in Search of Itself* (New York: Greenwood Press, 1988); Peter Brown, *Minority Party: Why the Democrats Face Defeat in 1992 and Beyond* (Washington, DC: Regnery Gateway, 1991).

[3] John B. Judis and Ruy Teixeira, *The Emerging Democratic Majority* (New York: Scribner, 2002). In the first few months of 2001, Republicans maintained procedural control of an evenly divided Senate due to the tie-breaking vote of Vice President Dick Cheney until the party switch of Vermont Senator James Jeffords threw control of the chamber to the Democrats. By 2015, Judis had changed his mind about the natural balance between the parties, concluding that the "emerging Democratic majority" had been transformed into an "emerging Republican advantage" (Judis, "The Emerging Republican Advantage," *National Journal*, January 31, 2015).

[4] Rove's quote from Dan Balz and Mike Allen, "Four More Years Attributed to Rove's Strategy," *Washington Post*, November 7, 2004, p. A01; see also Fred Barnes, "Realignment, Now More Than Ever," *Weekly Standard*, November 22, 2004, www.weeklystandard.com/Content/Protected/Articles/000/000/004/916rlnyg.asp.

The election of Barack Obama to the presidency, initially in concert with a fortified Democratic congressional majority, similarly encouraged some analysts to proclaim the dawn of a new era of liberal ascendance in American politics.[5] This conclusion seemed initially credible due to Obama's success in drawing particularly strong support from social groups that were projected to constitute a growing share of the electorate for decades into the future, including racial minorities, unmarried women, and members of the millennial generation – dubbed the "coalition of the ascendant" by Ronald Brownstein of *National Journal*.[6] Obama's reelection despite a sluggish national economy in 2012 revived this line of analysis, even compelling the Republican National Committee to charge an internal commission called the Growth and Opportunity Project with the task of identifying strategies to bolster the party's appeal among younger voters and Latinos in order to increase its competitive position in future presidential contests.[7] Yet Republicans had recaptured control of the House of Representatives in the interim by gaining 63 seats in the 2010 midterm elections and would soon retake the Senate as well. With the party also achieving significant gains in state governorships and legislative seats, the claim that Republican candidates faced a debilitating challenge in attracting popular support during the Obama years retained a veneer of plausibility only when applied to the presidency to the exclusion of all other offices and was thoroughly refuted by Donald Trump's victory in 2016. Whereupon the Democrats, so recently crowned the party of the future, were once again accused of fatally losing touch with the typical American voter – and so the cycle continued.

Rather than anoint either party as the natural electoral majority, it seems much more accurate to characterize the contemporary era as primarily distinguished by consistently strong and well-balanced national competition. The parties were separated by an overall popular vote margin of no more than 8 percentage points in five of the six presidential elections and 12 of the 13 House elections between 1992 and 2016; a

---

[5] For example: George Packer, "The New Liberalism," *New Yorker*, November 17, 2008; Michael Lind, "Obama and the Dawn of the Fourth Republic," *Salon*, November 7, 2008, www.salon.com/2008/11/07/fourth_republic/; Lanny J. Davis, "The Obama Realignment," *Wall Street Journal*, November 6, 2008, www.wsj.com/articles/SB122593028681903153.

[6] Ronald Brownstein, "Obama Buoyed by Coalition of the Ascendant," *National Journal*, November 8, 2008.

[7] The report that emerged from this effort is available at apps.washingtonpost.com/g/documents/politics/republican-national-committees-growth-and-opportunity-project-report/380/.

majority of both presidential and House elections during that time were decided by 5 points or less. Neither party has held more than 60 percent of the seats in either chamber of Congress since 1994, with Republicans maintaining an edge in congressional membership of 51.9 percent to 48.1 percent in the House and 50.5 percent to 49.5 percent in the Senate over the subsequent 24 years. Control of Congress has been open to legitimate contestation in most recent elections; of the 11 congressional elections between 1994 and 2014, six produced a change of partisan majority in one or both chambers.

To be sure, the spatial distribution of party support in the mass public can interact with electoral rules and institutions to provide one side or the other with an easier shot at national power. The Republican Party currently holds an underlying advantage in congressional elections due to the more efficient distribution of Republican voters across state and district boundaries. The results of 2016 suggest that this partisan imbalance might potentially extend to presidential elections as well, if the geographic coalition assembled by Donald Trump, who amassed 74 more electors than Hillary Clinton despite losing the national popular vote by more than 2 percentage points, is sustained by future Republican candidates.[8] This pro-Republican tilt can prove decisive from time to time in narrowly tipping control of national institutions to the GOP despite a modest popular preference for the Democratic opposition, but it is not steep enough to insulate Republicans from defeat when the national conditions become sufficiently unfavorable to their party.

In today's political climate, neither side maintains a "lock" on either the executive or legislative branch.[9] The four elections between 2004 and 2010 produced a sequence of outcomes exemplifying the closely matched partisan competition of the present era: (1) unified Republican control of the presidency and Congress (after 2004); (2) divided control between a Republican president and Democratic Congress (2006); (3) unified Democratic control of both branches (2008); and (4) divided control separating a Democratic president and Senate from a Republican House of Representatives (2010). The midterm elections of 2014 resulted in yet a

---

[8] These electoral college figures do not account for the seven electors in 2016 who violated their pledges to support either Trump or Clinton. Five Democratic electors in Hawaii and Washington cast their ballots for people other than their party's nominee, as did two Republican electors from Texas.

[9] See Alan I. Abramowitz, "Long-Term Trends and Short-Term Forecasts: The Transformation of US Presidential Elections in an Age of Polarization," *PS: Political Science and Politics* 47 (April 2014), pp. 289–292.

fifth configuration, in which Republicans achieved control of both legislative chambers while the White House remained in Democratic hands; two years later, Trump's surprising victory restored unified party control once again. The future emergence of a stable national majority able to establish long-term dominance over both Congress and the presidency would indeed represent a notable discontinuity with the volatile fortunes of both parties in contemporary elections.

It is below the national level – among individual regions, states, and congressional districts – where electoral locks are not only present but increasingly abundant. The relatively even overall balance of the parties masks the proliferation of dependable local, state, and regional bastions on both sides at the expense of marginal "battleground" constituencies. Across large expanses of geographic territory, either the Democrats or the Republicans enjoy a sufficiently decisive popular margin of support to give their nominees a prohibitive advantage in both presidential and congressional elections. Even some of the nation's most populous and socially diverse states now arguably lack fully functional two-party competition – for example, a Republican candidate last won a statewide race in California in 2006 and in New York in 2002, while a Democrat has not been elected statewide in Texas since 1994.

The formerly widespread phenomenon of the "personal vote," which once encouraged members of Congress to cultivate broad popular support across party lines by demonstrating their dedication to local issues and concerns, by delivering federal benefits and subsidies to their home states or districts, and by exhibiting stylistic compatibility with their constituents, has now almost entirely faded into history. Today, voters motivated overwhelmingly by national partisan loyalties and policy preferences will often tolerate significant personal faults in their congressional representatives rather than replace them with members of the disliked partisan opposition. Even nominees of the minority party who take pains to portray themselves as ideological centrists find it difficult to escape association with their party's more divisive national reputation and leadership.

U.S. Representative John Tierney, a Democrat from Salem, Massachusetts, sought a ninth term in office in 2012 despite his entanglement in a bizarre personal scandal involving an illegal Virgin Islands gambling ring run by his two brothers-in-law. Although his wife pled guilty to tax fraud in connection with the scheme, for which she served a 30-day jail sentence in 2011, Tierney publicly claimed ignorance of the entire affair – even as one of his wife's brothers told the press that "Tierney is the biggest liar in the world. He knew everything that was going on in my family for years. He sat with bookies at Fenway Park."[10]

Perceiving a rare opportunity in a normally solid blue northeastern district, House Republicans recruited a high-quality challenger to Tierney in Richard Tisei, an ideologically moderate and openly gay former state legislative leader. Tisei appeared for a time to enjoy electoral momentum; a late September poll by the *Boston Globe* found Tisei running six percentage points ahead of Tierney, while the Tisei campaign released an internal poll claiming a double-digit lead.[11] The challenger also received the traditionally liberal *Globe*'s endorsement for the seat – a rare achievement for a Republican congressional candidate in Massachusetts.

By the end of the campaign, however, the voters of the 6th District opted to reelect Tierney by a narrow margin; though they may have held little personal affection for their congressman, his constituents ultimately preferred an ethically compromised Democrat to a strong Republican challenger. As one district resident later told a reporter, "Richard Tisei is not a bad guy, but if you vote for him, you're also voting for [Republican House speaker] John Boehner."[12] Tierney was ultimately removed from office by Massachusetts voters two years later – not at the hands of a Republican opponent, but instead by losing the Democratic primary to challenger Seth Moulton, a Harvard-educated ex–Marine Corps officer and Iraq War veteran who easily prevailed in the general election.

Residents of Red America now demonstrate comparable devotion to the ascendant party in their own geographic region, even when the candidate's personal character is similarly open to question. In the weeks before the 2012 election, press accounts revealed that Republican congressman Scott DesJarlais, a former physician representing middle Tennessee's rural 4th District who had defeated a four-term incumbent Blue Dog Democrat by an 18-point margin two years before, had "engaged in sexual relationships with patients, medical center co-workers and a drug company

[10] Jess Bidgood, "Family Ties to Gambling Re-Emerge in House Race," *New York Times*, July 3, 2012, www.nytimes.com/2012/07/04/us/politics/john-tierneys-family-ties-re-emerge-in-house-race.html.

[11] Michael Levenson, "Richard Tisei Leads Rep. John Tierney in Poll," *Boston Globe*, October 1, 2012, www.bostonglobe.com/metro/2012/09/30/tisei-leads-tierney-globe-poll/wYWKkqXd1KaIpIW5lF8AVN/story.html. Tisei's poll is available at images.politico.com/global/2012/10/ma_cd_06_-_exec_memo_-_oct_12th.html.

[12] Shira T. Center, "John Tierney Survived 2012. Now What?" *Roll Call*, April 9, 2014, atr.rollcall.com/john-tierney-primary-race-he-survived-2012-now-what/.

representative" while married to his ex-wife.[13] DesJarlais, an avowedly pro-life social conservative, had also pressured one patient with whom he was romantically involved to terminate her pregnancy, as confirmed by a recording of the conversation.[14] Despite these embarrassing revelations, DesJarlais prevailed over his ideologically moderate Democratic challenger, state senator Eric Stewart, by 12 points in the 2012 election, and narrowly escaped defeat in the 2014 Republican primary before winning another House term the following November by 23 points. (DesJarlais was reelected yet again by a 30-point margin in 2016.) As veteran congressional elections expert Stuart Rothenberg observed about the current era, "even damaged candidates can limp through because it's gotten so partisan."[15]

For the vast majority of congressional incumbents, a serious electoral threat is now much more likely to arise in a party primary than a general election. This is particularly true for Republican members of Congress, who have often in recent years faced opposition from primary challengers who accuse them of insufficient party loyalty. With most electoral constituencies leaning strongly toward one party or the other, and with American voters increasingly reluctant to cross party lines to vote for (or against) a candidate on the basis of ideology, competence, personal scandal, or other considerations, the electoral incentives faced by officeholders increasingly reward philosophical purity and partisan styles of governing.

In one sense, the American party system has become electorally nationalized. Constituents of individual members of Congress routinely use their ballots as a biannual proxy vote for – or against – party leaders such as the president and speaker of the House. With the national parties at sufficiently comparable strength that the majority in one or both legislative chambers often hangs in the balance from one election to the next, congressional voting in the United States thus increasingly resembles parliamentary elections in other democracies

[13] Jaime Fuller, "Rep. Scott DesJarlais Engaged in Multiple Extramarital Affairs. He Still Might Win Thursday," *Washington Post* blog "The Fix," August 7, 2014, www.washingtonpost.com/blogs/the-fix/wp/2014/08/07/rep-scott-desjarlais-engaged-in-multiple-extramarital-affairs-he-still-might-win-thursday/.

[14] Michael McAuliff, "Scott DesJarlais, Pro-Life Republican Congressman and Doctor, Pressured Mistress Patient to Get Abortion," *Huffington Post*, October 10, 2012, www.huffingtonpost.com/2012/10/10/scott-desjarlais-abortion-pro-life_n_1953136.html.

[15] Jonathan Weisman, "Races for House Offer Little Suspense but Lots of Odd Back Stories," *New York Times*, October 27, 2012, p. A11.

– though within a distinctive constitutional structure that allows for frequent divisions of partisan control between chambers or across branches of government.

In another way, however, the parties have become more regional in character. The popularity of each side's issue positions and national leadership now varies significantly from one end of America to another. Both Democratic and Republican candidates find it increasingly difficult to appeal to voters outside their party's geographic home base, leaving large sections of the nation firmly in the hands of one or the other partisan camp. The growing nationalization of policy agendas and party reputations has provoked increasingly divergent popular responses in the Northeast and in the South, or in the coastal West and the interior West, regardless of the specific candidate or electoral environment of the moment.

Scholarly investigations conducted during the 1970s and 1980s often concluded that incumbent members of Congress had managed to achieve a sufficiently strong personal following to largely shield themselves from the shifting winds of party politics. But recent elections have repeatedly produced significant collective swings in one partisan direction or another, dislodging dozens of sitting officeholders and convincing many others to retire rather than risk defeat themselves. Only three of the 13 elections between 1968 and 1992 resulted in a net partisan change of more than 20 seats in the House of Representatives – a total that was equaled in the three consecutive elections of 2006 (30-seat Democratic gain), 2008 (21-seat Democratic gain), and 2010 (63-seat Republican gain). In these "national wave" elections, held in an age of unyielding popular frustration with the direction of the nation, citizens used their congressional votes to express disapproval of the performance of the incumbent president – whether Republican George W. Bush, as in 2006 and 2008, or Democrat Barack Obama, as in 2010 (and, later, 2014).

Yet these partisan shifts have only further widened the existing regional divide. Just as the Democratic congressional gains during Bush's second term decimated the remaining bloc of moderate Republicans representing northeastern or Pacific Coast states, the Republican victories during the Obama years solidified the party's advantage in the South and interior West at the expense of centrist Democratic Blue Dogs. Today, most congressional incumbents face little serious competition in general elections not because they enjoy strong personal popularity in their home states or districts, but because they represent dependably "red" or "blue" constituencies and have the right party label next to their name on the ballot.

The American party system has never been more nationally integrated, yet the regional distinctiveness of the parties' contemporary electoral coalitions has simultaneously reached its highest peak in nearly a century. The Democratic and Republican party labels each inspire a consistently friendlier reception in some corners of the nation than in others; these differences are more than large enough in a first-past-the-post electoral system to render most territory safe ground for the candidates of a single party. Citizens are increasingly united across geographic lines in viewing congressional races through the lens of national partisan competition, but the inhabitants of red and blue regions have increasingly reacted to this nationalization by making opposite choices in the voting booth. Across America, a converging set of political stimuli has thus produced a diverging array of popular responses.

POLARIZATION AND REPRESENTATION IN THE TWENTY-FIRST CENTURY

The ongoing scholarly dispute over the degree of political polarization in the contemporary American public offers two sharply contrasting accounts of the relationship between the policy preferences of voters and the actions of elected officials. To analysts who view the electorate as collectively moderate and pragmatic in its political inclinations, the progression of ideological polarization among partisan officeholders has severed the bonds of representation connecting citizens to their leaders. A voting public that is "closely but not deeply divided" has been deprived of options at the ballot box that correspond to its political views and has thus been relegated to choosing between two unpalatable extremes. Exercises in political punditry that describe a "great divide" or "culture war" in the population at large therefore mistake the dogma of party elites for the preferences of the wider electorate.

Other scholars have responded to this line of analysis by contending that the polarization evident among politicians in fact mirrors a similar rift among the voting public. In particular, they claim, the most politically attentive and engaged stratum of the citizenry has demonstrated a steady partisan and ideological divergence that has reinforced the parallel trend among party leaders. Rather than producing widespread disaffection and apathy, this development has stimulated a recent growth in rates of mass electoral participation by raising the stakes of partisan conflict. Although polarization may lead to unwelcome consequences such as frequent stalemate in government and regular eruptions of open acrimony between

Democrats and Republicans, it is nevertheless legitimately grounded in the changing behavior of the American populace.

Each of these perspectives is cogently argued, effectively supported with ample empirical evidence, and appealingly succinct in its conclusions, provoking a lively and informative debate over the past decade among students of American politics. Yet neither side can fully account for the findings presented here. The relationship between the polarization of political elites and the preferences of the mass public is neither a simple correspondence nor a complete "disconnect," but rather represents a complex interaction that requires recognition of the substantial power of electoral institutions that intermediate between citizens and their representatives.

Scholars who doubt the existence of mass polarization often describe a philosophically centrist general electorate that frantically seeks fellow moderates to enthusiastically reward with its votes – an objective that, in this telling, is systematically thwarted by the stubborn insistence of Democratic and Republican activists and primary voters on nominating relatively extreme candidates. The dearth of moderate officeholders in contemporary politics thus reflects insufficient supply in the face of strong popular demand. This argument attempts to account for the prevalence of liberal Democrats and conservative Republicans in public office while simultaneously exempting the American public from responsibility for the perceived scourge of elite polarization. But it cannot explain why voters have become less likely over time to support the moderate candidates who do manage to advance to the general election. Even centrist congressional incumbents, who enjoy a number of inherent advantages over challengers, have suffered a declining reelection rate since the 1970s; in most cases, voters who have removed them from office have replaced them with ideologically doctrinaire successors from the opposite party.

If we assume for the moment that most citizens indeed hold relatively moderate – or, at the least, ideologically inconsistent – views, it is still clear that they have come to weigh party affiliation much more heavily than ideological positioning when choosing congressional candidates, resulting in a more partisan and ideologically divided legislative branch.[16]

---

[16] For evidence that many citizens commonly classified as moderates in scholarly analyses in fact hold a number of nonmoderate (but ideologically incoherent) opinions, see Douglas J. Ahler and David E. Broockman, "Does Polarization Imply Poor Representation? A New Perspective on the 'Disconnect' Between Politicians and Voters," working paper, July 26, 2015, stanford.edu/~dbroock/papers/ahler_broockman_ideological_innocence.pdf.

The recent occurrence of several consecutive nationalized elections generating large shifts in the partisan distribution of congressional seats proved particularly treacherous for moderate incumbents, thus furthering the progression of elite-level polarization. The 2006 congressional midterms, which produced Democratic majorities in the House and Senate as a direct response to the declining popularity of President George W. Bush, inflicted especially harsh electoral punishment on the moderate wing of the Republican Party, whose members were less supportive of Bush's policies than their conservative colleagues but who represented electorally vulnerable "blue" constituencies and thus required a nontrivial level of Democratic support to remain in office. Bush's diminished political standing in 2006 largely reflected popular dissatisfaction with his policy in Iraq after nearly four years of war, yet one of the electoral casualties that year was Lincoln Chafee of Rhode Island, who had been the only Republican in the Senate to vote against authorization of the Iraq invasion in 2002 (while 29 Democrats had voted in favor) and who had refused to endorse Bush's reelection two years later. Similarly, public disapproval of the Affordable Care Act, Barack Obama's controversial health care reform initiative, contributed to the heavy losses suffered by the ruling Democrats in the 2010 midterm elections, which included the defeat of fully half of the 34 House Democrats who voted against the ACA earlier that year (four additional Democratic opponents retired and were succeeded by Republicans).[17]

These results do not reveal that voters actually prefer ideological extremity to moderation when party affiliation is held constant; both Chafee and the House Blue Dogs who broke with Obama's health care reform plan undoubtedly would have fared even worse at the polls had they proclaimed their fervent support of the presidential policies that had alienated a majority of their constituents. Whether or not the American public indeed holds collectively moderate views, however, it does not reliably rise to the electoral defense of like-minded representatives competing against more ideologically extreme challengers from the opposite party. For decades, southern and interior western electorates have steadily replaced Democratic centrists with Republican conservatives, while inhabitants of the Northeast and Pacific Coast have demonstrated a growing preference for liberal Democrats over moderate Republicans.

---

[17] Brendan Nyhan, Eric McGhee, John Sides, Seth Masket, and Steven Greene, "One Vote Out of Step? The Effects of Salient Roll Call Votes in the 2010 Election," *American Politics Research* 40 (September 2012), pp. 844–879.

This trend extends to presidential voting as well; "New Democrat" and native Arkansan Bill Clinton did not succeed in carrying the South and interior West in his 1992 presidential campaign, while self-styled "maverick" Republican John McCain similarly failed to make significant inroads among the voters of Blue America when he sought the presidency in 2008. The resurgent regionalism evident in the contemporary party system cannot simply be explained as the response of an ideologically innocent mass public to the presence of polarized choices on federal ballots, nor can Downsian models of spatial competition premised on the predictable support of voters for the most ideologically proximate candidate account for the electorate's contribution to the polarization of the parties in government.[18]

If the citizens of Red and Blue America were exhibiting rapid divergence in their respective policy views, the growth of geographic polarization in federal elections and resulting ideological polarization along regional lines in Congress would appear to constitute a direct process of democratic representation at work. However, the collective positions of voters on both economic and social issues have not become significantly more differentiated across geographic boundaries during the past 30 years, even as dramatic regional gaps have emerged over the same period in the results of partisan elections and the ideological positions of congressional incumbents. Instead, the key development at the mass level has been the broadening scope of policy-related partisan competition, which has extended to encompass social and cultural issues while retaining, and even strengthening, the traditional party divide on economic matters. Regional electorates do not disagree more today on these issues than they did in the 1980s, but their existing differences have become more electorally salient – thus widening the disparate partisan alignments now visible in presidential and congressional voting at the subnational level. Rather than interpreting the emergence of significant geographic variation in electoral outcomes as the consequence of corresponding ideological divergence (with voters in the blue states moving to the political left while their red-state counterparts collectively shift to the right), the evidence instead suggests that contemporary regional divergence represents a growth in the association between voters' existing views and their choice of candidates and parties.

---

[18] Jacob S. Hacker and Paul Pierson, "After the 'Master Theory': Downs, Schattschneider, and the Rebirth of Policy-Focused Analysis," *Perspectives on Politics* 12 (September 2014), pp. 643–662.

The complicated relationship between the preferences of voters and the behavior of elected officials extends to two other questions that have remained under dispute for much of the last two decades: (1) whether significant political differences exist between the denizens of Red and Blue America; and (2) whether a "culture war" rages in the American electorate. Mass polarization skeptics commonly emphasize the substantial overlap in public opinion that exists from one region to the next, arguing that deep divisions do not exist between the views of red-state and blue-state residents. This is a largely accurate characterization when applied to the distribution of political orientations in the public at large; one recent study by Ryan Strickler concluded that "there is substantially more common ground than difference" when comparing the political opinions of survey respondents residing in Democratic and Republican locales.[19]

Yet such arguments risk ignoring the serious macro-level political consequences of even small variations across geographic boundaries in issue positions, party identification, and candidate preferences. While a few "purple" states and House districts remain closely divided and highly competitive, the vast majority of the nation has become electorally secure for either Democratic or Republican candidates – not because all Californians have become ideological liberals and all Texans have likewise converted to conservatism, but rather because the existence of winner-take-all rules allows even a relatively narrow majority to establish unshakable dominance over a particular electoral constituency. Once this primacy is achieved, the minority party lacks an institutional channel to exert political influence – even if it commands the support of 45 percent or more of the constituency's voters. The contemporary parties would undoubtedly be less polarized if southern Democrats and northeastern Republicans still held office in large numbers as they did in previous generations, but the need to place first within a number of discrete geographic units in order to win political power has become an increasingly formidable impediment to the proportionate representation of these regional factions. Polarization in American politics is significantly exacerbated by the presence of an electoral apparatus that systematically overrepresents both conservative red-state Republicans and liberal blue-state Democrats while providing neither population with an incentive to reach

---

[19] Ryan Strickler, "A 'Sorted' America? Geographic Polarization and Value Overlap in the American Electorate," *Social Science Quarterly* 97 (June 2016), pp. 439–457, quote on p. 453.

across party lines whether on the floor of Congress or back home among their constituents.

The term "culture war" is a transparently hyperbolic characterization of contemporary political conflict, as many scholars have effectively demonstrated. Notably, views on economic issues remain powerful in determining the partisan preferences of voters, while many Americans continue to voice contradictory or ambivalent opinions on cultural matters. Yet the desire to combat the culture war "myth" should not lead political observers to deny the emergence of social issues as a significant and enduring secondary axis of policy difference between the parties – a development that has been particularly important in accounting for the diverging partisan alignments of Red and Blue America.[20] For example, voters' religious affiliations and degrees of religiosity now exert considerable influence over their partisan identification and choice of candidates; the Pew Research Center found in 2015 that white evangelical Protestants had come to prefer the Republican Party by a margin of 68 percent to 22 percent, while religiously unaffiliated voters now leaned toward the Democrats by 61 percent to 25 percent – a 40-point gap that equals the magnitude of the more long-standing difference in the partisan preferences of whites and African Americans.[21] While cultural liberals and cultural conservatives are not truly at "war," they are increasingly lining up on opposite sides in the ongoing electoral competition between the two major parties.

In summary, it is clear that the relationship between the polarization of elected officials and the choices of the mass public is remarkably complicated. But why should we expect otherwise? The process of citizen representation in the United States is itself inherently complex, with an extensive series of distinctive – and, in some cases, internationally unique – procedural characteristics. A large and diverse population faces the limited electoral choices supplied by a two-party system; the party winning the most popular votes nationwide may be denied the presidency or control of either congressional chamber; presidential nominees can receive a state's entire cache of electors by winning a bare majority of the statewide vote (or, in a multicandidate race, even less than a majority); a Senate class elected in response to the performance of a departing president

---

[20] See Jeffrey M. Stonecash, Mark D. Brewer, and Mack D. Mariani, *Diverging Parties: Social Change, Realignment, and Party Polarization* (Boulder, CO: Westview Press, 2003).

[21] Pew Research Center, "A Deep Dive into Party Affiliation," April 7, 2015, www.people-press.org/2015/04/07/a-deep-dive-into-party-affiliation/.

will remain in office during the entirety of the successor's term in the White House and for two additional years after that; Wyoming (2010 population: 563,626) receives an equal number of seats in the Senate as California (2010 population: 37,253,956); the nature of winner-take-all elections renders a state or congressional district nearly as electorally noncompetitive when the majority party holds a 55–45 advantage as when the partisan split is 80–20 or wider; a party with geographically concentrated supporters will face a systematic disadvantage in House elections compared to a party of equal size with more efficiently distributed adherents; the electoral college encourages presidential candidates to restrict their active campaigning to a small fraction of the nation; the procedures of the Senate allow the minority to obstruct much of the legislative action favored by the ruling party – all of these attributes and more depart from "pure" democratic majoritarianism to varying degrees, yet they each play critical roles in translating the votes of citizens into the composition of elective institutions and the development of public policy.[22]

Given this rampant, fundamental, constitutionally based complexity, any complete answer to the question of whether the American public is responsible for initiating or encouraging any particular large-scale trend in partisan or electoral politics is unlikely to be a simple "yes" or "no." Because many scholars, journalists, commentators, and citizens now view the ideological polarization of the parties as a troubling development with serious negative implications for the health and functionality of government, ascertaining the causal roots and reinforcing trends of this phenomenon is often treated as tantamount to the assignment of moral culpability. Yet the considerable institutional convolution of the American system should caution against such a view, even for those who fear that polarization exerts a destructive influence on the nation's politics. Small variations in mass behavior can produce much larger macro-level effects, changes over time in the geographic distribution of voter support can lead to significant political consequences even in the absence of intent on the part of citizens, and historical events often leave institutional residue that endures long after the context that originally created them has faded from view. Acknowledging the inherent complications that arise from the interaction between the behavior of voters and the mechanics of American political institutions may not leave us with a tidy or viscerally satisfying conclusion, but it boasts the advantage of

---

[22] Robert Dahl, *How Democratic Is the American Constitution?* (New Haven, CT: Yale University Press, 2001).

accurately characterizing the nature of democratic representation in the United States.

POLARIZATION, PARTIES, AND POLITICAL DYSFUNCTION: A FINAL WORD

The numerous examples of fallacious prognostication cited at the beginning of this chapter should inspire a degree of humility when extrapolating past electoral or partisan trends into the political future. But the phenomenon of party polarization is much more deeply rooted and longer-lived than the outcome of any particular election or performance of any individual president, and assuming its continued survival is thus a correspondingly safer bet. The presence of two parties of comparable national strength, with each side standing for a distinct ideological perspective, social group coalition, and regional base, seems to represent a natural state of political equilibrium that, once established, is difficult to dislodge. Polarization even displays self-reinforcing tendencies, as Mark D. Brewer explains:

Party elites became polarized ... followed over time by the mass public, as it perceived and reacted to the cues the elites were providing. It is also crucial to recognize that this process quite likely feeds off itself – elites polarize on issues, causing increased polarization among the mass on these same issues, which in turn fuels further elite polarization as politicians (who are after all elites) react to the views and demands of constituents and voters. This dynamic assists us in making sense of the highly polarized politics that currently exists in the United States.[23]

For many analysts, the rise of polarization is a deeply worrying development. These critics view the political leaders of the present day as frequently belligerent, inflexible, small-minded, and prone to excessive pandering to a small population of vocal extremists – especially in comparison to previous generations of public-spirited statesmen made even more heroic in retrospect by the rosy glow of historical nostalgia.[24] As Daniel DiSalvo observed in 2012:

Contemporary divisions appear all the more insidious, coming as they have on the heels of a high point in intraparty factionalism that reduced interparty tensions.

---

[23] Mark D. Brewer, "The Rise of Partisanship and the Expansion of Partisan Conflict Within the American Electorate," *Political Research Quarterly* 58 (June 2005), pp. 219–229, at 219.

[24] See, for example, Ronald Brownstein, *The Second Civil War: How Extreme Partisanship Has Polarized Washington and Polarized America* (New York: Penguin, 2007).

According to many pundits, increased polarization is a threat to the maintenance of American constitutional democracy. They claim that partisan rancor has the potential to undermine American institutions and so thoroughly alienate citizens as to destroy key habits of citizenship. Yet most analysts came of age in a highly distinct factional period that muted polarization. What they take to be the norm is in fact atypical ... In fact, government is returning to levels of polarization ... that prevailed from the 1870s through the 1920s.[25]

Yet this more measured, historically informed perspective has yet to win adherence among polarization's fiercest critics. And, as is often the case when political ills are diagnosed, observers looking to identify the source of the malignancy have landed on what they believe to be the guilty parties, as it were. Most political reform proposals that are intended to reverse the progression of polarization prescribe a solution of weakened partisan power, including changes to the primary election system that abolish the practice of party nominations (as in the "Top Two" or jungle primary variant instituted in California by a 2010 ballot proposition touted as an antipolarization initiative) and antigerrymandering restrictions (motivated by the assumption that party-dominated redistricting procedures create safe seats that encourage the election of strong ideologues). An alternative approach, adopted by the interest group No Labels, attempts to combat polarization by bestowing the label of "problem solver" on certain members of Congress who are said to favor "common-sense, common-ground solutions" to the nation's challenges, hoping that conflict-weary voters will use such endorsements as cues to guide their balloting choices in place of the usual popular reliance on party affiliation.[26]

Unless such measures can reverse the multidecade progression of polarization – and there is little empirical evidence to suggest that they would have a meaningful impact even if widely implemented – many contemporary commentators have concluded that the American political system faces a bleak future due to the obstacles posed by polarized parties to the effective operation of the federal government.[27] The tendency

---

[25] Daniel DiSalvo, *Engines of Change: Party Factions in American Politics, 1868–2010* (New York: Oxford University Press, 2012), pp. 184–185.

[26] No Labels Problem Solver Caucus, www.nolabels.org/problem-solvers-caucus/.

[27] On the illusory relationship between gerrymandering and polarization, see Nolan McCarty, Keith T. Poole, and Howard Rosenthal, "Does Gerrymandering Cause Polarization?" *American Journal of Political Science* 53 (2009), pp. 666–680; on primary election reforms, see Eric McGhee, Seth Masket, Boris Shor, Steven Rogers, and Nolan McCarty, "A Primary Cause of Partisanship: Nomination Systems and Legislator Ideology," *American Journal of Political Science* 58 (2014), pp. 337–351.

to blame the growth of polarization for government dysfunction – and, in turn, to blame party leaders and activists for the growth of polarization – is especially common among analysts who deny the existence of widespread ideological extremity in the mass public, thus exempting the broader electorate from responsibility for the governing problems that polarization is said to create. Chief among these difficulties is the prevalence of legislative stalemate under conditions of divided government, due to the lack of ideological overlap and bipartisan spirit now evident among federal officeholders. If the parties were weaker and more internally diverse, it is argued, leaders could more easily build cross-partisan coalitions in order to enact appropriately centrist legislative solutions to the important challenges facing the nation.

Complaints about the limited responsiveness of the government to the demands of the day are perennially widespread in the United States, and often contain substantial truth. Yet it is important to recall that previous generations of scholars frequently blamed gridlock on insufficient, rather than excessive, party strength. Adherents of greater party "responsibility" in the 1940s and 1950s argued that internal factionalization frustrated efficient policymaking by undermining the discipline of the ruling party, depriving its leaders of the practical governing majority necessary to enact the national platform endorsed by the American public. More recently, the parties of the 1970s and 1980s were frequently criticized for failing to inspire sufficient enthusiasm in the mass public to produce unified government, leaving a declining party system at the mercy of a candidate-centered politics that prevented either side from claiming a popular mandate for a coherent policy agenda or implementing it with dispatch.

Citizens, journalists, and scholars alike have long blamed party politicians for the lamentable prevalence of "gridlock" or "stalemate" in the functioning of elective institutions, but the roots of these supposed ills lie not in the parties but in the structure of American government itself. The much-celebrated array of constitutional checks and balances, when combined with other structural characteristics such as staggered terms of office and the apportionment of the Senate, represent the true primary obstacle to rapid and ambitious government action at the federal level. Instances of bipartisan cooperation can, and still occasionally do, overcome these mechanical barriers to legislative productivity, but it is unrealistic to expect modern political parties to accommodate them as a matter of course. The ideologically indistinct party system of the mid-twentieth century was an unstable anomaly resulting from the combined legacy of two massive historical events – the Civil War (in the South) and the Great Depression (nationwide) – and would have been exceedingly difficult to sustain in the long term under any circumstances. Nor was the relative absence of partisan polarization in previous decades sufficient to guarantee political placidity in a broader sense; contemporary complaints about the divisive remarks of politicians or uncouth antics of cable news talking heads appear hollow in comparison to the atmosphere of social unrest, scandal, and assassination that characterized the 1960s and early 1970s – an era now too often treated in retrospect as a golden age of relative comity.

To be sure, the parties bear substantial responsibility for both the progression of polarization and the accompanying impediments to effective governance. The operation of Congress, in particular, has been transformed by resurgent ideology and partisanship in ways that are not necessarily conducive to well-considered policymaking.[28] But the pursuit of governmental responsiveness, like that of democratic representation, implicates not only the party system but the larger electoral and constitutional structure in which the parties are embedded. As we have seen, many previous political experts raised similar concerns about the insufficiently responsive and representative nature of American government during periods when the relative strength, ideological cohesiveness, and geographic coalitions of the Democrats and Republicans differed dramatically from their current state.

Affixing sole blame to the parties for the perceived political deficiencies of the moment, though a practice that seldom falls out of fashion, fails to appreciate the extent to which the actions of party leaders are shaped by institutional constraints and electoral incentives alike – as especially illustrated by the example of contemporary polarization in an age of resurgent regional divisions. The American political system allows for the disproportionate election of liberal Democratic and conservative Republican officeholders, with most of these incumbents representing states or districts in which their party now holds a majority that, though not overwhelming, is secure enough to insulate them from serious challenge in general elections. It should hardly be surprising that such an institutional configuration proves conducive to the emergence

---

[28] Thomas E. Mann and Norman J. Ornstein, *The Broken Branch: How Congress Is Failing America and How to Get It Back on Track* (New York: Oxford University Press, 2006); Mann and Ornstein, *It's Even Worse Than It Looks: How the American Constitutional System Collided with the New Politics of Extremism* (New York: Basic Books, 2012).

and persistence of ideologically polarized parties. The current debate over polarization in the United States would benefit from a more extensive and forthright recognition of the ways in which constitutional and electoral elements have contributed to the rise of polarized parties and exacerbated some of its most dysfunctional consequences. Implementing foundational reform to the American political system is not immediately feasible – and may not, after careful study, even turn out to be desirable – but an honest acknowledgment of the contemporary difficulties that stem from the institutions and rules that Americans often treat as undebatable inevitabilities would be a more productive activity than simply pining for the return of a bygone style of weakened partisanship.[29]

A more extensive consideration of the historical evolution of the American parties also draws helpful attention to the unavoidable existence of tensions between competing goals and values. For example, the rising levels of party unity that often frustrate bipartisan cooperation under conditions of divided government also enhance the potential for legislative achievement when a single party holds unified control, such as those that occurred during the middle four years of the George W. Bush presidency and the first two years of Barack Obama's administration. Were the parties to revert to their previous factionalized ways, periods of one-party rule might prove less favorable to the objective of ambitious policy productivity, leading in turn to renewed calls for greater party "responsibility" to overcome this newly identified problem. It is not necessary to prefer a climate of polarization to one of cross-party coalition building in order to recognize that every historical twist and turn in the transformation of the American parties (and their respective geographic constituencies) over the past century has been accompanied by substantial dissatisfaction with the party system and an extensive roster of proposed remedies. The implementation of attempted solutions to large-scale political problems, while sometimes beneficial on the whole, seldom occurs without introducing new imperfections elsewhere in the system, and any future amelioration of polarization or its consequences will likely follow a similar pattern characterized by inevitable trade-offs.

Until the emergence of such a development, the continued growth of polarization is thus likely to result in a pattern in which legislative

---

[29] See David Karol, "American Political Parties: Exceptional No More," in Nathaniel Persily, ed., *Solutions to Political Polarization in America* (New York: Cambridge University Press, 2015), pp. 208–217.

prolificacy is more dependent than before on either the Democratic or Republican Party gaining and holding control of both elective branches of government. A nationally balanced and geographically polarized party system renders this alignment more difficult to achieve, but more likely to produce significant policy change during the periods when it does occur. Of course, the increasing use of the filibuster by the Senate minority – now a virtually automatic practice – can obstruct or moderate the policy agenda of the majority party even during periods of unified government. However, the unilateral elimination of the filibuster's applicability to judicial and executive nominations by the ruling Senate Democrats in 2013 offers a precedent for the abolition or modification of the supermajority requirement for cloture in a future Congress, and it may only be a matter of time before one party or the other will be seriously tempted to remove this remaining obstacle to its procedural autonomy.

At the same time, there is no guarantee that the enactment of the ruling party's agenda will be received positively by the electorate, which can then freely register its dissatisfaction in midterm elections by returning the government to a state of divided partisan control (as indeed occurred in 1994, 2006, and 2010). The prospect of either the Democrats or the Republicans maintaining a long-term cross-branch majority is relatively remote under conditions of regional polarization, due to the rough parity of the parties' national strength and the difficulty that each side now faces in making significant inroads within the sizable electoral base of its opponent. While voters routinely express generalized frustration with partisan stalemate or governmental unresponsiveness, they usually prefer divided government and the resultant procedural gridlock to the unfettered reign of a single disliked or distrusted party.

Under what circumstances might the party system become less geographically polarized in the future? Previous historical shocks to the existing alignments of the parties have come in the form of serious national emergencies (such as the Great Depression in the 1930s) or the emergence of newly salient political issues that cut across existing party coalitions (such as civil rights in the 1960s).[30] Such developments can be difficult to predict in advance, and truly transformational events may not occur for many decades. Even the Great Recession of 2007–2009, often considered to be the worst economic crisis to befall the United

[30] James L. Sundquist, *Dynamics of the Party System: Alignment and Realignment of Political Parties in the United States*, revised edition (Washington, DC: Brookings Institution, 1983).

policy concern

States since the Depression itself, failed to fundamentally reorder the coalitions of the parties or relegate the party in power (in this case, the Republicans) to minority status for longer than two years. The extension of partisan conflict to a greater number of policy domains over the past several decades also leaves few remaining issues with the capacity to initiate a cross-cutting cleavage and thus precipitate a new national realignment.[31]

Alternatively, the subjects that now play the largest role in reinforcing regional differences between the mass parties – religion, sexual politics, and moral traditionalism – could fade in the future as a key dimension of party conflict. From today's perspective, such a development seems unlikely to occur soon; if anything, the growth of geographic polarization has inspired party leaders to further emphasize their differences on cultural matters. With little remaining hope of extending their electoral reach to socially conservative constituencies such as the Old South and rural West, Democratic officials now feel free to energize their base in Blue America by accusing their Republican opponents of precipitating a "war on women," while Republican candidates who now likewise concede the urban North and coastal West in national elections can attempt to mobilize their own loyal supporters elsewhere in the nation by countering that Democrats are in return waging a "war on religious faith." Yet a narrower focus on economic interests by party leaders to the relative exclusion of social issues might well reduce the degree of regional variation in electoral outcomes from its current level, once again widening the scope of the geographic battleground.

Absent such developments, the regionally polarized party system appears well equipped to remain intact for years to come. In fact, the red-versus-blue alignment of party support in the American electorate is likely to become even further entrenched in the future, as state-level elections have increasingly come to mirror the familiar geographic pattern of partisan outcomes now consistently present in presidential and congressional voting.[32] The evolution of the two parties over the past century from loose patchworks of state and regional factions to philosophically coherent and nationally organized coalitions has not eradicated the

[31] Geoffrey C. Layman and Thomas M. Carsey, "Party Polarization and 'Conflict Extension' in the American Electorate," *American Journal of Political Science* 46 (2002), pp. 786–802.
[32] Daniel J. Hopkins, "The Increasingly United States," paper delivered at the Annual Meetings of the American Political Science Association, Washington, DC, August 2014.

enduring variation in opinions and values that continue to distinguish citizens who inhabit certain regions of the country from those who reside elsewhere. Such differences, though they may at times be overstated, are yet strong enough to ensure that most electoral constituencies maintain a loyally "red" or "blue" partisan hue, keeping the American political system itself locked in a state of perpetually simmering partisan conflict.

Index

abortion, *See* issues, social and cultural
Abramowitz, Alan I., 10, 36–37, 41, 118,
    146–147
Abrams, Samuel J., 36
Affordable Care Act, 151, 152,
    170, 223
AFL–CIO, 1
Alabama, 50
Alaska, 8, 27
Aldrich, John H., 70, 112–113
American Federation of Teachers, 1
American National Election Studies, 85,
    100, 109, 115, 117, 119, 129, 130,
    137, 140
American Political Science
    Association, 78–79
The American Voter, 76, 85
Americans with Disabilities Act, 94
Ansolabehere, Stephen, 35, 125
Arizona, 199, 202
Arkansas, 8, 56, 109, 110, 201
Armey, Dick, 112, 162
Ashcroft, John, 207
Atlantic Monthly, 32
Atwater, Lee, 105
Austin American–Statesman, 140

Bailey, Josiah, 74
Barone, Michael, 34
Barrow, John, 170
Bartels, Larry M., 69, 97, 124, 127
battleground states, 1–7, 45–57
Baucus, Max, 170

Beck, Glenn, 34
Begich, Mark, 22
Bennett, Robert W., 54
Bentsen, Lloyd, 92, 180
Bevill, Tom, 92
Biden, Joe, 4
Bipartisan Campaign Reform Act,
    154, 165
Bishop, Bill, 140
Blue Dogs, 22, 167–172, 218,
    220, 223
blue states, 8, 9, 32–35, 57–60
"blue wall," 210–211
Blumenauer, Earl, 43
Blunt, Roy, 207
Blute, Peter, 161
Bob Jones University, 41–42
Boehner, John, 44, 165, 218
Boll Weevils, 167
Bonamici, Suzanne, 43
Boston Globe, 218
Boyd, Allen, 169
Breaux, John, 92
Brewer, Mark D., 228
Brooks, David, 32–34
Brown, Scott, 22, 171
Brown, Sherrod, 207
Brownstein, Ronald, 215
Buchanan, Pat, 122–123
Bumpers, Dale, 92
Burnham, Walter Dean, 69
Busby, Horace W. Jr., 104
Bush v. Gore, 31, 32

Bush, Barbara, 122
Bush, George H. W.
  as candidate in 1988, 103, 138, 153,
    195, 201
  as candidate in 1992, 108, 121–123,
    153, 214
  as president, 84, 93, 94, 108–109,
    157, 158
Bush, George W.
  as candidate in 2000, 30–32, 35, 40, 47,
    61–62, 200
  as candidate in 2004, 6, 54, 203, 210
  as president, 5, 18, 22, 25, 123, 127,
    151, 164, 169, 214, 220, 223, 232
Byrd, Robert, 170

C-SPAN, 189
California, 19, 21, 24, 28, 48, 49, 52, 53,
    83, 103, 109–111, 113, 141–142
Campbell, Ben Nighthorse, 112
Campbell, James E., 83
candidate-centered campaigns, 87–89,
    96, 230
Carmines, Edward G., 69
Carsey, Thomas M., 119, 126, 142
Carter, Jimmy
  as candidate in 1976, 48, 52, 81, 83,
    106, 108, 109, 114, 151, 153
  as candidate in 1980, 81, 151, 201
  as president, 19, 94
Case, Clifford, 92
Casey, Robert Sr., 121
Castle, Mike, 163, 166
Caughey, Devin, 75
Chafee, John, 92
Chafee, Lincoln, 166, 223
Chamber of Commerce, 152
Chambliss, Saxby, 151
Cheney, Dick, 157
Chiles, Lawton, 92
Chinni, Dante, 34, 55
Christian Coalition, 120–122
Christian Science Monitor, 105, 123
church attendance, 117–120, 137–139
civil rights, *See* issues, racial
Civil Rights Act of 1964, 81, 82, 95, 150
Civil War, 66, 150, 231
Clean Air Act, 94
Clinton, Bill
  as candidate in 1992, 19, 68, 107–111,
    113–114, 116, 121, 139, 154, 156,
    197, 201–203, 208, 224

  as candidate in 1996, 154, 156, 161,
    197, 201
  as president, 18, 32, 111–112, 123,
    159–161, 164, 167, 168
Clinton, Hillary, 1–2, 4, 5, 7, 8, 21, 42, 49,
    122–123, 127, 138, 154, 195, 197,
    201, 202, 210–212, 216
Club for Growth, 162, 163, 166
Coats, Dan, 207
Colbert, Stephen, 5
Collins, Gail, 5
Collins, Susan, 167
Colorado, 56, 110, 199, 201, 202
conflict extension, 126, 142–143, 145
Congress, 73–76, 86–95, 112–113,
    146–192
congressional elections, 57–60, 85–87
Congressional Quarterly, 104
Connecticut, 113, 152–154, 196
Conrad, Kent, 170
Conservative Coalition, 74–75
Conservative Opportunity Society, 157
Conte, Silvio, 92
Contract with America, 160
Converse, Philip E., 36
Cook, Rhodes, 104
Coolidge, Calvin, 68
Cox, Chris, 190
Crotty, William, 88
Cruz, Ted, 180
cube rule, 39
"culture war," 14, 36, 37, 122–127, 143–
    145, 225–226. *See also* issues, social
    and cultural

Damore, David, 141
Davis, John W., 67
DeConcini, Dennis, 180
DeFazio, Peter, 43
Delaware, 27, 196
DeLay, Tom, 112, 162–164
DeMint, Jim, 43
Democratic Congressional Campaign
    Committee, 168
Democratic Leadership Council,
    106–108, 156
Democratic Party
  divisions within, 12, 73–80
  moderates in, 91–92, 106–108, 167–172
  problems competing for presidency,
    100–107
Democratic Study Group, 79

Dent, Charlie, 165
DesJarlais, Scott, 218–219
Destler, I. M., 104
Dewey, Thomas E., 76
DiSalvo, Daniel, 228
District of Columbia, 2, 8, 9, 46, 153, 196
divided government, 18–21, 23, 25, 70,
    89–95, 232–233
Dole, Bob, 112, 161
Dorgan, Byron, 170
Dornan, Robert, 189–190
Downs, Anthony, 158, 166, 224
Dukakis, Michael, 103, 104, 107, 109,
    110, 116, 138, 156, 195, 201

economic issues, *See* issues, economic
Economist, 123
Edwards, George C., 54
Edwards, John, 203
Eisenhower, Dwight D., 76, 85, 150,
    156, 198
election of 1960, 51–52
election of 1964, 80–81
election of 1968, 81–83
election of 1972, 46, 89
election of 1984, 39, 46, 89
election of 1988, 104, 107
election of 1992, 19, 107–111, 121–123,
    202–203
election of 1994, 19, 58, 111–113,
    159–160
election of 2000, 30–32, 37, 40,
    47–48, 61–62
election of 2004, 6
election of 2006, 164, 220
election of 2008, 5–6, 164, 220
election of 2010, 152, 165, 220
election of 2012, 4, 8–9, 20, 39
election of 2014, 165
election of 2016, 1–2, 6–9, 42, 49,
    210–212
electoral college, 2, 7, 17, 38, 51–57,
    210–212, 216
Emanuel, Rahm, 168, 172
Endangered Species Act, 94
Everson, David H., 88, 93

Family Ties, 105
Farhi, Paul, 34
Federalist Party, 66
Feingold, Russ, 207
Fenno, Richard F. Jr., 86–87

filibuster, 78, 233
Fiorina, Morris P., 10, 36, 37, 125, 146
FiveThirtyEight, 26
Flake, Jeff, 180
Florida, 9, 30–32, 35, 61, 199, 201
Flynt, Jack, 157
Focus on the Family, 121
Ford, Gerald, 52, 83, 153
Ford, Wendell, 92
Fox News Channel, 5, 34
Fox, Michael J., 105
Frank, Thomas, 123, 124
Franken, Al, 170
Frederick, Keith, 106
Frist, Bill, 112

Galston, William, 102, 104, 105
Garrett, Scott, 162
gay rights, *See* issues, social
    and cultural
Gelman, Andrew, 125
General Social Survey, 134, 137
geographic polarization, *See* polarization,
    geographic
Georgia, 150–152, 199, 202
Gephardt, Richard, 105
gerrymandering, 181, 183–184,
    209–210
Gilchrest, Wayne, 163
Gilded Age, 67
Gimpel, James G., 12, 34, 55, 194
Gingrich, Newt, 112, 157–161, 168
Glaeser, Edward L., 45
"God gap," 117–120, 137–139
Goldwater, Barry, 80–81, 150,
    151, 153
Gooch, Donald M., 119
Goodwin, Doris Kearns, 33
Gordon, Bart, 169
Gore, Al, 30–32, 35, 40, 47, 61, 108, 109,
    154, 200–203
Gore, Tipper, 202
Gowdy, Trey, 44
Graham, Lindsey, 43
Grant, U. S., 67
Grassley, Chuck, 207
Great Depression, 65, 68, 72–73, 79, 97,
    231, 233–234
Great Recession, 233–234
Great Society, 80, 103, 106
Green, Bill, 92
Guffey, Joseph, 74

Hadley, Charles D., 107
Hagan, Kay, 22
Harkin, Tom, 207
Harris, Katherine, 61
Hastert, Dennis, 162
Hatfield, Mark, 92, 180
Hawaii, 8, 27, 106
Heitkamp, Heidi, 171
Heritage Foundation, 43
Herring, Pendleton, 77
Highton, Benjamin, 137
Himes, Jim, 154
Hollings, Ernest "Fritz," 92, 170
Holman, C. B., 111
Hoover, Herbert, 68
House of Representatives, 17, 38, 78–79,
     156–170, 172, 177, 179, 189–190,
     204–205
House Rules Committee, 79
Humphrey, Hubert, 52, 82, 102

Idaho, 8
Illinois, 26, 48, 49, 52, 83, 103, 110, 111,
     206, 208, 209, 211
immigration, 141–142
incumbency advantage, 86–87
Indiana, 109, 206, 209, 210
Interior West
   definition of, 26–28
   politics of, 12–14, 19, 198–202
Iowa, 9, 53, 54, 203, 207, 210
Iraq War, 150, 164, 191, 223
Issa, Darrell, 190
Issenberg, Sasha, 52
issues
   economic, 16, 73, 75, 80, 99–100,
      124–139, 224, 226
   racial, 73–75, 80, 81, 82, 91, 95,
      141–142, 150, 151, 233
   social and cultural, 14, 16, 24, 32, 36,
      99–100, 114–140, 142–145,
      153–154, 168, 194, 197, 198, 201,
      224, 226, 234

Jackson, Jesse, 107
Javits, Jacob, 92, 180
Jenkins, Ed, 92
Johnson, Lyndon B., 7, 80, 82, 83, 104, 153
Johnson, Nancy, 164
Johnson, Ron, 207
Johnson, Tim, 170
Judis, John B., 197, 214

Kamarck, Elaine Ciulla, 102, 105
Kansas, 27, 124
Karnes, Kimberly A., 194
Karol, David, 93
Keaton, Alex P., 105
Kelly, Megyn, 5
Kennedy, John F., 52, 80
Kentucky, 27, 48, 49, 110, 201
Kerry, John, 6, 152, 154, 203, 210
Key, V. O. Jr., 69, 77, 95
Knuckey, Jonathan, 128
Kolodny, Robin, 163

La Follette, Robert M., 68
labor unions, 1, 73, 101, 129
Landon, Alfred M., 72
Landrieu, Mary, 22, 170
Latino vote, 141–142
Layman, Geoffrey C., 119, 126, 142
Lee, Frances E., 67, 180–181
Letterman, David, 32
Levendusky, Matthew S., 41
Levin, Carl, 207
Lewinsky, Monica, 32, 123
Lieberman, Joe, 203
Lincoln, Abraham, 67
Longley, Jim, 161
Lott, Trent, 112, 164
Louisiana, 8
Lugar, Richard, 166

Madigan, Edward, 157
Madison, James, 25
Maine, 2, 72, 142, 198
Manchin, Joe, 171
Manley, John F., 74
Marlantes, Liz, 123
Marshall, Jim, 151–152, 154–155, 177
Maryland, 19, 27, 50, 110, 111, 113, 196
Maslin, Paul, 105
Massachusetts, 24, 46, 50, 111
Mayhew, David R., 68, 69, 86–87, 94
McCain, John, 6, 170, 224
McCarthy, Kevin, 190
McClintock, Tom, 190
McCloskey, Pete, 92
McConnell, Mitch, 112
McGovern, George, 84, 102
McGovern, Jim, 161
McKean, Dayton David, 77
McKinney, Stewart B., 153
Medicaid, 80

Medicare, 80
Merkley, Jeff, 43, 180
Metropolitan areas
  politics of, 194–199, 208, 214
Michel, Bob, 157–158
Michigan, 9, 52, 208, 210
Midwest
  definition of, 26–28
  politics of, 26, 202–212
Miller, Gary, 138–139
Miller, Warren E., 119
Mills, Wilbur, 92
Minnesota, 46, 206, 210
Missouri, 8, 26, 56, 206, 209
Moderates
  disappearance of in Congress, 146–149,
    172–182, 206–207
Mondale, Walter, 102, 104, 107, 109, 156
Monroe, James, 80
Montana, 26, 110, 201
Moore, Stephen, 162
Moulton, Seth, 218
Mourdock, Richard, 166
Mulvaney, Mick, 44
Murkowski, Lisa, 166
Murphy Brown, 121

Nagourney, Adam, 123
National Election Studies, *See* American
  National Election Studies
National Journal, 215
National Republican Congressional
  Committee, 162
National Rifle Association, 152
National Right to Life Committee, 152
Nebraska, 2, 27, 50
Nelson, Ben, 170
Nevada, 53, 142, 201
New Deal coalition, 65, 71–72,
  81–82, 87
New Democrats, 106, 107, 109, 111, 224
New Hampshire, 53, 54, 142, 196, 197
New Jersey, 19, 21, 83, 103, 109, 111, 113,
  142, 196
New Mexico, 54, 201
New York, 19, 21, 48, 49, 52, 53, 106, 111
New York Times, 105, 108, 115, 123,
  165, 202
Nixon, Richard
  as candidate in 1960, 51–52
    as candidate in 1968, 52, 81–82, 87,
      103, 153

  as candidate in 1972, 46, 103, 153
  as president, 58, 83, 93, 94, 101, 102,
    106, 113, 158
No Labels, 229
NOMINATE scores, 43, 172, 180, 190
North Carolina, 201
North Dakota, 72
Northeast
  definition of, 26–28
  politics of, 8, 12, 14, 129, 194–198
NPR, 33, 34
Nunn, Sam, 92

O'Donnell, Christine, 166
Obama, Barack
  as candidate in 2008, 5–6, 54–55, 131,
    152, 154, 164, 183, 195, 210, 215
  as candidate in 2012, 4, 5, 9, 21, 39,
    116, 131, 141, 154, 183, 195, 197,
    201, 203, 208, 210, 211, 215
  as president, 18, 22, 23, 25, 44, 62,
    123, 127, 151, 165, 168–170, 220,
    223, 232
  as Senate candidate in 2004, 62
Occupational Health and Safety
  Act, 93–94
Ohio, 2–7, 9, 26, 35, 48, 49, 52, 103, 106,
  203, 208, 209
Oklahoma, 27, 50, 83
Operation Rescue, 121
Orange County Register, 141
Oregon, 41–44, 111

Pacific Coast
  definition of, 26–28
  politics of, 8, 12, 14, 111, 194–198
Pantoja, Adrian, 141
parties
  decline of, 12, 84–89, 97
    divergence of on social issues,
      114–127
    electoral parity of, 3, 18, 67, 215–217
    realignment of, 69–71, 87, 213
    and representation, 11–12, 144–145,
      221–228
    resurgence of, 12, 16–19, 64–66, 70,
      71, 97–98 *See also* Democratic
      Party, Republican Party
partisan sorting, 16–17
Partisan Voting Index, 176, 177, 183, 185
party responsibility, 76–80, 89, 230
Pelosi, Nancy, 152, 169, 170

Pennsylvania, 9, 26, 35, 52, 103, 106, 110, 197, 198
Pepper, Claude, 74, 75
Percy, Charles, 92
Perot, H. Ross, 108, 110
personal vote, 181–182, 217
Peters, Ronald M. Jr., 160
Peterson, Collin, 169
Pew Research Center, 226
Phillips, Kevin, 81–82, 103, 214
Pickle, Jake, 92
Planned Parenthood of Southeastern Pennsylvania v. Casey, 120
Polarization
  geographic, 3, 7–17, 19, 21–22, 32–63, 127–139, 172–182, 189–192
  in government, 9–10, 17–18, 21–22, 25, 146–149, 155, 172–182, 221–235
  of voters, 7, 9–17, 36–37, 40–45, 221–228
Polsby, Nelson W., 24, 53, 74
Poole–Rosenthal scores, *See* NOMINATE scores
Poole, Keith T., 172
Pope, Jeremy C., 36, 41
Populist movement, 67
Portlandia, 42
Progressive Policy Institute, 102
Proposition 187, 141–142
Pryor, Mark, 22
purge campaign of 1938, 74, 75
"purple" states, 35–37, 201–202. *See also* battleground states
Pursell, Carl, 92

Quayle, Dan, 121–122
Quayle, Marilyn, 122
QVC, 33

racial issues, *See* issues, racial
Ranney, Austin, 77
Reagan, Ronald, 81, 94, 101, 102, 104–106, 113, 158, 167, 191
  as candidate in 1980, 84, 103, 153, 195, 201
  as candidate in 1984, 39, 46, 103, 153, 195, 200
realignment, *See* parties, realignment of
Reconstruction, 66, 97, 150
red states, 8, 9, 32–35, 57–60
Reed, Ralph, 120

Regions
  declining importance of in 20th century, 95–98
  definition of, 26–28
  historical alignment of, 66–71
  polarization of, 57–60, 189–192
Reiter, Howard L., 129
religion, 117–120, 137–139, 226
representation, 10–18, 144–149, 221–228
Republican National Committee, 215
Republican Party
  in Congress, 156–167
  divisions within, 75–76
  former presidential advantage of, 82–84, 101–107, 214
  moderates in, 92, 161–167
  structural advantage of in congressional elections, 21–23, 149, 155–156, 182–188, 208–210, 216
residential sorting, 140
Ripley, Randall, 93
Robb, Chuck, 92
Robertson, Pat, 120, 122
Rockefeller, Jay, 170
Rockefeller, Nelson, 153
Rodden, Jonathan, 35, 125
Roe v. Wade, 114–115, 120
Roll Call, 163
Romney, Mitt, 4, 21, 39, 55, 141, 165, 195, 200, 201, 203, 211
Roosevelt, Franklin D., 71–76, 83, 103
Rosenthal, Howard, 172
Rothenberg, Stuart, 219
Roukema, Marge, 162
Rove, Karl, 5, 214
Rowland, J. Roy, 151
rural areas, politics of, 193–194, 198–203, 208, 211
Ryan, Paul, 4

Sasser, Jim, 112
Saunders, Kyle L., 37
Schantz, Harvey L., 97
Schattschneider, E. E., 69, 78, 79, 96
Schneider, William, 103, 104
Schofield, Norman, 138–139
Schuknecht, Jason E., 12
Schumer, Chuck, 180
Scott, Austin, 152
Scott, Tim, 43

Senate, 17, 38, 78, 166–167, 170–172, 177, 179–180, 186–187, 190–191
Serrano, Jose, 183
700 Club, 120
Shanks, J. Merrill, 119
Shays, Chris, 154–156, 163, 165, 177
Shelby, Richard, 112
Sherman, William Tecumseh, 150
Shuler, Heath, 168–169
Simpson, Alan, 112
Sittenfeld, P. G., 4
Skelton, Ike, 169
Smith, Chris, 165
Smith, Gordon, 190
Snyder, James M. Jr., 35, 125
social issues, *See* issues, social and cultural
Sorauf, Frank J., 96
South
  definition of, 26–28
  Democratic rebuilding attempts in, 105–109, 111
  historical alignment of, 67–68
  party change in, 89–92, 94, 111–114, 128, 139, 158–159, 162, 170, 198–199
  politics of, 12–14, 19, 198–202
South Carolina, 8, 41–44
Specter, Arlen, 166
Sperling, Godfrey Jr., 104
split–ticket voting, 12, 18, 19, 21, 68, 70, 84–89, 92–95, 102
spoiler effect, 39
Spratt, John, 169
Stanley, Harold W., 107
Starr, Kenneth, 32
states, polarization of, 45–57
The Stepford Wives, 153
Stewart, Eric, 219
Stewart, Jon, 34
Stimson, James A., 69
Stonecash, Jeffrey M., 129
Strickler, Ryan, 225
suburbs, politics of, 103–105, 109–110, 193, 195, 197
Sundquist, James L., 69
Super Tuesday, 107
Supreme Court, 31, 114, 120
swing states, 1–7, 45–57

Taft, Robert, 76
Taylor, Zachary, 83

Tea Party movement, 44, 165, 166
Teeter, Bob, 105
Teixeira, Ruy, 197, 214
television, 86, 89, 96
Tennessee, 109, 110, 201
Tester, Jon, 171
Texas, 8, 48, 49, 52, 53, 106, 199
Thurmond, Strom, 75, 81, 90
ticket–splitting, *See* split–ticket voting
Tierney, John, 217–218
Tisei, Richard, 218
Title ix, 94
Toomey, Pat, 166, 167
Truman, Harry, 76, 83, 103, 109
Trumka, Richard, 1
Trump, Donald
  as candidate in 2016, 1–2, 4, 5, 7–9, 21, 42, 49, 55, 62, 138, 154, 165–166, 195, 198, 200–202, 210–212, 215, 216
  as president, 44, 127, 198
Tuesday Group, 163
Tuten, James Russell, 150

unified government, 18, 20–21, 232–233
urban areas, *See* metropolitan areas
Utah, 8, 24

Vermont, 50, 72, 83, 142
Vinson, Carl, 150
Virginia, 56, 83, 142, 197, 201, 202
Voter News Service, 30
Voting Rights Act, 91, 94, 167, 183

Wallace, George, 151
Walmart, 33
Ward, Bryce A., 45
Warren, Elizabeth, 22
Washington, 19, 21, 111
Washington Post, 34
Watergate scandal, 58, 83, 191
Wattenberg, Martin P., 88, 96
Weber, Vin, 157
Webster v. Reproductive Health Services, 120
Weicker, Lowell, 92, 153
Weingarten, Randi, 1
Wellstone, Paul, 207
West Virginia, 8, 24, 27, 110, 201
White, Theodore H., 52
Wildavsky, Aaron, 53

Wilson, Joe, 44
Wilson, Pete, 141
winner–take–all electoral rules, 11, 13–15,
    38–45, 50–54, 212
Wisconsin, 9, 106, 203, 210
Wright, Jim, 157

Wurzelbacher, Samuel Joseph, 6
Wyden, Ron, 43
Wyoming, 26

Zelizer, Julian E., 73